DATE DUE

Alc

Cradle

Alcohol

Cradle to Grave

Eric Newhouse

An imprint of Idyll Arbor, Inc.
39129 264th Ave SE, Enumclaw, WA 98022

Cover and interior photographs: Larry Beckner ©1999
Cover design: Pat Kenny
Editor: Kenneth A. Lucas

ISBN 1-930461-04-6
ISBN-13 9781-930461-04-8

This book is gratefully dedicated to all those courageous people who shared their darkest secrets with me in the hopes of helping others conquer alcoholism.

To the Great Falls Tribune, and particularly Publisher Jim Strauss, who gave me the opportunity to investigate a community problem.

And to God, without whom none of this would have been possible.

CONTENTS

Preface   v

January   How alcohol permeates a community during the day.   1
February   Genetic reasons why alcohol is a medical disease.   29
March   Fetal alcohol syndrome: how drinking harms
           children.   49
April   The alcoholic makes the whole family sick.   67
May   Teenage keg parties and college binge drinking.   89
June   Readers tell us that drinking fuels domestic violence. 117
July   Drunken drivers destroy lives.   133
August   Alcoholism is epidemic on Indian reservations.   143
September Alcohol abuse keeps people off the job and in
           hospitals.   169
October   Nearly all of Montana's prisoners are addicted to
           alcohol or drugs.   187
November   Alcoholism costs the state of Montana more than the
           university system.   203
December   How do we treat this disease?   227

Postscript   253
Bibliography   269

PREFACE

Montana spends more money paying for the hidden costs of alcohol abuse than it does in educating its college-age youth.

That is a damning statement, but I know it to be true. It was the primary conclusion in a yearlong series of newspaper stories that I wrote in 1999 for the *Great Falls Tribune* that won the Pulitzer Prize for explanatory reporting in 2000.

While I can't prove that the same is true in every state, I doubt that any is much different.

That series of stories is the basis of this book, but I've also added material that should be of interest to journalists and others—why we undertook such a huge project, how we did it, the ethical issues that we wrestled with, and how we resolved them.

The stories ran once a month for a calendar year, so I've left the month as the chapter title. But the topic breaks down into two minor and two major themes.

The first minor theme is a chapter exploring the prevalence of alcohol in our community, a small town (about 60,000 people) that straddles the Missouri River. It was named after the Great Falls of the Missouri, which forced the Lewis & Clark Expedition to take a long hike two centuries ago. But a second river flows through the town, and it was one that I wanted to explore—the river of booze trucked into town each day and sloshed down each night in the town's many watering holes.

The second minor theme is a chapter explaining that alcoholism is a medical illness, and the genetic makeup of some people renders them unusually vulnerable to it. This turned out to be more important than I could have known. It removed much of the stigma of alcoholism and gave people the freedom to discuss their problems. With the exception of children, we had resolved to use names and photos in this series. I didn't realize it at the time, but this chapter made that possible.

The first major theme is the human cost of alcohol abuse, and it ran from March through August. This is why we called the series, and the book, *Alcohol: Cradle to Grave.* Every newspaper editor and reporter sees the flotsam and jetsam of that unrecognized river of booze: the divorces, lost jobs, battered wives and children, crime, drunken drivers, car wrecks, medical bills. It's just that we're all so accustomed to this debris underfoot that we rarely wonder why it's there—or if it's necessary.

The second major theme is the economic costs of alcohol abuse. I came to call them *hidden* costs. These were things like workplace absenteeism due to hangovers, welfare payments to alcoholics, medical costs of elective drinking, and crime (DUIs, assaults, etc.). The costs of crime alone include damages, cops to catch the drunks, prosecutors and judges, courts and prisons.

Instead of looking at a bunch of different bandages, I wanted to show the single gaping wound.

Several years ago, in a series of articles, the *Great Falls Tribune* explored unsolved murders on one Montana Indian reservation. All were alcohol-related, and most were unsolvable because all the witnesses were too inebriated to cooperate. Those stories stuck in the mind of *Tribune* Executive Editor Jim Strauss.

I, in turn, had been watching the national tobacco settlement unfold in the late 1990s and had been impressed with the way the lawyers had tied together the social and economic ramifications of smoking. Why hadn't the newspapers provided that perspective, I wondered.

Then I realized we had a perfect opportunity to do the same thing with alcoholism.

So I came before a meeting of *Tribune* editors in the early fall of 1998 with a conventional proposal: four or five major stories on alcoholism that would run over the course of a week. But no one could agree on what those four or five stories should be— there seemed to be many important things that were falling by the wayside.

With no decision, I came away disappointed that no one seemed to like the idea.

A couple of weeks later, Strauss surprised me by asking whether we could tackle the whole issue in a 12-part series, one part a month for a year. I was elated and told him yes, absolutely.

By the end of that afternoon, I sketched an outline. We fine-tuned it a little, but it essentially stood for the next year. Vision and planning were one key to the success of this project. Another was our community. Great Falls isn't much different than any other city in America, but it's still small enough that you can examine a local problem minutely.

And the *Tribune* is the state's newspaper, still trusted in the hearts and homes of its loyal Montana readership. That was critical to a project in which we would ask alcoholics to share some of their darkest secrets with 40,000 readers. To make their stories believable, we knew we would have to quote people by name—and use their photos on the front page of our newspaper.

To those who had the courage to trust us with their stories, I owe an immense debt of gratitude. Just think of how you would feel if someone like me came up and began asking the most personal of questions about behavior you had been accustomed to hiding.

Dirk Gibson and Dr. Dan Nauts of Benefis Healthcare, as well as Rod Robinson at Gateway Recovery Center, made that job easier by telling their patients that alcoholism is an illness, and they shouldn't be ashamed to be ill. They often helped find people willing to talk to me on the record and encouraged them to do so.

Another huge debt is to the *Great Falls Tribune*, which has given me permission to reprint the bulk of the stories. This book will provide a much wider audience for my work.

And my colleagues at the *Tribune* deserve a lot of credit. Jim Strauss had the vision to recognize an important project. Assistant Managing Editor Linda Caricaburu read rough copy and suggested improvements, News Editor Carrie Koppy oversaw production, and Také Uda designed many of the pages. Finally, there is Larry Beckner, the former photo editor whose striking photographs accompanied each of the stories—we logged many miles together, happily and enthusiastically.

I'm also indebted to a panel of experts who advised me from the fall of 1998 through the development of this series. They helped us shape the series from the beginning, then were available to work with me on stories within their expertise. The panel included

- Marcia Armstrong, then addictions treatment officer for the Montana Department of Public Health and Family Services in Helena
- Rod Robinson, former executive director of Gateway Recovery Center
- Dirk Gibson, former addictions abuse coordinator for Benefis Healthcare
- Wava Goetz, a local family counselor
- Les Stevenson, executive director of Opportunities Inc., the clearing house for social services in Great Falls
- Chris Christiaens, former state senator and director of the Prerelease Center
- Gail Cleveland, then special education director for the Great Falls Public Schools

- Tammera Nauts, former school system counselor for at-risk youth and employee assistance program administrator for teachers. She's also Dan's wife
- Chris Reilly of VRI, the local employee assistance program
- Former Police Capt. Larry Renman

Finally, I'm grateful to the Hazelden Foundation, first for working so closely with me on treatment models, then later for printing the hardcover edition of this book; and to Idyll Arbor, Inc. publisher Tom Blaschko for printing this softcover version.

JANUARY

Alcohol flows through every life, directly or indirectly.

Most people drink in moderation; others abstain. Those who abuse this dangerous, but legal drug pay a severe price to their health, their finances, their family lives, their social lives, and their jobs.

My challenge was to determine the size of this river. I decided to do it by examining its impact on our community in a single day. Here's how this day went.

5:30 A.M.

I start before dawn on a cold December morning at the Great Falls Rescue Mission, which has been called the last stop before the graveyard for those unable to handle their addictions. The lights go on at 5:30 A.M.

"About half of our clients abuse alcohol, and about half abuse drugs," says Glenn McCaffrey, director of the Rescue Mission. "They drink, gamble, do drugs."

On this particular morning, the Mission houses five transients and seven regulars working off their room and board.

"Most of these people get government checks of some sort, and when those checks run out later in the month, we begin to see them in greater numbers," says McCaffrey.

Breakfast is at 6 A.M. Today it's grits and eggs; clients are expected to help clean up the cafeteria and sweep out the dayroom before they head out.

"A few are actually looking for jobs," says McCaffrey, "but most of the professionals will be out collecting cans to get the money for alcohol or drugs. But we have a rule here—if you come back intoxicated, you forfeit your bed."

8:00 A.M.

By county ordinance, there can be no sale of alcohol between 2 A.M. and 8 A.M., so that's the earliest the bars can open. The old Maverick Bar in downtown Great Falls once began its happy hour at 8 A.M. for the night shift workers; by the early morning hours, it would be a rowdy place. Frequently, there's a line at the back door of the Lobby Bar in downtown Great Falls.

8:15 A.M.

Tom, a former ranch hand from Miles City, is sitting on a bench in the Rescue Mission, already drunk and waiting for his morning coffee. Considering the Mission's rules, how did he spend the night there?

"I didn't," he says. "I usually spend the nights out."

But the gray-tiled dayroom is a dry place, so Tom periodically slips out into the alley where he has a cache of beer waiting for him.

"I pick up cans," he says. "If I go all day, I usually can get around 30 pounds."

That's $7.50, and Tom says he spends most of it drinking beer with his friends.

"Tom is what I call a suicidal drinker," says McCaffrey. "He just drinks himself to death every day. I've watched him deteriorate over the past few years."

That's an unfortunate reality at the Mission, where success stories are rare. In fact, Tom died on the sidewalk outside the Rescue Mission about eight months after my visit.

"This is the last stop for most of these folks," McCaffrey says. "They're almost literally one yard from hell."

Unfortunately, people are reaching that last stop sooner.

"One thing that really worries me is that we're beginning to see a lot of 18- to 25-year-olds here now," says McCaffrey.

8:30 A.M.

Then I join Officer Mark Thatcher of the police department's DARE squad, who is standing before Vi Figarelle's class at Blessed Trinity Catholic School, preparing to talk about the evils of alcohol, drugs, and gangs.

But first, he opens a box of questions from the nineteen fifth graders:

- *Do you ever arrest anyone who doesn't want to be arrested?*
  "Most people don't want to be arrested," responds Thatcher, remembering in particular a 16-year-old drunk who wanted to avoid being charged with minor-in-possession.

    "I put him up against the car to frisk him, but he took off and ran from me," he remembers. "I chased him and tackled him, but during the scuffle, he bit me on the inside of the leg. Another officer joined me at the scene and we subdued him and threw him in the back of a police car," says the officer. "Then he spit in my face and kicked out the rear window of my police car."

- *Do many people abuse drugs and alcohol?*
  "I know quite a few people who take drugs and a lot of people who drink too much," says Thatcher.

- *How about police officers?*
  "I don't know of anyone who takes drugs, but I do know a few who drink a little too much," he responds. "I don't think they're alcoholics, but they may let the stress of their jobs get to them a little too much."

9:00 A.M.

More drinking generally means less working, but those figures aren't easy to come by.

The Great Falls School District reports a daily employee absenteeism rate of about 3.8 percent: 61 absent out of a work force of 1,580.

There's no way of knowing how many of these are alcohol-related, but one American in 10 has a drinking problem, and two-thirds of them hold jobs.

Employees dependent on substances such as alcohol have two to three times the normal absenteeism rate, according to VRI, the employee assistance firm.

9:15 A.M.

The Cascade County Tavern Association board of directors was to meet at the office of its executive director, John Hayes, on North Star Boulevard, but none of the board members show up this morning.

Hayes has prepared a report, however, reporting that the association's major fund-raiser the week before raised $12,000, most of which would go to support local charitable activities.

"We average ten to twelve calls a week for donations," says Hayes. "Our board meets once a month to send checks to those we feel we should help.

"Our emphasis is on kids," he says. "For example, we usually help the St. Vincent DePaul Society with their annual outing that takes about 40 kids up to a camp near Monarch.

"That costs $1,500 to $2,000 each year, and we finance most of it," he adds. "They make the kids pay a buck apiece, and we make up the difference."

On this Friday, the tavern association received two requests for charitable donations, and it wrote checks for $250 to St. Vincent's and $400 to the food bank, says Hayes.

9:30 A.M.

Business is already booming at the Lobby Bar.

Half a dozen folks are at the bar, a handful are gambling, and three people are locked in a serious discussion at a back table, with twelve-ounce glasses of red beer in front of them.

"They're lined up at the door when I open at eight," says manager and former owner Tara Fatz.

"I have quite a few seniors who come in for coffee and some who come in to drink," she says. "We call it the 'Soaps and Suds Hour' because we're all watching the big-screen TV."

10:00 A.M.

A dozen people straggle into a room on the second floor of Opportunities Inc., for their weekly Alcoholics Anonymous meeting.

There are 64 meetings in Great Falls each week. Typically, they open with members introducing themselves by first name and admitting their alcoholism. Then they go around the room, discussing current problems and the 12-step recovery program.

At this meeting, however, members are nervous about my presence and ask me to leave, so I do.

10:30 A.M.

I head over to Gateway Recovery Center, where a distraught mother has just been in to ask center Director Rod Robinson for "help and hope" in treating her fifteen-year-old daughter who is hooked on alcohol and marijuana. Her mother hopes she will find her way back to her family. Right after that, says Robinson, a former patient "just stopped in to say thank you" for helping him get his life and family back together again.

11:00 A.M.

I also visit Municipal Court, which is just winding down in the basement of the Great Falls Civic Center. "I'd guess that more than half of our caseload is alcohol-related," says Kory Larsen, an assistant city attorney. Later, he looks up the number of court appearances that morning—thirty-one of them—and finds that eighteen obviously involve alcohol.

11:15 A.M.

I find it important not to demonize saloon keepers, so I hook up with Paul Horning, a bartender with the Half Time Sports Bar who teaches a course in responsible alcohol consumption. He's visiting with Viki Gallagher, owner of the Frontier Bar, about the TIPS program under which bars can get a 15 percent break on their liability insurance.

"We're trying to promote responsible consumption of alcohol," says Horning, explaining that the classes cover how to deal with underage drinkers, fake ID cards, and bar liability issues.

"One of the biggest problems our new bartenders have is how to tell someone they're cut off without creating a great big hassle," says Gallagher.

"It's never easy, and sometimes there will be hassles," Horning responds. "But we'll show your bartenders how to kill 'em with kindness, and we'll do some role-playing to help them learn. We'll also show you some ways to slow customers' drinking down."

Before the discussion is over, Gallagher has agreed to enroll half the Frontier Bar's alcohol servers in the program, which is locally underwritten by Devine Brothers Distributing and Anheuser-Busch.

11:45 A.M.

Back downtown at the Largent School, Tammera Nauts is compiling a list of school district students who have been charged with being minors in possession of alcohol (MIPs).

Through the end of October, 619 students have been written up, compared to 491 at that time a year before.

"At the rate we're going, we're projected to have 766 MIPs this year," says Nauts. "Last year, we had 593."

NOON

"Here comes trouble," sings out Jack King, proprietor of Bert & Ernie's Saloon and Eatery, as I stop for lunch. He's standing behind the bar, a glass of beer in each hand, so I ask how much alcohol his luncheon crowd consumes.

"Give me a moment to think about that," he says and heads off to deliver the beers. When he returns, he has an exact count.

The restaurant has 45 tables, he says, and 40 are full. Only four of them have alcohol on the table, and half of those tables are occupied by retirees.

"People are drinking less, but that really doesn't affect us as much because this is a restaurant, not a bar," says King.

"In the past, someone might have two drinks with lunch," he adds. "Now it's usually one."

1:00 P.M.

Two aides and one teacher are finishing feeding lunch to one student and beginning the afternoon special education class at Loy Elementary School.

The six students, ages 6 to 11, are severely and profoundly cognitively delayed, which is the new buzzword for mentally retarded. One sits at a high chair, howling, another in an easy chair rocking, and the other four surround a teacher who is trying to help them pick out a picture of a tree in her textbook.

There are 1,327 special education students in Great Falls, with disabilities ranging from speech defects to severe retardation.

Although the Centers for Disease Control in Atlanta have said that mothers' drinking during pregnancy is the leading cause of mental retardation, only a few children in our school district have been formally diagnosed with Fetal Alcohol Syndrome (FAS).

"I suspect the problem is with the diagnosis," says Gail Cleveland, who is in charge of special education programs. "It requires mothers to admit that they've been drinking during pregnancy," she explains. "So they deny it, and the physicians don't press the issue."

1:30 P.M.

I stop by our local hospital, Benefis Healthcare, but admissions records don't show the cases in which alcohol contributed to illnesses such as cirrhosis of the liver, heart problems, premature births, or accidental injuries.

But the hospital does have a sophisticated program for treating alcoholism, the Addiction Treatment Center, and a group session is winding down in a small conference room with a one-way-glass window that allows counselors to keep track of the half-dozen patients. Benefis has a couple of padded rooms for patients seriously out of control, but today they're empty.

In fact, there's no one in the detoxification program or receiving inpatient care. Normally, there are three to five patients in detox and a couple more receiving inpatient treatment, says Dirk Gibson, the hospital's addictions abuse coordinator.

Nine patients are spending the day in the hospital for counseling, but go home at night, and another forty-four adults and fifteen adolescents are receiving outpatient treatment for alcoholism.

There are also thirty-two people ordered by the courts to attend DUI classes at the hospital.

"We aren't the only ones offering these classes," Gibson adds. "There are probably sixty people in DUI school at any given time in Great Falls."

Dr. Dan Nauts, the program's medical director, says Montana's per capita alcohol consumption isn't so high, but it is more concentrated.

"We have a lot of heavy drinkers," he says. "The levels on the breathalyzers far exceed what I was used to in Washington State."

He is used to the problems, but surprised they still remain problems. "If all these problems are so obvious, why haven't we done more to solve them?" he asks.

3:00 P.M.

As schools get out, the Heroes and Neighbors Down at the Schools (HANDS) programs get going across town.

More than 900 elementary school children are enrolled in the program, which is designed to give students a safe learning environment from the end of school until their parents get off work.

"We're trying to provide a program that's better for the child than going home or being out on the streets," says its director, Ann Hagen-Buss, as she sits at a table in the Riverview School and plays a game of sequential numbers with six-year-old Andrew Carter.

Later, a group of fourth and fifth graders join Hagen-Buss at the table. Asked if they are aware of teenaged drinking, all nod.

"My sister's in twelfth grade, and she smokes and drinks," says one of the students.

The U.S. Department of Public Health and Human Services (HHS) reports that 65 percent of Montana's adolescents experiment with alcohol before they reach fourteen and that high school students binge drink (five or more drinks at a single sitting) at twice the rate of adults.

For that reason, Hagen-Buss wants to expand HANDS into the middle schools.

"This would be a place for them to hang out, use the libraries or the computer labs or the sports equipment, or just do some of the activities that interest them," says Hagen-Buss.

"But if they just want to hang out and listen to music, that's better than being out on the streets," she adds.

4:30 P.M.

By now, the Lobby Bar is doing a thriving business, with drinkers shoulder-to-shoulder at the bar.

"We're just here to have a beer and gamble," says Loren Carrier, an out-of-work cook from Tacoma, Washington.

"I've only been here a month, but I hooked up with a woman who did me wrong, and I've been drinking for three weeks now," he says.

At a table near the front window, an off-duty bouncer named Trevor J. Pasha is drinking with a friend and discussing the bar scene they both know.

"I've seen some people get about ten feet tall and belligerent when they drink," he says, "but other people kind of go into a coma and don't talk to anyone. Funny things get funnier and sad things get sadder.

"I've seen some bar fights, but not many injuries," he adds. "Most people are too drunk to do much damage to anyone. When you put those guys out, it's kind of like pouring out a kettle of chicken soup."

Up at the bar, Tara Fatz is preparing a tray of sandwiches and chicken wings to feed anyone who's hungry.

"I always feed them on a Friday night to protect our regulars from getting DUIs," she says. "I'm real proud that we've only had one DUI that I know of in nine years of Friday nights."

4:45 P.M.

With schools out, district administrators get some daily figures on drug and alcohol use in the schools.

There were 183 kids in group sessions, most of them for drug and alcohol dependency problems, and another 84 in individual counseling sessions.

Seven students were written up for illegal possession of alcohol on Friday, according to Tammera Nauts, and one was dismissed from school for using marijuana.

5:15 P.M.

During Happy Hour, I am introduced to Ellis and Ilse McLean, who are sitting at a table in Jaker's Restaurant, dining out and celebrating their 44th wedding anniversary.

"My husband doesn't drink anymore, but I'm having a glass of wine with my dinner," says Ilse with a captivating smile. "Two, in fact."

A native of Germany, she appreciates a good Riesling. And she has pronounced views on teaching young adults to drink responsibly.

"I think young people should learn to drink at home on special occasions," she says. "In Germany, we give children a little glass with water in it so they can join in the toasts. Later, we might add a little wine to their water.

"If children aren't allowed to have something, they automatically want it," she explains. "They should learn to drink responsibly at home."

5:40 *P.M.*

After leaving Jaker's, I check in with the Police Department. In the parking lot, Officer Patrick Brinkman tells me of a call he just handled, a party in a home in which the owners were out of town.

"One of the people said he had permission to be in the house, but we couldn't verify that so we asked them all to leave and we secured the house," says Brinkman. "They were all pretty intoxicated."

That's relatively common for night-shift cops.

"On this particular shift, I would estimate that 70 to 80 percent of our business is alcohol-related, whether it is family disturbances, DUIs, or parties," says Officer Mike Stimac, with whom I'll be riding for the next few hours.

6:55 *P.M.*

There's an early flurry of activity. A middle school student walking up 5th Street North with his friends is shot with a pellet gun by a passing motorist.

Minutes later, another man is wounded slightly a few blocks away, jumps in his own car, gives chase, and gets a license plate number. When officers make an arrest, they find beer in the car, but no indication that either the driver or the alleged shooter had been drinking it.

8:00 *P.M.*

Robinson tells me that during an intensive outpatient alcohol dependency session at Gateway Recovery Center, one of the eleven patients told the group that she finally felt safe and hopeful that her life could change for the better.

8:28 P.M.

Officers are called to 504 42 Ave. SW, where they find William Patrick Bailey bleeding profusely from the head and left eye.

"He and his friend had been drinking all day, and then they got to arguing so I hid all the knives," says his girlfriend, Shawna Odegard. "But the other guy grabbed a carving fork and just kept stabbing and stabbing and stabbing him in the head."

Stimac checks the home for the assailant, finds no one, and begins working on Bailey's wounds. Bailey, sitting in front of a half-empty 18-pack of beer, wants none of it.

"I don't want to press no charges," he declares repeatedly. "I just want to kill that boy."

As medics try to persuade Bailey to go to the emergency room so that he doesn't lose sight in his punctured eye, suddenly another man staggers into the kitchen.

"It's him," screams Odegard. "He's the one who did it."

Stimac brushes me aside and is on the other drunk like a flash, whirling him against the doorjamb, patting him down for weapons, and handcuffing him.

"Are you going to arrest me?" asks the suspect, thirty-one-year-old James L. Roach. "I just flipped out. He made me do it."

Roach bursts into tears as he's led to a squad car for booking on an assault charge.

"This is one of these houses where we come a lot," says Stimac on the way to the hospital. "And it's always alcohol-related."

Later, it turns out that Bailey is a false name, and the stabbing victim is identified as William Patrick Bird.

9:50 P.M.

Two teenagers at a high school prom are charged with MIPs after one of them vomits on the dance floor and officers find an open 18-pack of beer in one of their vehicles.

10:15 P.M.

Two squad cars scramble to the First Avenue Bridge after a caller advises the dispatcher that he saw a woman being chased down the street in front of the Lido Bar, and that she was abducted and thrown in a blue and white pickup truck, which was heading for downtown Great Falls.

No truck matching that description crosses the bridge, and when I checked with a bartender at the Lido, she says she knows nothing of an altercation outside the bar.

11:00 P.M.

Police dispatchers begin receiving calls that vandals have spray-painted homes, cars, and property in a four-block area on the West Side.

More than thirty people are victimized by the vandalism. When an eighteen-year-old man is arrested on Monday morning, he tells police he was intoxicated when he went on the spray-painting spree.

11:10 P.M.

Officer Stimac is still mulling the parting words of a Benefis emergency room technician, who had been complaining about the lack of a drunk tank in the city. As a result, the ER technician said, many drunks who can't be discharged are left occupying hospital beds until they sober up enough to allow them to be safely released.

"A lot of the bigger cities have drunk tanks," says Stimac, turning his squad car off Fox Farm Road onto 10th Avenue South, "but does that condone a drunk's actions?

"There's no incentive to stay sober if you know you've got a warm place to stay for the night and maybe even breakfast when you sleep it off.

"But it is a problem," Stimac adds. "What are we supposed to do with a drunk who really just needs to sleep it off?"

11:15 P.M.

There's a call to a teen drinking party in Prospect Heights. Three officers arrive with their lights off and park their squad cars around the corner from the party.

As they walk down the dark street, two young men—one with an open beer in his hand—leave the house. One officer stays with them and the other two sprint for the house, where the kids are already spreading the alarm.

Officers suspect some of the teens, and probably some of the beer, escaped through a back door. Ultimately, there's not enough evidence to make any arrests.

11:45 P.M.

Four intoxicated males are reportedly fighting in an alley on the lower South Side, but they have left the scene by the time three squad cars get there.

11:55 P.M.

It's another call for a fork stabbing at 504 42 Ave. SW. Officer Stimac can't believe it, but he's rolling fast with lights flashing and siren sounding. There's an ambulance and EMT personnel in a fire truck right behind the squad car.

When he hits the scene, though, it's a different problem: two women brawling in the doorway of the house we had left just a couple hours earlier.

"She got mouthy with me, and I punched her," says one of the combatants.

The other woman asks an officer if he'll give her a lift to Cindy's Bar, just around the corner.

MIDNIGHT

Officer Stimac checks in briefly at the police station. In the first six hours of his shift, he has handled eight calls—and all but one involved alcohol in some way.

"That's about the average I had anticipated," he says, "but the probability of alcohol-related calls increases as we get closer to closing time."

12:15 A.M.

As Stimac checks in at the station to fill out his reports and catch a bite of supper, I figure I'll check out the bar scene, now winding down. Joe's Place, up near the Holiday Village Shopping Mall, is tame by comparison. Several dozen people are drinking, chatting, gambling, but no one is out of control.

"It's been fairly quiet in here tonight," says the bartender, Tom Knutson.

12:30 A.M.

Just down the street, it's a little livelier at the Other Place, another bar. The music is a little louder and the crowd a little bigger. One patron with a point-and-shoot camera wanders through the bar, capturing the action.

"Hey, cut that out," snaps a guy in a baseball cap who has been hugging a woman by the bar. "Man, you're gonna get us both killed."

1:30 A.M.

But the J-Bar-T across from the fairgrounds is packed, and Alibi, a Billings band, is playing some old favorites.

The dance floor is full. One blonde is relatively formal in a low-cut, black velvet dress with a heavy silver necklace and high heels. Another is fashionably informal with her red vest unbuttoned to show her lacy black brassiere and the elaborate tattoos on her chest and shoulders.

Hot off the dance floor, a young man in a white cowboy hat stands beside a woman perched on a barstool. She glances around, then begins unbuttoning his denim shirt and nuzzling his chest. Embarrassed, he flushes and begins to back away.

Beside them, a middle-aged man is asleep, the brim of his black cowboy hat just resting on the bar. Beside his head is his beer bottle.

"We're going to let him sleep until we close," says the barmaid, Laurene Lawson. "Then we'll escort him out of here, make sure he's OK, and get him a cab if he needs one."

With that, the band winds it up for the evening and the lights come on.

On Friday, December 11:

City police handled 18 complaints involving alcohol, including five disturbances, four improper parties, three intoxicated individuals, three pellet gun shootings in which beer was found in the vehicle, one DUI, and one MIP.

County police received three alcohol-related complaints, including two fights and one MIP.

Of thirty-one appearances before Municipal Court, eighteen obviously involved alcohol, according to the City Attorney's office.

Seven students were cited as minors in possession of alcohol. Another 267 students were being counseled for substance abuse problems, mostly relating to alcohol.

Benefis Hospital's Addiction Medicine Center had nine patients in daytime counseling for alcoholism, plus another fifty-nine receiving outpatient care. There were also thirty-two drivers in the hospital's DUI program.

Fourteen people were receiving inpatient treatment for alcoholism at the Rocky Mountain Treatment Center, with another three receiving outpatient counseling.

At Gateway Recovery Center, sixty patients received group or individual counseling for alcohol dependency, including nine from the Department of Corrections or its boot camp.

"There's a point where you have to exercise self-control," says Page Lutes of Bozeman, looking down at the sleeper. "When you can't maintain control, you've lost it. And it takes a lot of control sometimes to maintain it."

Off the dance floor comes a younger couple. They begin to arouse the sleeper. Finally, they get him to his feet and begin to lead him out of the bar.

About halfway to the door, however, he lurches into a young woman and pinches her butt.

Without hesitation, she whirls him around, crouches down, and bites the label off the rear pocket of his jeans. Laughing, she stands with the label between her teeth.

Outside the bar, the sleeping drinker comes to life in the chilly night air. He's Knute from Jordan, Montana, he announces.

As the parking lot begins to clear, I asked Knute if he is going to be driving home. I certainly wouldn't want to be on a highway anywhere near him.

"It's too far to drive home tonight," says the young lady who has been helping Knute out of the J-Bar-T. "So we'll take him to a motel tonight.

"And tomorrow," she adds, "we'll probably start all over again."

BARS IN GREAT FALLS

Another way to look at the river of alcohol that flows through our town is to look at the industry itself, at the number of people who make their living from its sale. "Taverns are a big part of the local economy," said Diane Jovick-Kuntz, who is president of the Downtown Business Association and owner of the Montana Bar on Central Avenue downtown. "The revenue we provide through gaming and alcohol taxes makes up about 18 percent of the city's budget," she said. "Without us, you might not have a police or a fire department."

Alcohol is an industry, and a big one in Montana. Liquor sales alone came to $46.5 million last year, and beer sales topped $100 million. There's no good estimate on the dollar volume of wine sold in the state since the Revenue Department taxes on volume, not sales. "There are a lot of people buying homes, cars, and groceries on this business in Great Falls," said John Hayes of the Cascade County Tavern Association.

In fiscal 1998, the state sold 1,125,678 gallons of distilled spirits, about half of which went into private homes.

Montanans also bought—and presumably consumed—367,600 barrels of beer and 2.7 million liters of wine.

The Montana Bar is just one of 105 drinking establishments in Great Falls. That includes thirty-three beer bars and another seventy-two full-service bars, including fraternal organizations like the Elks, Moose, and Eagles Clubs; the Veterans of Foreign Wars; the officers' club at Malmstrom Air Force Base; the city golf courses; the Dodgers ballpark; and the airport bar.

Overall, about 3,000 people are employed in bars and restaurants, with a payroll close to $19 million, according to Hayes. "When our kids come home from college, they gather in the bar of their home town," said Mark Staples of Helena, legal counsel for the Montana Tavern Association. "Friends get together in the local bar. Taverns have sustained themselves since territorial days as part of the culture of our state."

BOOZE IN MONTANA

The state health department reported recently that only 2.3 percent of the Montanans it surveyed had never taken a drink. In the past year, the survey found that 78 percent of the respondents have consumed alcohol. And in the past month, more than 58 percent of those surveyed said they have used alcohol.

That puts Montana somewhat above the national average. Sixteen percent of Americans say they have never used alcohol. Montana has about 1,800 bars and restaurants, which employ roughly 20,000 people. "And they are also the first place anyone goes for a charitable contribution in their town," Staples said. "We're a part of their society, sponsoring a softball team or a charity dance of some other fund-raiser," he explained. "The retail outlets have profits that go out of state faster than they clear your credit card, but Montana bars are owned by Montanans, and that money circulates through our local economies."

State tavern owners want it known, however, that they promote drinking only in moderation. Paul Horning of the Half Time Sports Bar is one of several certified trainers teaching periodic courses to instruct bartenders and servers in state law and industry self-regulation. Called the TIPS program, it helps bartenders recognize when a patron has had too much to drink and instructs him or her in how to slow that drinking down—or cut it off entirely—without creating too much of a hassle.

"My biggest fear is to have someone who is intoxicated get on the road and get into an accident," said Jovick-Kuntz, whose father bought the Montana Bar in 1975. "I tell my staff that if there's a problem, it can come back to harm the bar and, in an age in which everyone sues everyone else, it can harm them personally as well. If there's any question," she added, "I tell them not to serve that person."

Still, Jovick-Kuntz wonders how far a bar's responsibility goes. "There's a big problem with self-responsibility that I don't understand," she said. "People make a conscious decision to come in and take a drink," she said, "but if they take too many, then it's our fault somehow."

DRINKING IN AMERICA

Actually, per capita consumption of alcohol has been declining in recent years, after decades of growth. In the years preceding World War II, alcohol use increased rapidly, then stabilized between 1947 and 1961. It increased again for the next two decades, then began to decline. In 1993, the average American over fourteen years old drank 2.17 gallons of alcohol a year, the lowest average since 1963.

Here's a listing of the top 10 states (including the District of Columbia) for alcohol consumption and the average amount of pure alcohol consumed by each individual in the state fourteen years of age or older.

1. New Hampshire 4.13
2. Nevada 4.00
3. Washington, DC 3.89
4. Alaska 2.88
5. Wisconsin 2.69
6. Delaware 2.66
7. Colorado 2.63
8. Florida 2.58
9. Montana 2.55
10. Louisiana 2.52

U.S. average 2.17

Source: U.S. Department of Health and Human Services

That makes alcohol a $100 billion business in America. In 1997, the nation's 476,000 licensed retailers sold nearly six billion barrels of beer, while 503 million gallons of wine were sold along with 328 million gallons of hard liquor, according to the 1998 BIMS Industry Analysis. That translates into sales of $53.2 billion for beer, $34.1 billion for spirits, and $13 billion for wine.

But drinking that much creates an even greater number of problems, according to HHS. Last November, it estimated the cost of alcohol abuse at $148 billion, and said governments typically pick up about half the bill for social, medical, and criminal consequences of excess drinking.

Which led me to one further question: What's the state's role in all of this? The answer: *Supportive.* Montana makes money on the sale of alcohol, and putting social Band-Aids on the injuries creates state jobs. Over the past decade, state government has made more than $200 million off the sale of alcohol in Montana. Ostensibly, the state's role has been to regulate alcohol, but the profit motive is never far behind.

"I question that we are seriously in the business of controlling alcohol consumption anymore," said state Sen. Eve Franklin, D-Great Falls. "Our current focus is revenue." That dichotomy can be seen in a pair of back-to-back statements in the 1997 annual financial report of the Revenue Department's Liquor Enterprise Fund:

"**Our Function:** As a control state, Montana believes that moderation can best be achieved by neither promoting nor encouraging the consumption of alcohol, but instead controlling it. ...

"**Benefits to Montanans:** Liquor sales provide a major source of revenue to the state of Montana, relieving taxpayers of a significant tax burden each year."

In fact, the state made $21.3 million off alcohol sales in 1977 and turned over about $6.2 million of it to local governments. Revenue from liquor taxes is distributed each year to cities, towns, and counties to be used for alcohol control, prevention, detection, prosecution, and rehabilitation projects. In 1997, for example, Great Falls received $243,723 for such programs, while Cascade was given $3,137 and Belt got $2,295. Cascade County received $21,500.

Franklin said that could be perceived as a fair balance. "If a third of that money goes to treatment and if you accept that Montana is in the alcohol business as a source of revenue, then we have probably reached some sort of balance," she said. "The larger question is whether the state should be in the alcohol business at all, and what would be the economic consequences if we were to get out of it," said Franklin. Last legislative session, there was a push to get the state out of the liquor business, but it failed—in part because lawmakers were reluctant to lose the state's middleman profit on selling alcohol.

How does the state of Montana make its money off alcohol?

In 1997, the state bought 4.2 million liters of liquor, marked the price up by 40 percent, and sold them at a profit of $4.7 million.

Then it collected an excise tax on that liquor to raise $6.2 million.

It collected another $1.7 million from the liquor licensing fees for its 102 agency stores, as well as $3.9 million for licensing other outlets, including Montana's 1,800 taverns and restaurants.

The state's beer tax collected $3.3 million and its wine tax added another $1.5 million.

Total take: $21.3 million.

POWERFUL LOBBY

But tavern owners also opposed the measure, said Dave Lewis, the governor's budget director. "Our argument was that we don't have to be in the distribution business if we can tax it, but the liquor industry wouldn't buy it," said Lewis. "The liquor industry liked the fact that the state was willing to carry its inventory," he said.

And Lewis said tavern owners, backed by both the alcohol and gambling industries, carry tremendous political clout these days. "Tavern owners and the gambling industry are the 1990s equivalent of the Anaconda Copper Company in lobbying the Legislature," he said. "They're doing nothing illegal, but they're so well organized and well financed that they can control this Legislature better than anyone else. The power of the tavern owners is astonishing," Lewis added. "I admire them for what they're able to accomplish, but it can be a little scary."

Montana legislators did, however, decide to sell off the former state stores in 1996, frequently to the same employees who had operated them for the state. That nearly halved the state liquor division's operating expenses from a little more than $3 million in 1996 to $1.76 million in 1997. Salaries dropped from $1.4 million to $688,000, and $182,500 in building rent virtually disappeared off the state's books.

STATE REGULATION

But Montana bucked one national trend. Virtually every other state that privatized its liquor outlets found increased consumption. Not Montana. Liquor sales dropped about 16 percent across the state from 1996 to 1997. In Great Falls, three state stores sold $4.3 million worth of alcohol in 1996, but sales dropped to $3.6 million in 1997 when they were in private hands.

The likely reason is that alcohol did not become more available under private hands because operating hours for the liquor outlets remained set by state law. "This is one of the vestiges of our state's blue laws, enacted 70 years ago as a way of controlling social behavior," said Franklin. "But today, this responsibility has been replaced by a revenue motive."

The liquor industry, however, sees state regulation as beneficial. "The structure of Montana's alcohol sector—which some decry as anachronistic—has in fact worked to provide jobs and business for an amazingly varied and broad spectrum," said Mark Staples, general counsel for the Montana Tavern Association.

"There are no 'ma and pa' businesses left these days, except taverns," he said, "and that's because the alcohol business is one of the few where vertical integration is not allowed. A manufacturer can't be a wholesaler or a retailer, a wholesaler can't be a manufacturer or a retailer, and a retailer can't be a manufacturer or a wholesaler," he explained. "No one can overwhelm and dominate everything else by buying up everything in sight."

In fact, state regulation has forced the tavern industry to retain an old-time charm, said Staples. "Part of the reason tourists come is because Montana still has a broad-based, down-home alcohol system instead of the monolithic and faceless system in other states," he said. "I think it's a very quiet but significant feature of Montana's society."

FEBRUARY

Now I needed someone who showed the effects of alcohol. Early in February, Dirk Gibson, supervisor of the Addiction Treatment Center at Benefis Healthcare, introduced me to Bill Broderson, an alcoholic who would turn into the unlikeliest of friends.

He was a skinny man with a lined, yellow face, big brown eyes, and hands that constantly shook. He looked to be in his 70s, but he was only 49. Broderson told me he woke up the other night in the detox unit of Benefis Healthcare, watching a shadow on the wall that looked like a gorilla. "It was a fat guy running around the ward naked in the middle of the night," he explained later. "So I got a nurse, and they locked him down."

Alcohol turned Broderson's life into a nightmare. But he's not alone. More than 120,000 Montanans range from problem drinkers to full-blown alcoholics, according to the state health department. Some have managed to quit drinking, but about 75,000 of them remain in need of treatment, it said.

That seems like a surprising number of people with drinking problems, but some of them are closet drunks who seem to function normally—as did Anne, who led a double life in Great Falls for years. Her story follows later.

It's not only the alcoholics who are affected by this disease. Family, friends, and co-workers all pay a price. It's estimated that one alcoholic has a direct impact on at least four other lives. Tammera Nauts know that cycle well. She's the addictions specialist for the Great Falls School

District, but she's also a recovering alcoholic who paid a big price for one drunken evening many years ago. Her story also follows later.

DISEASE OF ALCOHOLISM

The American Medical Association (AMA) defines alcoholism as a chronic, progressive disease, which appears to be genetic because it can usually be traced up a family tree. It starts innocently with a couple of drinks, but they affect people very differently. Some feel fuzzy and removed, while others experience almost a sense of euphoria. Those who get the rush are predisposed to alcoholism, a disease that can have devastating physical, spiritual, psychological, emotional, and occupational consequences. Ultimately, this disease ends in denial and fear—along with death, if it goes untreated.

Right now, Broderson faces a life or death choice, if indeed it is his choice. He had lost 25 pounds and was down to 137 as he sat in the Benefis detox unit. His hands were shaking, his liver was shot, and his eyes were as round and glassy as a calf's. "He is not trying to drink himself to death," said Gibson. "He just can't stop."

In fact, Broderson has been through the state's chemical dependency centers in Galen and Butte more than fifty times. He can't count the number of other thirty-day treatment programs to which he has been committed. Alcoholism is considered a medical illness, but Broderson has no job or insurance. And treatment isn't cheap. Benefis writes off the cost of Broderson's detoxification treatment, which runs $400 to $500 a day. Most of the Montana Chemical Dependency Center funding comes from a state tax on alcohol, but an average visit can still cost a person $3,000 to $4,000.

Mandated Treatment

Broderson's medical costs have been substantial, but he isn't alone. Caregivers talk of one alcoholic in Billings who has been through forty-seven treatment programs in the past six years.

"We're mandated by statute not to turn anyone away due to an inability to pay," said Roland Mena, chief of the state's Chemical Dependency Bureau in Helena. "Unfortunately, a small minority of our clients makes this a lifestyle—they learn to use the system. But every once in a while, something clicks and we can turn one of our chronic alcoholics around," he added, "and that makes it all worthwhile."

There are reasons for Broderson's uncontrollable drinking. His childhood was stressful, and alcoholism runs in his family. His parents divorced when he was six, he said, and he ended up in the Deaconess Children's Home in Helena.

"When I came home on one of my visits, there was a stranger sitting in the kitchen," he said. "He turned out to be Frank, my new step-dad." Frank turned out to be Broderson's ticket home, though. "After she [his mother] got married again, she got me out of there," Broderson said. "But they were mostly in the bars, so I was by myself."

At fourteen, Broderson started drinking. He dropped out of school, lied about it, and spent as much time as he could on the golf course with a twelve-pack of beer tucked away in his cart.

"There was always alcohol in his home," said state Rep. Hal Harper, D-Helena, Broderson's best friend during junior high. "I think he just got sucked down the tube." By his twenties, Broderson was having blackouts—"I woke up in Idaho once and had no idea in hell how I got there"—but he didn't think he had a problem. "We fed him whenever he showed up, but we never gave him money," said Harper. "Companionship only goes so far, though, and when he needed another drink, he'd take off."

Through the years, Broderson has made many attempts to quit drinking, he said. At one point, he had been sober for a year, and things were looking up. He had been admitted to MSU-Northern's School of Nursing, had been given a grant to cover his tuition, and had worked a deal to paint rooms in exchange for food and lodging.

Then a friend invited him out and bought him a soft drink, but drank a beer in front of him. "I thought if he could have a beer, I could have one, too," Broderson said. "But after one beer, I wanted another. In the course of a week, I had sold my Volvo, my fishing gear, and most of my possessions."

Having blown his chance at a nursing career, he has been living downtown on food stamps, doing odd jobs, and scraping by, until a few weeks ago when he tried to commit suicide. "I just gave up," he said. "I'm not contributing anything. I'm just taking up space."

Even as he sat in the hospital, though, Broderson was craving whiskey. "I need a shot," he said softly. "There's a guy on my shoulder who keeps saying no, but the guy in red on my other shoulder, he has a louder voice or something."

It's frustrating, said Gibson, the unit supervisor, not to be able to break though with treatment for chronic alcoholics like Broderson. "We'll provide him with the best medical treatment in the most respectful way we can, all without any charge, and we'll continue providing that treatment each time he comes back. Our problem with him has been the follow-through on his treatment," he added. "The way he's going, he's drinking himself to death."

Harper sees it as a human tragedy. "If he could have gone down a different road, who knows what he could have done. He was smart, popular with the girls because he was so cute. He could have done pretty much anything he put his mind to. But now," Harper added, "it's just amazing he's still alive."

That raised a lot of questions in my mind. First, what was it that made him different? How do the Brodersons of the world live if they can't work? And what would become of him? I told Broderson I would like to check back with him every month that year. He thought about it, shrugged, and said, "Why not?"

A THREE-DOLLAR BILL

Between five and ten percent of all Americans are either alcoholics like Broderson or are dependent on alcohol. Between 60 and 70 percent of them work full-time, go to school, raise families.

Why do they drink? There is no single cause of alcoholism, but scientists are getting closer to an answer. "Drunks beget drunkards," said Plutarch, the Greek historian, nearly 2,000 years ago. Now doctors are discovering the truth in that statement.

Some people are more prone to alcoholism than others, and it can be traced in families. In Denmark, scientists found that the sons of alcoholics were about four times more likely to be alcoholic than sons of nonalcoholics. "Being raised by either nonalcoholic adoptive parents or biological parents did not affect this increased risk," said Drs. Robert Anthenelli and Marc Schuckit in the *American Society of Addiction Medicine* magazine.

There's no specific gene that's responsible, but researchers have found differences in the levels of a couple of key chemicals in the brain.

One is dopamine, a substance that creates natural highs as part of the brain's reward circuit. Its primary function is to stimulate people to do the things that are good for their survival. Thus, people experience a euphoria accompanying sex, good food, and exercise.

But for some people, alcohol tricks the reward system into producing dopamine, giving them a sense of euphoria that comes with being drunk. Ultimately, alcohol takes over the reward process, dominating the production of dopamine to the exclusion of healthy activities. But the reward also begins to taper off over time, forcing people to drink more to get the same sense of well-being.

In all people, alcohol addles our thinking by interfering with the neurotransmitters in the brain's cognitive center. But alcoholics have a greater problem. With the cognitive center unable to override pleasure center demands, it's more difficult for an alcoholic to listen to reason and stop drinking.

"If I have one beer, I have to have sixty," said Broderson. "Especially if you're buying."

One theory is that people predisposed toward alcoholism are born with abnormally low dopamine levels, leaving them lacking the joys that others experience naturally. "I always felt like a three-dollar bill in a world of one-dollar bills," said Rod Robinson, director of the Gateway Recovery Center and a recovering alcoholic.

But that first drink changes everything for such people. "I knew I was home," said Mike Misener, another recovering alcoholic in Great Falls. "For the first time in my life, I felt like I fit right in."

Studies show that dopamine levels drop when alcoholics stop drinking, making it particularly difficult for them to swear off booze. Most alcoholics also find themselves with low levels of serotonin, the mechanism that tells most people when to stop drinking. Serotonin is produced as a response to a food or an activity, telling the brain to stop eating potato chips, for example. But alcohol doesn't seem to trigger the serotonin buildup in some people.

One alcoholic remembers spending Christmas Eve unable to leave a bar, even though he wanted to be home with his family on that special night. "After that first drink, I just couldn't force myself to leave," he said.

For that reason, most treatment of alcoholism requires abstinence. Doctors have discovered that alcoholics have different brain waves than others, with a markedly smaller and slower P-300 wave, which seems to be related to impulsivity. When they found the same abnormality in the young children of alcoholics, they proved that it wasn't caused by prolonged exposure to alcohol. Now they speculate that it could be used as a diagnostic tool to predict a predisposition to alcoholism.

Another possible diagnostic is the presence of an enzyme known as MAO (monoamoxidate) in the blood. Type 1 alcoholics, who have the milder form of the disease, have MAO levels very similar to non-alcoholics. But type 2 alcoholics, who begin drinking heavily as teens and who are most severely affected by it, have significantly lower levels of MAO in their blood. This is sometimes called early-onset alcoholism.

People's bodies also break down alcohol differently. Women, for example, get higher than men on the same amount of alcohol, in part because they generally weigh less. But it's also because their stomach enzymes aren't as effective in breaking alcohol down, allowing more of it to enter their bloodstreams.

About half of all Asians seem to lack an enzyme that breaks down alcohol in the liver. "After imbibing alcohol, affected individuals develop higher blood acetaldehyde levels with associated flushing, tachycardia, and a burning sensation in the stomach," said Drs. Anthenelli and Schuckit. "Not surprisingly Asians missing this isoenzyme are less likely than others to drink heavily and appear to have a lower rate of alcoholism."

Alcoholism, as an illness, is very similar to diabetes, said Robinson. Alcoholism involves an inability to process alcohol, while diabetes is an inability to process sugar. Like alcoholism, there are two types of diabetes: early-onset diabetes, which requires daily shots of insulin, and adult diabetes, which is less severe.

Both are chronic and progressive, meaning that they will continue to worsen without treatment. "With both alcoholism and diabetes, if I don't adjust my diet and lifestyle, they will kill me," Robinson said.

But genetic differences aren't the only cause of alcoholism. "It is likely there are multiple roads into the heightened alcohol risk," said Drs. Anthenelli and Schuckit. "Some individuals develop their alcoholism in part through very high levels of impulsivity... but others increase their risk for alcoholism through a low level of response to alcohol," which leads them to drink more to get the same high as their friends.

"It is not likely that a single gene explains the alcoholism risk, but that it is multiple genes interacting with the environment," the doctors said.

A DISEASE OF THE BRAIN

If alcoholism is a genetic illness, you would think that scientists could replicate the problems in lab animals. And, in fact, they have. Scientists are learning a lot about alcoholism by watching lab animals get drunk.

"Researchers have shown that after an animal's acclimation to alcohol's adverse taste or smell, the drug can become a reinforcing, self-administered substance for several species, including monkeys, rats, and mice," said the U.S. Department of Health and Human Services in its ninth special report to Congress in 1997.

For example, scientists now can prove that the disease is genetic. They can breed rats that crave alcohol, are indifferent to it, or hate it. Researchers set up a system in which rats were required to press a lever to get a drink, and they found the alcohol-craving rats were ten times more likely to press the button and take a drink.

The results, HHS said, showed "An association between a genetic predisposition for high alcohol intake and greater motivation to work for alcohol."

The reason appears to be significantly different levels of two key chemicals—dopamine and serotonin—in the rats' brains. Dopamine is a chemical produced in the brain that scientists believe enhances pleasure.

In some rats, alcohol doesn't seem to affect normal dopamine levels. But alcohol-craving rats seem to start with a dopamine deficit, then use alcohol to stimulate the chemical.

Ultimately, the brain depends on alcohol for production of dopamine, making withdrawal doubly difficult.

Serotonin is another chemical produced in the brain in reaction to a food, drink, or activity. It tells us that we have had enough pizza or soft drinks, for example. In some animals, however, alcohol doesn't appear to trigger the serotonin's "had enough" effect. "Alcohol-preferring rodent lines exhibit marked differences in brain serotonin content compared with lines selected for alcohol nonpreference or aversion," said the health department.

Scientists also found that lab animals appear to drink to relieve anxiety.

Rats that have consumed alcohol are more likely than sober rats to venture into elevated mazes or carry on normal social interactions in unfamiliar and brightly lit environments.

They have also found other factors in animal drinking:

- "Fight-stressed submissive mice" exhibit increased alcohol consumption during challenges to the social hierarchy.
- Rats drink more if they have subordinate social status or early social isolation.
- And in rhesus monkeys, the emotional stress of social separation during adolescence increases drinking patterns during adulthood.

"Both adverse rearing environments and prolonged exposure to social stress or social isolation are potential determinants of abnormal drinking," the health department reported. "Such findings in animals are important for understanding environmental factors, such as family structure and child-rearing practices, that may enhance the risk of developing drinking problems or alcohol dependence in humans," it said.

As further proof that a craving for alcohol can be chemically induced, scientists have found they can use chemicals to block drinking in lab animals. One chemical, for example, blocks alcohol from boosting dopamine levels. Low dosages of fluphenazine stop rats from drinking alcohol-laced water, but not pure water, according to the American Society of Addiction Medicine (ASAM).

Another drug has been found to have the same effect on some animals and humans. "The limited data so far suggest that Naltrexone acts to reduce the pleasure that a dose of alcohol produces, so a transient lapse to drinking is less likely to progress to a complete relapse," it said.

Researchers also were curious about alcohol withdrawal. They cut off booze to alcohol-dependent animals and watched dopamine levels in their brains drop. Then they gave the animals a chance to get drunk again. "The animals were allowed to self-administer ethanol (alcohol) during this withdrawal, and they self-administered just enough ethanol to return dopamine levels back to normal," according to ASAM.

Termed the "alcohol deprivation effect," it said rodents, monkeys, and humans were inclined to relapse after periods without alcohol. "Even more intriguing, this alcohol deprivation effect can be blocked by chronic administration of the anti-relapse drug acamprosate," said the addiction medicine society.

Acamprosate has been used in France for years and has just been licensed for use in Great Britain and the United States (in 2004) under the trade name Campral. "Although its mechanism of action is not yet fully clarified, acamprosate appears to, in part, act at a modulatory site on the NMDA receptor [in the brain]," the society said. "This may explain its perceived clinical action to reduce craving for alcohol and so improve the long-term outcome of abstinence."

Alcohol typically blocks the N-methyl D-aspartate (NMDA) receptor from releasing neurotransmitters that create anxiety. Without treatment, withdrawal from alcohol causes increased anxiety levels.

Such experiments teach us how alcohol affects humans, said Gibson of Benefis Healthcare. "One of the important benefits of animal experiments is that they remove the moral question from alcoholism. They show that alcoholism is a medical illness. Therefore, people suffering from this disease should be treated with compassion and respect."

SHORT-TERM RELIEF

But Robinson, a friend and colleague of Gibson's, believes those suffering from the medical process are among a small minority of alcoholics.

"I firmly believe that 80 percent of what I deal with daily is learned behavior," said Robinson, sitting in an office off the lobby of the Gateway Recovery Center.

He noted research showing that 59 percent of recovering alcoholics blamed their relapses on boredom, anger, loneliness, or depression; 40 percent said they were having problems with relationships; and 35 percent told counselors that they were stressed by financial problems.

"Stress, or dysfunctional stress, is one of the main reasons for use," said Robinson. "People want to alter their mood, and alcohol can give you a short-term euphoria. If you can't make a car payment, you can get some short-term relief from that anxiety by buying a bottle of booze," he added. "Of course, when you wake up the next morning, your problem may be three times worse."

And in addition to genetics, alcoholism is learned behavior in alcoholic families, said Robinson. "My father never stacked up to what he believed he should have," said Robinson. "He became an alcoholic and passed the same expectations on to me—and I did the same. Some of us were fully alcoholic before we ever took our first drink," he added. "All that we were missing was the substance."

Anne, a grandmother who has been diagnosed as psychologically addicted to alcohol, illustrates a less visible alcoholic. A member of Alcoholics Anonymous, she asked me not to use her last name. I respected her reason, but it was one of the few times we agreed to withhold an identity.

I had known her for several years without ever suspecting she had a problem with alcohol. She was outgoing, efficient, and unflappable with the public, even when she was handling four phone calls and a balky computer. Her drinking problem stemmed from her childhood, but she hid it too easily for too long.

"I was an only child with an alcoholic father who never showed his emotional side at home," she said. "He and my mother had nothing going, so she smothered me; my father ignored me," she said. "I was getting mixed messages, and never felt like I fit in."

Drinking was a way of fitting in for Anne, but that feeling dried up the next morning when she dried out. "Many alcoholics drink because they're lonely," said Anne. "I call it the hole-in-the-soul disease because there's a void in your life that you're always trying to fill."

Anne said she spent her life trying to please others while ignoring her own needs. "Many of our feelings are fear-based," she said. "Fear turned outward becomes anger. Fear turned inward becomes depression.

"But I was in denial about my fear," she said, "and that made me a terrible wife. Neither my husband nor I ever knew who I was because I was changing so fast trying to become what I thought my husband wanted." It didn't work. After three suicide attempts came a divorce. After two DUIs came a recovery program.

But even a psychological addiction is hard to kick.

"I spent a lot of my early recovery in pain," she said. "I'd want a drink so bad. I'd look at the clock and say, 'God, let me stay sober for the next five minutes.' A lot of days, I got through five minutes at a time."

It was also important for her to examine the psychological causes for this illness. "I spent a lot of time trying to peel away my excuses and my defenses," Anne said. "It was like peeling an onion. But when I finally got to the bottom, 98 percent of the time I realized that I was driven by fear that I was inadequate. And I'd bet that holds true for most alcoholics."

RATES OF ALCOHOLISM

Rates of alcoholism are very difficult to prove because it's impossible to estimate the extent of alcoholism with any degree of accuracy.

The best guess is that about 10 percent of all Americans—and 15 percent of all Montanans—are alcoholics or booze abusers. About 14 million Americans, or nearly 10 percent of the adult population, can be considered alcohol dependent or alcoholic, according to Health and Human Services. The National Institute on Alcohol Abuse and Alcoholism (NIAAA) put its estimate a little higher, at 17 million people.

In Montana, however, the percentages are even higher. After a survey of adults in 5,500 households, the Montana Addiction and Mental Disorders Division of the state health department reported that 15.8 percent of the state's residents have lifetime alcohol or other drug disorders.

And it said that 8.6 percent of the population had experienced an alcohol or other drug disorder within the previous eighteen months.

That means that more than 120,000 Montanans are problem drinkers (dependent on alcohol) or full-blown alcoholics, while about 75,000 of them remain in need of treatment, according to the state health department.

"I suspect Montana has a higher rate of alcoholism because we have higher rates of alcohol consumption," said Marcia Armstrong, addictions treatment officer with the state health department. The U.S. Department of Health says Montanans have the ninth highest per capita level of alcohol consumption in the nation.

"YOU'VE HAD ENOUGH"

At 8:30 A.M., Blue was drinking coffee in the Lobby Bar, but he slurred his words and staggered as he walked to the bathroom.

"No more for you," bar manager Tara Fatz scolded him.

A downtown bar, she said, is like a family. People drop in all day because they're lonely, and she takes care of her regular customers. If they drink too much, she'll cut them off.

Tara Fatz pours an early morning drink at the Lobby Bar in Great Falls.

"We have chameleon drinks," said Fatz. "We give them a shot of water with a splash of Coke, and some get real drunk on it. Or I'll talk to people and tell them to quit drinking because they'll get a DUI or their wives will tear their hair out."

People don't need to get drunk to have fun in a bar, she added.

"There was one old guy in here yesterday, and I got on him real bad," she said. "I told him he couldn't drink because he would gamble and lose all his money, and he's on a fixed income. So he didn't drink and he didn't gamble," she said. "Instead he went out and bought me a porcelain hummingbird. What it's really about is you have to care about people."

Blue tugged at her elbow. "Can I just get a drink?" he asked. "Nope," she said.

Suddenly, the back door opened and Chuck the Cowboy strode in. At seventy-six, he's a sturdy, sun-bronzed character under a black hat.

"Blue, you old coyote," he yelled. "You get into some bad meat?"

"We've been friends for forty-five years," Blue explained. "He can't beat me at pinochle, but we get along just great."

"Nobody bothers Blue or they mess with me," agreed Chuck, wrapping his hand around the first beer of the morning.

"I know I can bang on his door any day of the week, tell him I need a place to sleep, and I'll be on his couch in a heartbeat," Chuck added.

"Regulars of the Lobby Bar take care of each other," agreed Fatz. She takes some of her patrons out hunting so they'll have food, she said; frozen packets of deer meat then become available when someone is having trouble living from paycheck to paycheck.

"Many of our customers are old, retired cowboys who can't read or write," she said. "I do all their paperwork for them, make their medical appointments, find homes for them. I'm a mom to all of them 'cuz most of them don't have any other family."

Almost on cue, Bobbie wandered in for his morning cup of coffee. Middle-aged, he lives on Social Security disability checks. He suffered brain damage, he explained, from oxygen deprivation at birth.

"I can't read or write," said Bobbie softly. "Tara helps me fill in the forms and do the paperwork and cash my checks. She does a lot for us all."

Back at the bar, Blue worked up his courage to make one last plea for alcohol, but Fatz shook her head. "You've had enough," announced Chuck, suddenly standing up. "And I'm taking you home." So Chuck the Cowboy grabbed the still-protesting Blue by the elbow and marched him out the back door and into the bright morning sunlight.

DEFINING ALCOHOLISM

Are these men alcoholics? It's hard to tell, but complicating the whole issue is the definition of alcoholism, which can differ among organizations.

The World Health Organization (WHO) uses one set of criteria, while the federal government uses another devised by the American Psychiatric Association (APA). Called the Diagnostic and Statistical Manual of Mental Disorders (DSM), the APA criteria defines an alcohol dependence syndrome based on a cluster of recognizable symptoms, such as impaired control over alcohol intake, tolerance for alcohol, and continued drinking despite personal, family, or occupational problems.

Other organizations, like Alcoholics Anonymous and the National Institute on Drug Abuse (NIDA), have developed simplified questionnaires to let people know of their own problems.

But a researcher with the Veterans Affairs Hospital in Seattle believes alcoholism can be tied directly to consumption. Kristin Bush, a daughter of Phil and Karen Korell of Great Falls, argued in an article last year in the *Journal of Internal Medicine* that a diagnosis of alcoholism can be based on how often people drank during the past year, how many drinks they had on a given day, and how frequently they put away six or more drinks in a row.

"We considered patients to be heavy drinkers if they drank more than fourteen drinks a week or five or more drinks on one occasion in the past or a typical month, based on the trilevel alcohol consumption interview," she wrote. "These criteria were based on evidence that men who drink above these levels have increased psychosocial or other adverse consequences of drinking," she concluded.

Others have a still simpler definition. "If you continue drinking despite recurring problems in your life," said Robinson, "you're a problem drinker."

SURVIVING ALCOHOLISM—BUT AT A PRICE

Tammera Nauts was just such a problem drinker. Her drinking started in her early teens when her family would party with friends after racing sailboats. She would sneak a beer or pour some liquor in a pop can. "I always felt like I was a little different," she said. "I never fit in. But when I drank, it filled a void and made me feel like I was a part of the crowd."

By the time she was in high school, she and her friends were drinking before school. "We'd park a couple of blocks from school and throw back a couple of beers before we went to class," she said.

That led to marijuana and amphetamines before she turned her life around—for the first time. "At eighteen, I got into Transcendental Meditation, became a vegetarian, didn't drink or smoke, didn't even use sugar," she said. "It was the epitome of a lifestyle I wish I could get back to today."

Three years later, she got a job in a restaurant with a great wine cellar and began drinking again. She also got heavily involved with cocaine.

Married at twenty, a mother at twenty-one, she soon went back to school and got a divorce.

"I knew there was something wrong—I was spiritually bankrupt, my body was breaking down, and none of my relationships were working out—but I never attributed it to alcohol," she said. "Talk about denial."

Then she began learning more about alcoholism while several of her drinking/using friends began disappearing into treatment. And the alcoholic mother of an alcoholic friend killed herself. That also killed Nauts's denial.

"That was the first thing that really opened my eyes to the power of alcoholism," she said. "So my friend and I began to look at our own drinking. Often, we'd do this over martinis or a bottle of wine," she added.

Discovery was painful. "I began to realize that alcohol held my family together," said Nauts. "Our connection to each other was that we drank together. I knew then that alcohol was a problem for me, but I refused to stop," she said. "Alcohol was my connection with my family, with all my friends. Losing that connection was really scary."

With each friend in recovery, she grew angrier at their betrayal of the booze-enhanced lifestyle. "I remember that I was sitting at my kitchen table with a bottle of bourbon, watching the sun go down and knowing that I had some hard choices to make," she said. "I could either find new friends and continue using, or I could stay with my friends and go through treatment. So I really kicked my alcohol and drug habit and was pulled screaming into recovery because I didn't want to lose my friends."

She has been in recovery for twelve years now and is a certified chemical dependency counselor, helping others avoid the problems she has experienced. Nauts considers herself lucky to have survived alcoholism, but she also paid a price:

Physically:
"The first time I got really drunk, I was fourteen," she said. "I drank eight shots of whiskey in half an hour, blacked out, and was raped.

"I didn't know what to do," she said, wiping a tear from her eye. "There wasn't much information available, and I didn't tell anyone. There was also the additional shame of having put myself in that position—I felt I was partly responsible for the rape.

"For the next four years, I used alcohol, pot, and speed regularly." In the latter stages of her disease, Nauts said, she lost her athletic body tone and experienced drug-induced anorexia.

Spiritually:
"I was spiritually bankrupt and looking outside myself for answers, both in substances and in alternative religions," she said.

Psychologically:
"I definitely suffered from depression and low self-esteem," she said.

Emotionally:
"I lost my husband and almost lost my daughter," she said. "I got to the point in my alcohol and cocaine use that I didn't want to be a parent or a wife anymore. I just wanted to go to school and party afterward. Nothing more."

Occupationally:
"I knew if I could hold my job together, I wouldn't be touched," she said. "Basically, I was just protecting my paycheck."

In retrospect, Nauts feels that conquering her illness has been good for her.

"In a lot of ways, I feel blessed to have had these experiences and to have survived them," she said. "Knowing that I could survive something so devastating and that I chose life makes me feel like I can do anything I set my mind to and that I can create any kind of a life I want to. It's very empowering, although I know there's a Higher Power who is lovingly supporting me," Nauts added. "I couldn't do this on my own—I'm just not that powerful."

MARCH

Establishing early on that alcoholism is a medical disease turned out to be more important than I knew. That freed people to talk with me. If they were ill, it took the shame away.

I noticed that immediately on the Fort Belknap Indian Reservation about 200 miles north of Great Falls, where I went to interview a specialist on fetal alcohol syndrome. Maza Weya, also known as Jill Plumage, turned out to be both an instructor and her own worst textbook example.

"When they put my [newborn] baby on my breast, I knew something was wrong, so I lifted my head to look at him," she told me, dabbing her eyes as she spoke. "And I could smell the alcohol on his breath," she said. "My baby was born drunk."

After years of drinking everything she could get her hands on, Maza Weya managed some years later to get sober. Her son wasn't so lucky, however. Scarred in the womb by alcohol abuse, he is abnormally small and suffers from permanent brain damage.

It's called fetal alcohol syndrome (FAS). Treating and caring for its victims is estimated to cost more, on the national level, than $2.5 billion each year. "Alcohol continues to be a bigger threat to larger numbers of children than any illicit drug known to man, including cocaine," said Ann Streissguth of the University of Washington's fetal alcohol unit. "In the 10 years since the Surgeon General recommended not drinking during pregnancy, there have been at least 70,000 children born in the United States with full FAS."

There's also a less severe form of the syndrome called fetal alcohol effects (FAE) that may affect twice as many babies. Some doctors also believe drinking by pregnant mothers may be a cause of attention deficit disorder, the hyperactivity condition that has been swelling public school special education classes.

Since 1979, the number of pregnant mothers who drink heavily has increased dramatically, according to HHS. Physical damage is possible for any child whose mother drinks during pregnancy, but counselors at Benefis Healthcare, the two treatment centers in Great Falls, and the public school district have a patient load that's predominantly Native American. "That's because Native [American] people are more comfortable with FAS and speaking about alcoholism, but when you leave the reservation, it's still taboo and there's a lot of denial," said Carlene Red Dog, former FAS coordinator on the Fort Peck Indian Reservation.

Fetal alcohol syndrome may affect three dozen babies in Montana each year—at a lifetime cost estimated at $1.4 million apiece. Since I planned to do only one segment of this series on Native Americans, I had hoped to interview a white mother and child, but every person I could locate turned out to be Native American.

Doctors can't make an FAS diagnosis without proof that the mother had been drinking, so they sometimes have a tough time attributing these disorders to alcohol.

But it was glaringly obvious to Maza Weya, an Assiniboine Indian whose name is translated as "Iron Woman." Alcohol had ruled her life since she first drank herself into a blackout at fifteen. "My twin brother excelled at everything," she said, "so I excelled at being an alcoholic."

Her drinking worsened after a marriage ended, and she left two children behind when she became infatuated with a man she met in treatment. "I ended up by going back to his small community in North Dakota with him," she said. "He was from a prominent white family, and I was the only Indian in town.

"There, I became a raging, raving alcoholic." She also became pregnant, and they fought and drank for eight months. Then, she said, she picked a fight as an opportunity to get drunk, and her baby's father was killed in a car wreck that night.

"I went into complete shock," she said. "One of the doctors gave me a big bottle of Librium, and I got a ticket home to Fort Belknap. I went to the basement of my parents' home and spent the next month eating Librium and drinking anything I could get my hands on."

After her son was born, Maza Weya didn't stop drinking. In fact, she said, doctors recommended she drink two or three beers a day in order to have better breast milk—and she took that as permission to keep drinking heavily. "But I don't blame anyone for that recommendation," she said. "Doctors didn't know as much about the effects of alcohol then."

After five months, her family intervened and took her baby to raise. She kept on drinking—everything from whiskey to Lysol spray, she said—and ended up on skid rows, in detox units, and in jails.

She remembers spending nights in the old Weiss Hotel in downtown Great Falls and still has a patched bed sheet to remind her of her fall from grace. "When they took my son, I told myself that I didn't give him birth with dignity, but I would be there for him later," she said. "And I couldn't do that either."

The end came when she received legal notification that her son had been adopted by her sister, and she hadn't been there for the adoption. "My last drink wasn't a can of beer or a shot of whiskey or a glass of wine," she said. "I found a bottle of perfume, and I drank it." Then she decided that she had to reform for herself, her children, and her family. Working through some 12-step sobriety programs, she began to turn her life around. She came back to the reservation to become a drug and alcohol coordinator in the school system and began to realize the damage she had done.

"My son is an exceptional person, but I noticed that in school he was just a little shadow against the wall," she said. "When he needed attention, he became the clown and everyone would protect him because he was so small."

Her son stands five feet tall and weighs about 95 pounds, she said. "Finally, I had to tell him that I had been drinking most of the time I was carrying him and that it affected him," said Maza Weya. "And he asked why I didn't love him enough that I wouldn't drink while he was inside me. He asked why I had made him so small when he wanted to be tall and strong. He asked if I had given him up because he wasn't perfect, because he was damaged.

"We were both crying," she said, "but all I could do was sit there and take it." Finally, she said, she told her son that she had to give him up to save his life, a concept he still struggles with. "I'm not proud of what I've done, but I'm not ashamed of it either," said Maza Weya. "I think God put me in this role for a purpose."

These days, Maza Weya is counseling women on the Fort Belknap Reservation about the dangers of drinking while pregnant, using her own life story as an example; she has a grant from the University of New Mexico. It's an uphill battle because it's a worsening problem—and not just for Native Americans.

FAS STATISTICS

The Centers for Disease Control in Atlanta (CDC) estimate that 1,200 infants are born each year suffering from fetal alcohol syndrome, which has been labeled the leading cause of mental retardation.

No amount of alcohol is safe for a pregnant woman to drink, but a recent study by researchers at the University of Washington found that 52 percent of the women surveyed had used alcohol at some time during their pregnancies, and another 13 percent had consumed five or more drinks on one occasion—a phenomenon known as binge drinking—during their pregnancies.

A team from Children's Hospital in Charleston, South Carolina, found that one-third of all children exposed to alcohol before birth will show physical damage. The most severe manifestations come from binge drinking, and it has been increasing sharply. In a study of 114,000 women in forty-six states, CDC found four times as many pregnant binge drinkers in 1995 as it had found in 1991.

"Binge drinking is becoming a more popular pattern of alcohol use among pregnant women," it noted. And it said that the number of diagnosed fetal alcohol syndrome children was six times greater in 1993 than it had been in 1979.

The best estimate now is that about two children per 1,000 births are afflicted with full fetal alcohol syndrome, while twice that many more have fetal alcohol effects. But the rates appear to be higher in Montana, said Cathy McCann, genetics counselor for Shodair Children's Hospital in Helena. "I would bet that more than 50 percent of the patients that we see are for the evaluation of fetal alcohol," she said.

Although the state health department doesn't keep track of fetal alcohol conditions, McCann estimated the FAS rate at three children per thousand and said it probably affects 30 to 40 newborns a year in Montana.

Analyzing her own hospital's data over a four-year period, 1995 though 1998, she discovered 59 FAS diagnoses, 356 FAE diagnoses, and 324 cases in which fetal alcohol exposure was suspected but not proven. "I think Montana is a little higher than the rest of the nation, but I would not attribute that to a higher proportion of Native Americans," she said. "I think drinking is a pastime that occurs in stressful, isolated situations.

"When you look at the fact that we are geographically and socially isolated, when you look at where we stand with wages and the numbers of second jobs, when you consider the relatively high cost of living compared to the salaries paid, I think all of these are stressors. I think there are more reasons here that contribute to drinking," she added. "Beyond [drinking], there isn't that much else to do."

FAS RELATED CHALLENGES

Alcohol affects different babies differently, and doctors have no explanation why. In addition, drinking at specific stages of pregnancy affects different phases of development.

"The face and head of a fetus are formed during the first three weeks," said McCann. "How many women know they are pregnant during that first three weeks? A lot of other major malformations can occur someplace in the first three- to eight-week period, including problems with the heart and development of the cranium. The central nervous system, including the brain, is developing during the first four-to-twenty-week period, so when the hardware of the brain is being laid down, there is a chance of its being laid down wrong due to early alcohol abuse," McCann said.

There are some specific conditions associated with fetal alcohol exposure, however.

One is small size. FAS babies are frequently born prematurely and grow more slowly. Skulls may be smaller than usual, eyes smaller, and the upper lip and nose smaller, as well. Many are retarded. More than half of the FAS patients in one recent study had an IQ of less than seventy.

And one of the symptoms of alcohol abuse is attention deficit disorder (ADD). "Attention deficits characterize 75 to 80 percent of the patients with FAS, contributing to the difficulty with classroom learning during the school years and to major problems with employment during adolescence and adulthood," said Ann Streissguth of the University of Washington. "A large proportion of patients with FAS/FAE have, in the past, become the responsibility of the community to raise and shelter because of the high rate of maternal death, termination of maternal rights, and abandonment of these children," she said.

Her colleague, Dr. Robin LaDue, a clinical psychologist at the University of Washington's fetal alcohol unit, told a seminar in Great Falls that approximately 69 percent of the mothers of FAS children die before the child's fourth birthday due to complications related to alcohol use.

FAS children are likely to fall behind in school at an early age and demonstrate increasing difficulty in handling abstract concepts like English and math. The University of Washington studied 661 fetal alcohol syndrome patients and found 70 percent had attention deficit disorders and nearly half had failed at least one grade in school.

More than half of the patients suffered from depression, and 80 percent of those older than twenty-one years were unable to live independently. They were frequently in trouble—35 percent had been jailed at some point—and 45 percent of them had demonstrated inappropriate sexual behavior.

More than a third of the fetal alcohol syndrome patients were themselves alcohol dependent, it said.

THE EGG LADY

Back on the Fort Belknap Indian Reservation, Maza Weya works to lessen the damage of alcohol. She's known as "the egg lady" because when she talks to school students, she pours grain alcohol on a raw egg at the beginning of her lecture. By the time she has finished, the egg is hardboiled.

"Fetal alcohol syndrome is 100 percent preventable," she tells them, "and it's 100 percent irreversible once you pour alcohol over the egg in your womb." She works to keep pregnant women sober, and she works with the children who have been victimized by alcohol abuse.

In all of their faces, she sees her own son. "I go to bed every night thinking about what I've done," she said, "and I'll go to my grave thinking about it. I'm not God and I wouldn't change my life," she said, "but I would change what I did to my son if I could."

I came back from Belknap emotionally drained. I don't believe I've ever done a tougher interview. Maza Weya broke into tears often, and I felt like it.

What can anyone do to protect the unborn child of a mother who is drinking? The answers include a range from education to counseling, treatment, and jail.

On the Fort Peck Indian Reservation, tribal officials are working on plans for involuntary treatment. "It's not against the law for women to drink so we can't incarcerate them," said Gary James Melbourne, director of the Fort Peck Tribal Health Department. "But it's a very serious ethical and moral issue."

Melbourne added that approximately eighty children and young adults on the reservation have been diagnosed with fetal alcohol syndrome, at a cost for custodial care estimated between $20,000 and $24,000 a year apiece. Prevention and treatment are the answer, he said.

Melbourne said the DUI Task Force, which he chairs, is drafting tribal legislation to provide involuntary treatment for pregnant juveniles at the Spotted Wood Treatment Center. And he said similar legislation for adults will be proposed as soon as an acceptable treatment center is in place. "If you don't have anything in code to protect a fetus, you have nothing to charge a drinking mother with," he explained. "But I don't want to go into the next millennium with these types of statistics," he added. "I want to turn this around, but it will require us to provide a treatment center first."

Montana state officials can recommend strategies to prevent fetal alcohol abuse, but there's nothing in state law to force a pregnant mother to stop drinking. State law does allow a judge to order treatment of an alcoholic who harms or threatens to harm another, but state health officials said there has been no precedent yet allowing them to intervene on behalf of an unborn baby.

South Dakota was the first state in the nation to pass legislation allowing judges to order drinking mothers-to-be committed to centers for treatment. "They should throw these women in jail and make them get four or five month's treatment, no question about it," said Dr. Lucy Reifel, a physician on the Rosebud Sioux Indian Reservation who adopted a child with fetal alcohol syndrome.

One law allows judges to confine pregnant women in detox centers. Another allows them to require up to nine months of involuntary treatment. And a third makes drinking while pregnant a form of child abuse. Harsher measures have been imposed in other places. On the Fort Belknap Indian Reservation, drinking while pregnant constitutes child abuse, which is a jailable offense, said Maza Weya.

In North Dakota, several drinking mothers-to-be were charged with assaulting their unborn children and jailed, but "their convictions were overturned by state and federal courts," said Dr. LaDue.

In a policy statement, the American Society of Addiction Medicine said jail isn't the answer. "The imposition of criminal penalties solely because a person suffers from an illness is inappropriate and counterproductive. Criminal prosecution of chemically dependent women will have the overall result of deterring such women from seeking prenatal care and chemical dependency treatment, thus increasing rather than preventing harm to children and to society as a whole," ASAM said.

Instead, it recommended programs to educate women about the dangers of alcohol; counselors could assist them in staying sober.

"Several reservations have fetal alcohol syndrome coordinators who can give women the education and support that they need," said Carlene Red Dog, who held that position on the Fort Peck Indian Reservation before moving to Bakersfield, California, to work with the Kern County Health Department. "If a woman is afraid of going to jail," added Red Dog, "she's going to stay out of the way of everyone who could be of help to her."

FIND THE PAUSE BUTTON

When I got back from Fort Belknap, I checked in with Broderson.

After getting out of the detox unit, he faces a life of poverty, loads of time to kill, and the everlasting lure of liquor. Doctors at Benefis Healthcare recommended in February that Broderson spend a month at the Montana Chemical Dependency Center in Butte, followed by eight or nine months in a halfway house to thoroughly dry him out.

But Broderson had been there more times than he can remember, and he was having none of it.

"Why bother?" he asked. "Most people go there [MCDC] because they're court-ordered. They do their twenty-eight days, get out, and get drunk again."

Instead, Broderson checked out of the hospital and went back to the house he shares with friends. "It's a nonstop party there until they all go to sleep," he said. There Broderson exists, rent-free, on $125 a month in food stamps. The woman who owns the house gets a disability check that goes for food, and the residents pool their resources to buy booze. "We

do the Frisco circle," he said. "When anyone gets some money, we all
pitch in."

Broderson left the Army years ago with a dishonorable discharge, so
there are no GI benefits. And the Social Security Administration is being
hard-nosed about providing him with disability benefits. "We understand
you have alcohol problems," it wrote him last month, "but we find you
are still able to do unskilled types of work." Broderson is skeptical about
that. "With my reputation," he said, "people who don't know me well
won't hire me."

With no money and equally empty days, Broderson spends a lot of
time walking around town and thinking. One of his regular stops has
become visiting me at the *Tribune*, which can try the tolerance of my
colleagues because he looks pretty rough around the edges and goes for
days, sometimes *many* days, without bathing. I generally take him
outside where we can sit and talk without creating an interruption.

As we talk, he often leans over and begins to speak directly into a
felt-tipped pen in my shirt pocket, as though it's a microphone. It's an
amusing joke, but I have a nagging concern that it may also reflect a
growing paranoia resulting from the damage to his brain by alcohol.
"I've got so much shit going on in my head," he said recently, sipping an
orange juice in the Lobby Bar. "Sometimes it builds up so much that I
want to take a drink just to hit the pause button."

In fact, he said, he would have added some vodka to the orange
juice, but the bartender, Tara Fatz, won't sell him hard liquor. In fact, she
and I have an agreement not to *enable* his alcoholism. It's a strange role
for Fatz, cutting him off after so many years of allowing him to drink
freely. While belated, it shows a commendable responsibility.

Other friends buy him booze, however. "I had a road trip with one
friend the other day and we hit every bar between here and Augusta," he
said. "And then we hit every one on the way back." But that's self-

destructive, and Broderson knows it. "I'd really like to stop drinking," he said. "My physical and mental health is shot."

I can see signs of that. He has been prescribed the anti-depressant drug, Paxil, which he can't afford. Sometimes I'll buy it for him, but I won't just give him the money to pay for it.

He has begun working with New Directions, a Great Falls-based component of the Golden Triangle Community Mental Health program, on an outpatient basis. There doctors promised to work with him if he would promise not to try to take his life again. He promised, although he sometimes has second thoughts when he considers the limited options that confront him at age forty-nine. "I wish I could find the pause button for this life, rewind it, and start it all over again," he said. "Or maybe just stop it altogether."

ATTENTION DEFICIT DISORDER

Since the symptoms are almost identical, I was also curious to know if there was a link between fetal alcohol effect and attention deficit disorder, the malady afflicting an ever-greater number of the nation's schoolchildren.

I found that although about 11 percent of our public school students are disabled, very few of them have been officially diagnosed with fetal alcohol syndrome. There are 1,334 special education students in Great Falls, but only eight with FAS. However, the American Medical Association has labeled alcohol abuse the nation's leading cause of mental retardation.

Gail Cleveland, who was in charge of the Great Falls School District's special education program, suspects that fetal alcohol syndrome too frequently goes undiagnosed. "It requires mothers to admit that they've been drinking during pregnancy," she said. "So they deny it, and the physicians don't press the issue."

"Many physicians don't want to stigmatize these children by labeling them," agreed Carole Kenner, professor of nursing at the University of Cincinnati, "and others do not want to anger affluent clients whose alcohol consumption is considered legal and socially acceptable." So some doctors believe that fetal alcohol children are merely diagnosed with attention deficit disorder, a non-pejorative condition that occurs frequently as a result of alcohol abuse.

"If you look at FAS behavior—hyperactivity, impulsivity, poor judgment, and inability to learn from past experience—it's the same criteria for diagnosing ADD," said Dr. LaDue, the clinical psychologist in Seattle who works with the fetal alcohol syndrome unit at the University of Washington.

"A lot of us feel that ADD is greatly over-diagnosed," said LaDue. One major difference, she noted, is that fetal alcohol syndrome requires a doctor to prove, or a mother to admit, alcohol use during pregnancy, whereas attention deficit disorder focuses solely on the symptoms.

In Great Falls, there is no specific category for ADD children. Instead there are three categories—emotionally disturbed, learning disabled, and other health impaired—into which attention deficit disorder children are regularly placed.

In the past nine years, the number of children in those categories has increased by 42 percent, from 513 in 1989-90 to 727 in 1997-98. The number of special education students increased from 1,058 to 1,337 in 1998, while the cost of educating them increased from $3.5 million to $4.8 million. Classroom teachers currently provide medication, generally Ritalin, to 577 students, said Cleveland.

Dr. Robert Hackford, a behavioral pediatrician at the Great Falls Clinic who deals frequently with attention deficit disordered children, said it's tough to diagnose the effects of fetal alcohol exposure.

"On a rare occasion, I might make that diagnosis," he said, "but my main approach is to try to identify the problems relating to treatment.

Specifically diagnosing fetal alcohol syndrome is less important for the treatment of the child than it is for the education of the mother. If a child has signs of attention deficit disorder, the child should be treated," he added, "and I would do that whether there was a diagnosis of FAS or not." But Hackford and other doctors also noted that attention deficit disorder may stem from causes other than prenatal exposure to alcohol.

"A child may come to us with behaviors very similar to alcohol-related problems, but there are other causes," said Cathy McCann, genetics counselor with Shodair Hospital in Helena. "A lot of kids come to us with a history of a dysfunctional family and potential abuse," she said. "The question then becomes whether the illness is caused by alcohol abuse or the home life that would normally have a kid bouncing off the wall. ADD can run in the family, but it also can have an environmental component," McCann added. "It can occur independently or it can occur in conjunction with alcohol."

Over the past decade, health officials have seen a dramatic increase in drinking, particularly binge drinking, among pregnant women. But they also say there's no point in making the mothers feel guilty. "It's important to realize that we can't be blaming moms who made a choice that was the best they could make at that particular time," said McCann. "Most moms who admit alcohol use during pregnancy have been under some extraordinary social and emotional stressors that can drive a person to drink."

LIVING WITH FAS

Drinking mothers can do tremendous damage, as I found when I talked with Melissa Clark, a twenty-two-year-old victim of fetal alcohol syndrome.

She was home alone in Great Falls when a man rang the doorbell. Although she didn't know him, she let him in. He walked into her bedroom and started to undress. Then he told her to take her clothes off too, and she did. When it was all over, she called her foster mother, Johnelle Howanach, who called the police. But officers wrote it off as consensual sex.

Not so, insisted Howanach. Clark's brain was damaged as a result of her birth mother drinking during her pregnancy, and she didn't know that having sex with a stranger is wrong. "People with fetal alcohol syndrome just don't have those boundaries," said Marilyn Kind, a friend who works with the developmentally disabled.

"They are easily victimized," agreed Bill Hayne of Lewis and Clark College in Lewiston, Idaho. "They can be standing next to someone at the bus stop, and they'll assume that person is a friend and will go with them. They are eager to please, very friendly, and it leads to a lack of boundaries," he added. "They don't know the difference between a friend and a stranger because they can't remember."

Learning boundaries is one of Melissa Clark's current tasks. "I have learned to say no to a lot of things," she said, "but I need someone to tell me when someone is not safe. I don't want to go out with anyone unless my mom is there because guys can take advantage of you big time real quick." After Clark told me her story, I was troubled. It illustrated the problems that FAS victims face, but I didn't want to print something that could come back to harm her. And although she was of legal age to grant an interview, I didn't want to take advantage of her.

So I wrote up the interview as though it was a news story, gave it to Clark, and asked her to discuss it with Howanach and Kind. The next day, we all sat in her living room, and Clark told me they had decided to go public with the story because it was true and because other people had to realize how severely alcohol could damage a baby's brain.

Clark also noticed her dilemma. She wants desperately to be independent, but she also knows that's not likely. "I jump in to do something, but I don't know what I'm doing," she said, "and it always turns out to be a disaster."

One of the first children in Montana to be diagnosed with FAS, Clark combines an impulsive nature with impaired judgment. And she gets tremendously frustrated when she can't do what she wants, when she can't do what others seem to do so easily. "I'm tired of people telling me what to do or putting words in my mouth," she told Howanach explosively during a recent interview. "I have my own opinions, and people aren't going to change my mind by putting words in my mouth," she snapped.

But under Howanach's gentle questioning, Clark admitted she lies at times. "A lot of these kids are tired of being twelve, fifteen, twenty steps behind anyone else and they'll lie to make themselves look better," explained Hayne.

Clark admitted she has stolen money. "If there's not a definite physical connection to somebody, they think it's OK to take it," said Hayne "It's not stealing. It's like me taking a newspaper off a chair in an airport—it isn't mine, but I assume it was left behind so it's OK to take it."

Clark makes up stories when she can't remember exactly what happened. "They forget because alcohol stirs things up in the brain so they'll make something up," said Hayne. And Clark worries about what will happen to her when Howanach is no longer around to guide and protect her.

For all her problems and worries, however, Clark is an amazing success story. When she was born Nov. 5, 1976, she was two months premature and weighed less than three pounds, two ounces. She remained in the hospital for thirty-nine days. According to her medical records, "Patient wasn't sent home earlier because the mother drinks a lot and I was scared to send it home."

On Feb. 3, 1977, Clark's doctor noted: "This patient was a markedly premature child, Mother was an alcoholic, drank a lot. This may have something to do with the child's condition at the present."

At a year and a half, Clark was diagnosed with what was then called fetal maternal syndrome. Social workers placed the child with Howanach in 1982, but said it wasn't likely she would be able to absorb an education. "She had an attention span of no more than a minute," said Howanach. "She was a truly hyperactive person—she was just swinging from the chandeliers."

But after years of hard work, Clark graduated from C.M. Russell High School and reads at about a sixth-grade level, according to her foster mom. "That was hard," said Clark. "My reaction time was different. I was in a special education class, but it seemed that all the kids were two or three steps ahead of me. They always seemed to have the answers when I didn't."

Some of Clark's progress was because her foster mom worked with her, using simpler teaching tools. FAS children do better with art, music, and tactile sensations than with abstract concepts like English and math.

And Howanach emphasizes structure, going over each step of a simple process: how to cook spaghetti, answer a phone, or do laundry. "I'd be in more than trouble without that structure," said Clark. "I'd be walking the streets or in the JDC [Juvenile Detention Center] or doing drugs if that support system wasn't there for me."

Stress is particularly hard for Clark to handle, as she found out when she got a job as a dishwasher. "I couldn't keep up with my job, and I broke two or three dishes," she said. "I was hanging in there for a while, but I kept getting behinder and behinder and finally I just crash-bombed."

Clark has also made contact with her birth mother in telephone conversations that were painful to both mother and daughter. "It was a lot more than I could handle," said Clark. "When she started to talk to me about her drinking, I went over the edge and had to give myself space to deal with my emotions. And she was crying so hard I couldn't really understand her."

Now Clark has started her own business—she walks dogs for a small fee. And she uses the money to further what has become her life mission: to educate the public about fetal alcohol syndrome.

Her message? "Having fetal alcohol syndrome makes you feel like an animal all penned up in a big cage with a chain around your neck," said Clark. "But when the cage door is opened and the chain drops off your neck, you're afraid to go too far from the cage. At least it's safe in there."

APRIL

Fifteen percent of all Montanans drink too much, according to state figures. Most of them have parents, spouses, and children, many of whom bear the brunt of the drinking.

In April, we asked our readers to tell us what it was like to live in an alcoholic household. Part of my curiosity was the kind of lifestyle that families were enduring, but it also was to determine how prevalent this problem was. To make it easier for people to share their stories, we promised not to use their last names or any small towns that would make them easy to identify.

I got scores of phone calls from people who wanted to get this burden off their chests. Here are excerpts from some of their responses.

"One night, I was out partying with friends at a dance and, for no reason, got really angry with a friend. I began to chew her out right there in public, but suddenly I started to listen to myself and realized to my horror that I sounded just like my mother. After that, it was a three-drink limit and then I was through. I didn't want to be exhibiting any more of that less-than-lovely behavior."

—Pam, northern Montana

"My big thing was protecting my children and never letting anyone know what went on in our house. That just increased our isolation. I was doing all the wrong things for all the right reasons."

—Maggie, Great Falls

"My parents were abusive to each other, physically and verbally. When he was in that condition, you never knew what he would do. I remember once him throwing a plate at my mother while she was holding the baby—it was just a miracle neither was hurt.

"My dad hurt my mom to where she was hospitalized and the police took him to jail. Three of us went to one foster home and two to another. The foster parents were related so we got to see each other. I think we were there about four months. I was eight at the time."

—Karen, north central Montana

"I had to maintain this appearance of normal life because the townspeople thought my husband was great, so I went to counseling, driving furiously 100 miles to another town after lunch and back home before the kids got out of school. Finally the psychologist said I should get a lawyer and force him into treatment.

"So I did. Through the lawyer, I forced him to go to California for treatment, but he wouldn't stay there so we came home."

—Marian, north central Montana

"I remember sitting on the front porch every holiday, waiting for daddy to come home from work and crying because he never came until too late. So many holidays, we never got to family festivities because he was always drunk."

—Beth, Great Falls

"My dad worked in a sawmill, and he used to tell me that lumberjacks worked hard and played hard. I remember he was driving home from work drunk once and went in a ditch. I told him if he could get it out, I'd drive the truck home.

"So I did it. I was about six. I remember turning the key on and off every time I needed to slow down to make a corner. Finally, I woke him up to help me make the last turn into our driveway."

—Darwin, Great Falls

"One evening as my dad was kicking and hitting my mom at the dinner table, I got up on a chair and poured a bottle of milk on my dad's head. I ran and hid in the alley. I knew that when he found me, the brush on my bottom would hurt, but that was OK. I had saved my mom, and that felt good.

"I was seven years old when I learned that taking care of others was more important than taking care of myself."

—Delores, Great Falls

"I grew up in a small town where everyone drank, so I never thought it was unusual for us kids to be sitting in the car in front of the bar, reading our comic books. But then we moved to town, and I noticed that the neighbors didn't have police cars in front of their homes, and they didn't have knock-down, drag-out fights like my parents, either.

"Now I don't want to fight like my parents, so when I feel a fight coming, my trick is to run into the bathroom, shut the door, turn the water on, and cry until I get a lump in my throat so big I can barely breathe."

—Matilda, Great Falls

"Everyone on my mom's side and probably all from my dad's side were alcoholics.

"The worst part was the house parties. A lot of people you didn't know were there, cussing, fighting, arguing. They'd go on all night long and all the next day. Us kids would just stay in the bedroom and play. Sometimes they would come into our bedrooms and call us names or hit us—and there was some sexual abuse, too.

"I'm an alcoholic myself now and I have house parties too, but not when my kids are around. I have three kids, and they stay with other family members or friends when I'm partying."

—Michelle, northern Montana

"I was called just about every name in the book and never knew why. It could happen just about every time of the day. There weren't too many good times.

"My stepfather would come into the house drunk. We had a new bathroom, and he would fill the bathtub up, sit on the commode, and put his feet in the bathtub with his cowboy boots still on. Then he would shout at me to come in and help him get his boots off and back on again. It was so stupid. He would just disrupt the whole household."

—Dee, Great Falls

"My father worked on the railroad, but when he'd come home, he would sit down at the kitchen table and drink blackberry brandy all weekend. He'd beat the bloody hell out of my mother, and my brother and I got a lot of beatings, too.

"I'm one of eight brothers and sisters. All of us are alcoholics, but six are in recovery."

—Diane, Great Falls

"My father was an alcoholic and my brother became one. He was the perfect child until I was born, then he let me have that role and he began acting out.

"My father was gone all week and drank all weekend, but he had a low tolerance and he was usually passed out by 7:00 P.M., which meant that he was unavailable to us on weekend nights when my brother might have ball games.

"My mother stayed with him twenty-six years, but died long before he did. That tells me that sometimes the enabler becomes sicker than the actual alcoholic."

—Candace, Great Falls

"Anger may be the main characteristic of alcoholism. They're hurt and angry about their childhood. They numb their pain with alcohol and then act out their anger or pain. I think many were abused children in one way or another.

"My husband was an abusive alcoholic, and I left our marriage because of it. Now I feel a tremendous peace as I allow myself to grow."

—Laura, Great Falls

"Sometimes I would grab the kids up, go out a window, and take off because my husband was in a tirade and I was afraid to remain in that house. One time, we went and spent some time at a lake. Another time we went to another town and stayed in a hotel for a few days. But I never told the children why. My mother told me never to talk against your husband, and it was too painful for me to discuss the reasons with my children. So that was damaging to them, not knowing why we had done these abnormal things."

—Marian, north central Montana

"Recess was always so hard because I didn't have boots or gloves, even in the thirty-below winters. My sisters showed some sense—they used to go steal gloves from the lost and found. I didn't think it was right to steal, but it sure wasn't right to go without either."

—Jennifer, Great Falls

"I've got two older brothers, two younger sisters, a younger brother, two uncles, two aunts, and both my parents who are all alcoholics. I'm basically the only sober one in the family.

"The reason is that I was raised out of the home, and I firmly believe that the social setting has a lot to do with alcoholism."

—John, Great Falls

"I married young and thought that I could change my husband by sheer will power, by having a baby, or by moving to another state. But he drank a lot, he had a lot of anger, and he was abusive. Within a few years, I believed I was going to die unless I got help."

—Lonnie, Great Falls

"I've repeated all the patterns. I married an alcoholic and didn't see it. I suffered all kinds of physical and emotional abuse. I divorced my husband because he would discipline my child by slapping her in the face. I guess, technically, that I married my own dad.

"You repeat that pattern because it's the only thing you ever know. It's absolute insanity, but you end up living with men who are alcoholics and who beat the crap out of you. You feel like a piece of crap because no one loves you. No one knows how gut wrenching it is, even now as an adult."

—Jennifer, Great Falls

"Alcoholics have so much guilt about what they are doing that they need to spill it out on others. For ten years, I kept hearing that if I had done things better, my father wouldn't need to drink. Finally, I began to believe it. I had this big button called self-doubt. All he had to do was push it and I was in another world, questioning my own behavior and off his back. And he felt that justified his going out and getting drunk again."

—Elizabeth, Great Falls

"Professionals need a stress break from the intense work they do, so I thought it was great for Fred to stop after work and relax a bit with the guys from the office. Little by little, the phone began to ring: 'I'll be a little late.' And little by little, no phone call and no Fred. When he did come home, you bet I was by the door waiting with the famous words: 'How could you? You promised me. . . .'

"The broken promises kept me both alive and crazy. I had to do something more so he'd stay home. What was wrong with me?

"When I'd ask, he'd tell me it was all my fault: I didn't like his friends, or I wasn't any fun any more.

"So I'd correct the spoken problems, and as soon as I did, a new list was added. So I tried harder. I became Supermom, Superwoman, anything to prove I was capable and worthwhile."

—Delores, Great Falls

"My mother was drunk every Christmas Eve through Christmas dinner throughout the entire childhood of my children.

"My kids didn't want my mom to come. They liked my father, who was a happy drunk and would just go to sleep.

"But my mother had a vitriolic temper and could be difficult to deal with. She would start in with each child and just berate every one of them.

"Finally, after 35 years of this, I said, 'Mom, you don't even like yourself, do you?' And she said, 'No, I don't.' She was taking out her self-hate on my children.

"My mother was flirtatious and had a few affairs through her years. I think her self-loathing came because she could not control her behavior or her jealousy."

—Pam, northern Montana

"While I was emotionally unavailable, my two daughters were next door being sexually abused by a grandfather in coveralls who was looking after them.

"I was too uninvolved to see the danger signs in my own kids for a year. I never realized why my own daughter was afraid to sleep alone at night."

—Jerry, Great Falls

"My son suppressed so much that he has driven himself inward. He's a real introvert. His personality changed a great deal because he had to suppress this part of his life that was so painful. My daughter was holding in so much anger that sometimes she exploded. And my youngest daughter was so dreamlike. They were all trying to escape a painful reality. And yet we looked so all-American from the outside. We were like an apple, beautiful on the surface but rotten inside."

—Marian, north central Montana

"I'm seventy-one now. I grew up with an alcoholic father. I'm still finding out what damage it did to me—and that's remarkable.

"College was the first time I allowed myself to realize that I had no confidence in myself. About fifteen years ago, I went back to school and took some psychology courses. I kept getting A after A after A, but I didn't

feel anything. Finally my professor said to me, 'You have to realize that you really can do this.' And that was a real shock to me."

—Virginia, Great Falls

"My dad has pretty much quit drinking, and we've made reconciliation. I'm elated at being able to experience life from the other side.

"The tradition is breaking in our family—and I give the credit to God. I also like the 12-step program because many people aren't spiritual, but they are willing to acknowledge that they need a Higher Power than themselves to rely on."

—Darwin, Great Falls

FAMILY SECRETS

There are a couple of main threads that run through the excerpts above. Therapists see four main characteristics in the families of alcoholics:

- **Rigidity**. Family members are thrust into inflexible roles as the alcoholic fails in his or her duties. And as the alcoholic becomes increasingly unpredictable, other family members have to assume those duties consistently. This rigid structure blocks emotional growth of the children.
- **Silence**. Members of an alcoholic family are ashamed of the drinking and don't talk with others about it. But they don't talk with other family members either about what's happening or about how they feel about it. By not discussing their feelings, they frequently are unable to identify them.
- **Isolation**. The family is a closed unit, protecting a dirty secret. It creates a myth that no one outside of the family would understand and that no one can be trusted. As the family isolates itself from others,

each member isolates himself or herself from other members—and ultimately from himself or herself.

- **Denial.** By refusing to admit a problem, the alcoholic and his or her family don't have to confront a need for change. As the family becomes more dysfunctional, the denial grows progressively stronger. Family members also deny feelings that result from the problems they deny.

"In one way or another, all of the roles that are played in the alcoholic family enable the alcoholic to continue to drink and act in a way that is both self-destructive and harmful to other members of the family," said Wayne Kritsberg, author of *The Adult Children of Alcoholics Syndrome.*

In addition to talking with our readers on the phone, I also accepted an invitation to attend a meeting of Al-Anon, an invitation that, unbeknownst to me, could have sabotaged this entire project.

The leader of the group, who had invited me, introduced me as a *Tribune* reporter. I added that I was there to learn, but that I would respect the tradition of anonymity and not use their last names. Then I pulled out a pen and notebook and began taking notes through the session.

As I walked out the door, I had a committee waiting for me. You aren't going to quote what we said in there, they asked me. Of course I am, I said. So they explained that another tradition of Al-Anon requires that what is said in a meeting room remain in that meeting room. So why was I even invited, I asked.

In the end, I explained that I would be willing to respect that tradition, as well, but that I felt the group had wasted several hours of my time. How could they make that up to me, I asked.

Ultimately, the group agreed they would meet with me that afternoon at a picnic bench in a local park and we would recreate the morning session away from the meeting room. As a journalist, I felt it was perfectly within my rights to print what I had been invited to witness, but I didn't want to inflict a new injury on people who had already been through so much. So I agreed to spend a couple more hours with them.

"Alcoholism is one of the few diseases I know of that consumes the entire family," said Kathy, whose has seen three generations of her family scarred by alcohol. That's why Kathy has been active with Al-Anon, a self-help group for families of alcoholics. Like Alcoholics Anonymous, Al-Anon enforces a strict code of anonymity.

There are 11 Al-Anon meetings each week in Great Falls where people can share experiences, seek advice, and offer support. Attendance may range from half a dozen to twenty-five or more members. Ages range from teens to grandparents. While many of the members are women trying to deal with alcoholic husbands, men also attend regularly.

One of the main messages is to quit being an *enabler*, or one who unintentionally helps the alcoholic continue drinking. Take care of yourself, members are told, but demand that the alcoholic take care of herself or himself.

"We all believed that we were being helpful by doing everything for an alcoholic, but they would be better off without that help," said Elizabeth, a local Al-Anon member who joined us in the park. "It's a false sense of caring if you always step in to fix things up for another person."

Members are encouraged to identify suppressed emotions, accept responsibility for the way they feel, and communicate freely. "It wasn't until I went to Al-Anon that I realized how crazy I had been acting," said Lonnie, also a local member. "And I wasn't the one who had been drinking."

Children who grow up in alcoholic homes are taught not to feel, not to trust, and not to talk, said Kathy. "You don't share what's going on in your home because you realize your schoolmates don't live in the same sort of home you do," she said. "There's no trust because there's no consistency in the life of an alcoholic—or his spouse, either, because her behavior is dictated by the alcoholic."

Changing such behavior isn't easy, said Dorothy, another local Al-Anon member. "Every time I got angry, someone else got angrier," Dorothy said, "and it wasn't worth it. So I stuffed my anger, but it came out anyway by damaging my health in different ways."

Everyone in the family is affected by the behavior of one alcoholic, said Kathy. "When one person is alcoholic, I believe the spouse becomes more ill than the alcoholic just to hold things together, to make a family a unit rather than being devastated by the disease."

Anger was a tension running through their household. "My dad was angry, my mom was angry at him, and I was angry at them," she said. That behavior carried over into adulthood, where she married an alcoholic who had stopped drinking several years before, but who hadn't changed the behaviors that lay behind his alcoholism.

"My obsession was making sure my alcoholic was OK," she said, "because that meant that me and the children were OK, too." Since her husband had quit drinking, her children grew up in a household in which there was no alcohol. But one of her sons became an alcoholic anyway, Kathy said.

"That was my catalyst to begin a program of recovery," she said. "And now my son is in recovery, too. Many of us in Al-Anon live with an alcoholic or the dry product and have very rewarding, peaceful lives, in spite of what is going on around us," she said. "I don't love my husband any less, but his disease has destroyed much of what a marriage is about."

CONFRONTING A FAMILY DISEASE

It turned out that the decision to respect the Al-Anon tradition was a critical one. I needed to talk with a couple of families—on the record—to detail what happened within a family when one parent was an alcoholic.

So I made arrangements to meet with two couples in a local restaurant. If I passed the test and inspired confidence, I would be invited to come to their homes, meet with their children, explain again why doing this story would be important—but also to talk about the dangers it posed before (hopefully) gaining consensus.

As I finished up the first conversation with Doug and Mary Keeler in the restaurant, Mary asked how the dispute with Al-Anon had gone. I was a little surprised that she even knew about it, but I explained what I had promised to do.

"I know," said Mary, grinning. "That's the only reason we're here tonight. If you had tried to screw those people over, no one in town would have talked to you again." All of a sudden, I could feel my heart thumping like a rabbit trapped in a garbage can.

Mary told me her kids remember finding empty beer cans on the coffee table in the afternoon and trying to rouse her. "She was sleeping a lot, and when I'd get home from school, I'd wake her up and ask what was for dinner," said her twelve-year-old son Brian. "And she'd say, 'What are you still doing here?' like it was still morning. I didn't know what was wrong with her," he added, "and it scared me."

Evan Ashby's son remembers being afraid to get in the truck with his father when his dad's speech was too slurred.

"I felt an incredible peace the day my husband lost his job," said Brenda Ashby. "I felt that the worst had finally happened and now all we could do was trust in God to take care of us."

Mary Keeler and Evan "Skeet" Ashby III are alcoholics, an illness shared by perhaps 15 percent of the adults in Montana, according to state health officials.

On average, an alcoholic directly affects the lives of four other family members, friends, or co-workers, according to the National Institute on Alcohol Abuse and Alcoholism. But it's the family that suffers most damage, says Rod Robinson, executive director of the Gateway Recovery Center in Great Falls.

Alcoholics focus on their drinking, often neglecting their families, he said. Most feel guilty about their behavior and take their anger at themselves out on their families through verbal, emotional, or physical abuse. They also neglect their family responsibilities, forcing spouses and children to take over some of their burdens. Experts say this leads to isolation, loneliness, insecurity, and anger.

Without treatment, the unhealthy family structure is likely to be passed on. Statistics show that children of alcoholics have a much greater likelihood of becoming alcoholics themselves.

Keeler's addiction to alcohol became serious when her kids went off to school and her husband, a long-haul trucker, was on the road. "I was bored," she said. "I started with a little beer, but in the last couple of years, it got pretty heavy." Housework was the first casualty. Dirty dishes littered the counters of her Sun Prairie Village home, and there were piles of dirty laundry. "I remember once Brian asked me to wash his gym clothes, and I did," said Keeler. "But I didn't dry them. He didn't ask me to do that."

Both kids were concerned about the amount of beer their mom was drinking. "We'd always take a cooler of beer on our trips and that scared me," said Brian. "I think the times that scared me the most were when she'd get a six-pack of beer in town, put it in the back seat and drink it on the way home," said Stacy, nine. "I was scared of accidents and of the cops finding out," she added. But there were no accidents, not even a ticket.

Keeler's world changed in Rapid City, South Dakota, as she was on a trip back from delivering a trailer home with her husband, Doug. They had gone out to dinner, had a few beers, and gambled a little. Then she lost it. "I started to have blackouts and hallucinations, to hear voices and see people who weren't there," she recalled.

"You were hollering and cussing at a candy truck," added her husband. Doug Keeler knew his wife needed help, so he put her back in the truck and headed home fast. "She was talking into a CD player that was turned off," he said. "She was talking to friends and people she knew through that turned-off CD player like it was a cell phone."

Doug Keeler checked his wife into the Benefis Healthcare Addiction Medicine Center, where doctors told him the hallucinations and delirium could have been fatal.

After seventeen days of inpatient treatment, she was released for outpatient care. Now the whole family is undergoing counseling and has enrolled in various 12-step support groups to help heal the wounds of alcoholism.

"I feel as though I've been given the opportunity to start life all over again," said Mary Keeler. "I have a new appreciation for all the things my family is doing now that I can participate in them sober."

Brian feels a burden has been lifted off of him because he isn't forced to do the housework his mother had been neglecting. "Mom's been getting up in the morning, driving us to the bus stop, helping me with my homework, and baking stuff with me," said Stacy. "And I'm not getting as angry as much with my mom."

"I'm looking forward to having a family life," said Doug Keeler. "I'm looking forward to going camping and having the whole family with me, physically and emotionally."

RECOGNIZING FAMILY ROLES

Since alcoholism affects the whole family, the treatment must involve them too, experts say.

When the alcoholic ceases fulfilling his or her role in the family, others have to assume the burden, explained Sandra Schwartz, a Benefis family counselor. The spouse of an alcoholic frequently becomes an enabler, picking up the pieces so the family can continue to function, she said. That enables the alcoholic to continue his or her destructive behavior.

"The oldest child frequently becomes the hero," added Schwartz. "He or she unconsciously recognizes a need for self-worth in the family and strives to provide it. The second child is often blocked because the oldest child is getting all the strokes, so he or she frequently acts out in the other way, rebelling and creating trouble," she said.

"With the positive and negative roles already filled, a third child may disappear from the family dynamic," she said, "becoming what we call the lost child." Another child may become the mascot or family clown, joking away the pain inside.

"These are all mechanisms for people to cope with the fear, loneliness, and shame that they feel," said Mary Ann DuBay, another Benefis family counselor.

"I think people begin to heal and break the cycle when they learn to value themselves," said Schwartz. "Alcoholism is very much a self-esteem issue."

But it's also a matter of personal discipline, as Evan Ashby III found after he left the Air Force. During his college career at Virginia Military Institute and during his seventeen years as a navigator aboard C-135 refueling planes, Ashby kept his drinking under control, most of the time, because his job demanded it.

Then in 1994, he retired from Malmstrom Air Force Base and found work fielding emergency road service phone calls. "Without that absolute commandment not to drink for twelve hours before reporting for [military] duty, I gradually began doing things I should not have done," said Ashby.

He didn't spend much time in bars, but he spent a lot of time at home with a big bottle of Scotch. "His speech would get slurry and I didn't want to be around him," said his eleven-year-old son, Evan Ashby IV. "He scared me."

"[My brother Evan] spent a lot of time in his room, reading books and watching movies," agreed eight-year-old daughter, Blair.

Young Evan remembers getting a glider on his birthday and asking his dad to help him put it together. "He told me, 'Maybe someday, but not today.'"

That was frustrating to Brenda Ashby, who let her anger build until it exploded in angry confrontations.

That's a familiar dynamic for family counselors, who tend to see anger growing in those forced to assume some of an alcoholic's family functions. Only the alcoholic can choose to stop drinking, and that's usually only when the pain of the consequences outweighs the pleasure of drinking.

Nothing worked to block Ashby's growing obsession with alcohol. He was downing about 3.5 liters—or 120 shots—of Scotch a week. That's about twice as much as he had been drinking during his Air Force days.

"One night, he had been drinking and his speech was slurred and he frightened me, so I went to hide under the kitchen table," said Evan. "Then the phone rang. It was my mom, and I told her dad was scaring me. She told me if he wanted to drive me anywhere, don't go," he said. "Get out of the house and run to your friend's house."

The drunken nights became half-drunken, hung-over mornings, and during one of them, a few days before last Christmas, Ashby was sent home from work to sober up. When he reported to work the next morning, he was fired.

"When we got home that afternoon, I found my husband three sheets to the wind, so I took my kids down to the basement and asked them if they noticed anything about their dad," said Brenda Ashby.

"I said dad looked really depressed and his speech was very slurred," said Evan.

So Brenda Ashby told the kids her husband had lost his job. Then she took the remainder of the bottle of Scotch to a friend's house and asked her to pour it down a drain. Finally she came home, gave her husband a mental health hotline number, and told him he needed help. "He made the call and asked for substance abuse," she said. "I was shocked—but really happy."

One way that the Addiction Medicine Center at Benefis Healthcare breaks through this behavior is with family group sessions, in which people who have hidden their problems for years learn finally that they're not alone.

"Almost without exception, women in our recovery groups heave a sigh of relief when they discover they can talk about their problems, that they can be accepted, and that there's hope," said Schwartz. "They also must learn to identify their feelings and express them in an appropriate, respectful, non-blaming way."

Treatment also gives children a safe haven in which to demonstrate their feelings. "Kids are amazing," said DuBay. "We do family sculptures and they show us physically what their roles are. A lot of truth comes out because it's a safe environment for role-playing. Frequently, addicts will be surprised at how others see them."

Sometimes, children can help their parents quit drinking, but usually only with the help of a trained intervention specialist. "Children have a wide emotional swing from fear to intense anger," said Rod Robinson of the Gateway Recovery Center, "but there's not much ground in the middle. They're fearful their parents will go away and stay away," he said, "and they're angry and hurt because they think a parent's drinking is their fault as is the fighting that results.

"It's an angry swirl of emotion," said Robinson. "Left to their own resources, they feel very helpless, very hurt and angry."

Without outside help, he said, children of alcoholics either adopt enabling roles or fall into drinking to punish themselves and others. Once family members understand the roles they play, counselors say, they can choose healthier, more normal ways of getting their needs met. DuBay said Benefis family counselors have had a 70 percent success rate over the past few years. "There's such great hope if we can get families to treatment," said Schwartz. "Families have an innate longing for peace, serenity, and healing, and we can help them achieve it here."

Four months of sobriety and treatment are making a big difference for the Ashby family. "It's been amazing," said Brenda Ashby. "I had forgotten the person I married, but that person is back now. His sense of humor has returned, and several of my friends have commented that they don't know my husband now."

The kids said their dad's isolation is disappearing. "Sometimes his voice gets louder and he starts to tickle us and stuff," said Blair. "He's been roughhousing with us more after treatment," agreed Evan. "I think it's a sign that he's feeling better inside."

For Ashby, sobriety has meant reconnecting with himself, relearning self-discipline, honesty, and religion in a wide-ranging series of family discussions. "Alcoholic insanity is doing the same thing over and over again, but expecting different results," he said. "It's denying consequences and outcomes. It's not rational behavior, but I did it for years and years," he said. "And I used to get so angry with myself for doing the same stupid things over and over again."

Now the family talks about moral values over dinner or in the car on the way to church. "The number of times I lied to myself and to others about my drinking is something I'm not proud of," Ashby said.

"Sacrificing those moral values simply makes no sense to me now that I'm sober."

That's a painful admission to make publicly. "This [interview] is for me, to get this off my chest," said Ashby. "And if someone else can learn from this, that's great. We have to share, to help others. Reaching out to help others helps me, too."

CHILDREN OF ALCOHOLICS STATISTICS

According to the National Clearinghouse for Alcohol and Drug Information, children of alcoholics:

- Are at high risk for having their own alcohol or drug problems.
- Often live with pervasive tension and stress.
- Have higher levels of anxiety and depression.
- Do less well in school.
- Experience problems with coping.

There are an estimated 28.6 million children of alcoholics in the United States, nearly seven million of them under the age of eighteen.

Among youth, almost three million are expected to become alcoholics. About half will marry alcoholics and are likely to duplicate the unhealthy family conditions in which they grew up, experts say.

♦ ♦ ♦

BRODERSON: MIA

As the month went by, I realized that Bill Broderson was nowhere to be found.

When I checked up on him, I found that, without an explanation, he had left the home in which he had been staying a week before. Left behind were his clothing and a few personal possessions. Missing were the household food stamps for the month and his former roommates had some harsh suspicions.

Before he left, Broderson had talked about the difficulty of remaining sober for someone whose body is unaccustomed to sobriety. "I can't turn my mind off," he said. "It's going all the time, driving me crazy."

Broderson had nothing to keep him busy—no job, no hobby, no income. "The shrink I've been seeing told me to take up golf or fishing," he said. "But how am I going to do that? I have no money."

Broderson had been receiving free outpatient counseling at New Directions, the Great Falls-based component of the Golden Triangle Mental Health program. "He's been doing real well," said Tara Fatz, manager of the Lobby Bar. "He has been in a couple of times, drinking orange juice."

But relapses are part of Broderson's life. He raked a friend's yard recently and was paid $4. "Just enough for a six-pack," he said.

So Broderson spent his pocket change on alcohol, rather than putting it toward a fishing license that would afford him entertainment and food. And he complained about his perpetual boredom.

"I used to read a lot, but my mind is gone now," he said. "What I read I just can't comprehend anymore. I promised my shrink that I wouldn't commit suicide, but those thoughts keep coming back to me," he added. "A lot of days I just wonder if there's any reason to keep on living."

MAY

Bill Broderson returned to Great Falls in May. But it was obvious that alcohol was taking a progressively greater toll on his health.

He spent a week in the psych ward of St. Peter's Community Hospital in Helena in the past month. And he's undergoing a series of tests to determine how severely he has damaged his liver after years of heavy drinking.

Broderson dropped out of sight suddenly a month ago, taking with him the food stamps he had contributed to a local household in return for free rent. The house was getting too crowded, he explained.

He hitchhiked to Helena, where he moved in with a friend and drank heavily until he was admitted to St. Peter's, although he has no money or insurance. "I just told them I'd pay them," said Broderson, knowing full well that he couldn't. But that's standard procedure for a guy who has been in and out of more than fifty treatment programs in Butte, Helena, and Great Falls.

Since he returned to Great Falls, Broderson has been staying at the Rescue Mission, which provides free shelter and food—but only to those who abstain from alcohol and drugs. "I've only had three beers in the past four days," he said.

But Tara Fatz said Broderson drank a lot of beer in her establishment in the first few days he was back in town. "He's looking pretty rough," she said. Broderson also admitted he was staying in the Rescue Mission because no one was willing to put up with his behavior. Bonnie, his former housemate, was so angry that he stole her food stamps she took his few remaining possessions down to the Salvation Army.

And Jolena, whom he calls his daughter, won't let him back in the house with her husband and two small children. "I might have taken things from them to buy booze," said Broderson, "but honestly, I don't remember."

A TEEN PARTY TURNED DEADLY

A week or so later, I was introduced to a teenager named Mike, who said his life was turned around by a kegger that nearly snuffed it out at sixteen.

"I've been clean ever since," said the high school sophomore, whose last name the *Tribune* wouldn't print because he was a juvenile. "And I've been doing stuff with my family, stuff that we never used to do before. It's brought us a lot closer together."

Keggers and house parties are a rite of spring for most Montana high school students. Proms and graduation ceremonies both traditionally trigger illegal teenaged drinking, so we timed our look at teen drinking to run in May.

Drinking is particularly dangerous for teens because they drink competitively, their bodies are unaccustomed to alcohol, and their developing judgment can be easily clouded. Several Montana teens die each spring in car wrecks after such parties. But Mike's brush with death came during a kegger on a mountainside one chilly night in March.

"Those kids were lucky," said Chouteau County Sheriff Doug Williams. "It was really close."

A friend, Tim, suggested a camping trip with five other friends; alcohol was on the agenda. Most of the teens had been drinking together nearly every weekend for some time. Tim brought a couple of coolers of beer. "I have no idea where it came from," said Mike, "but sometimes people buy it for you." They began drinking about 5:00 P.M. as they set up their tents on the edge of a prairie in the Highwood Mountains, Mike said.

About four hours later, they were feeling no pain. Suddenly, seven carloads of partying seniors showed up, and the whole atmosphere changed. "We had a fire about as big as a dining room table, and one kid had a set of fifteen-inch speakers on his car," Mike said.

"It got real loud, and there was plenty of beer," he added.

Some of the sophomores went back to their tents, but Mike and Tim stayed up to party with the seniors. "I was trying to keep up with them," he said, "but I'd found a bottle of vodka beside the fire and I had switched to that."

Tim passed out about 11:00 P.M. and nearly fell in the fire. He was placed in his tent. Shortly afterward, Mike blacked out, but he fought being put in a tent because he was afraid he was about to puke all over it. The sheriff's department hit the party about half an hour later, tipped by a suspicious parent, and found two dozen drunken teens around a blazing fire. Snowdrifts were studded with chilling beer cans.

"Everybody ran and threw their beer cans away," said Mike. "There were a couple of [marijuana] bongs there, and someone threw one in the back of the new truck I had just bought," he said, "so it got impounded." That's what Mike was told, anyway. He doesn't personally remember anything of the bust. He was unconscious and nearly dead.

"The first teen I found was face down," said Chouteau County Sheriff's Deputy John Oeleis. "When I touched him, he was cold. I thought he might have been dead, but I finally got a very faint and rapid carotid pulse on him." Oeleis rolled Mike over, found his face and mouth were filled with mud, and cleaned out his airways so that he could breathe.

"I don't know how he was breathing," said the deputy. While he was trying to bring Mike back to life, Oeleis heard a gurgling noise in a nearby tent and thought someone was choking. "I had trouble getting in because the tent had partially collapsed and the second youth was lying against the door," the deputy said. "He was lying on his back with a puddle of vomit on his face, partially held in by the fabric of the tent."

The deputy rolled Tim over and cleaned out his mouth so he could breathe without choking. "He was totally covered with vomit, and he was very cold because he was lying on the fabric floor of the tent, which was no warmer than the ground," Oeleis said. "Medical personnel felt their chances of survival were not good."

Deputies called for the Mercy Flight chopper to air-evacuate the teens out, but later sent them by ground ambulance to Benefis Healthcare in Great Falls. Five other teens were apprehended, but the rest splashed through the creek, ran up a hillside, and escaped. Sheriff Williams said his deputies confiscated the liquor, then built up the fire and left because they were afraid the wet teens might freeze in the woods if officers remained on the scene.

"I woke up in the hospital and saw my parents," said Mike. "They were just glad I was alive." Later, Mike's parents grounded him for six months after he got his truck back. He pleaded guilty to minor in possession of alcohol and possession of drug paraphernalia in Fort Benton, was fined $345, and ordered to receive alcohol counseling. "I didn't think any of this could ever happen to me," he said. "Almost dying, getting my truck taken away, it just isn't worth it."

TEEN DRINKING STATISTICS

"Kids are starting to drink in the fifth and sixth grades," said Candace Atwood, an addictions therapist for ChemCare Associates, Inc. "And most parents just dismiss it, thinking, 'Yeah, we drank too when we were kids.' But these are totally different times." said Atwood. "They're starting so much earlier, and they're drinking so much more."

Atwood, who runs the county's minor in possession of alcohol counseling program, said teens steal alcohol from their parents, shoplift it from stores, are given it by older friends or brothers or sisters, or pay transients to buy it for them.

"And there are tons and tons of fake IDs that kids make," she added. "These aren't just the problem kids, but the 'cream of the crop' kids." Because their bodies are still developing, the kids experience alcohol more severely than adults. "They're drinking lots more than adults and their addiction rate is twice that of adults," said Atwood. "When they start drinking as teenagers, it takes less time for them to become addicted than it does for adults."

A survey of 15,455 Montana eighth, tenth, and twelfth graders showed about one quarter of the students have never taken a drink, but nearly the same percentage admitted they have used alcohol on forty or more occasions.

Half of them told researchers they would take a drink if offered, even though they know it's wrong. And the vast majority doubt they would get caught by the police or their parents. Fifty-nine percent said they took their first drink before they were fifteen.

That's a major concern because the National Institute on Alcohol Abuse and Alcoholism says kids who begin drinking before the age of fifteen are four times more likely to become problem drinkers. More than 40 percent of those who begin drinking before fifteen become alcohol dependent at some point in their lives, it said.

ESCAPING THE PAIN

"My mom was an alcoholic, so I've been drinking as long as I can remember," said Allison Bayne, a sixteen-year-old sophomore at Great Falls High School. In foster homes since the age of five, Bayne said she used drugs and alcohol as a way of escaping the pain—but knew it was a selfish way to escape.

"I'd find myself drifting apart from my foster family, not wanting to be a part of it, not focusing on my school work, just being selfish," she said. However, that method of escape is all too common, Bayne said.

"At my age, kids drink to get drunk," she said. "Society isn't exactly wholesome and homes aren't what they used to be, so a lot of kids drink to forget their problems and their pain. And a lot do it to get sex—they say they slept with so-and-so, but that it's OK because they were drunk," she said. "Being drunk can be an excuse to do all kinds of bad things."

The Great Falls Youth Risk Survey found that a third of the city's middle school students had had five or more drinks of alcohol in a row on at least one day in the previous month. Finally, increasing numbers of teens are being charged with minor in possession of alcohol these days. There were 696 MIP charges filed in 1998, up from 593 the year before and 582 in 1996.

TEENS IN COURT

Tuesday afternoon is minor in possession (MIP) day in Municipal Court, and it transforms the Civic Center. Teens sit on the steps outside waiting for their parents, or they crowd the courtroom in the basement waiting to appear before Judge Nancy Luth.

"I got busted for drinking in a motel after the senior prom," said Christina. "I called my mom and asked her to come get me, but she said she couldn't because she'd been drinking, too." That was Christina's third conviction for minor in possession of alcohol. "I keep telling her she's got to learn to quit getting caught," said her mom. "When I was her age, I was a lot faster."

On one recent Tuesday, about thirty kids and their parents packed the courtroom. Most had been charged with minor in possession of tobacco, but at least five of the kids had been charged with alcohol possession. Nicole was one of the few to be represented by an attorney, who had negotiated a plea bargain under which she would plead guilty to three MIPs over the past year and promise to remain in high school if prosecutors would drop three other outstanding MIPs.

"Six MIPs is uncommon, but it's not rare," explained Tony Lucas, a city attorney.

Judge Luth told Nicole she had a major problem. "You need to take a hard look at your drinking," said Luth from the bench. "When you are sixteen years old and you blow a .206 into the machine [more than twice the legal intoxication limit for an adult], you need to get a grip on your life."

Nicole was fined $660, ordered to perform forty hours of community service, and warned of the consequences of continued drinking when she turns eighteen in another month. "If you get another MIP, I guarantee you that you will go to jail," said Luth. "There will be no hesitation on the part of this court to send you there."

Judge Luth is no shrinking violet, and she doesn't hesitate to challenge a defiant attitude.

Jennifer told the judge she had been caught drinking in a car after she had told her mother that she would be at a going-away party at which there would be no alcohol. "You lied to your mother," said Luth, "and I think you owe her an apology." Jennifer mumbled she was sorry without looking at her mother.

"I've got a ten-year-old son who can apologize more sincerely than that," snapped Luth. "Please tell your mother you've been irresponsible, you're sorry, and you won't do it again." Jennifer did, but she left the courtroom with an angry flush to her cheeks.

"We see all kinds of kids in here," said Lucas after court. "Some are just kids who are doing kid stuff. But some are sixteen-year-olds who blow a .26. And that's usually a sign that they've been drinking a lot for a long time."

Low-Level Consequences

Our legal system can actually harm juveniles by being too easy on them, some authorities say. Just look at the numbers, says Atwood, who runs the counseling program for minors in possession of alcohol. Last year, nearly 700 juveniles were cited for MIPs in Cascade County.

"But hundreds of kids who were picked up for underaged drinking never bothered to go to court," said Atwood. "They know the system, and they know that if they don't obey the rules, there are no consequences. They might get a contempt citation, but there are no warrants out for their arrest," Atwood explained. "So if they don't get into trouble again, they're home free."

The same rule applies to kids who go to court and are ordered to undergo MIP counseling. If they don't show up or don't complete the program, again there are no consequences, she said.

Of 700 violators, only about 200 actually finish the MIP classes, said Atwood. "That's the frustration we have with the system," she said. "MIP is considered a low-level crime. But if we held them accountable at this level, I think we'd see a huge decrease in crime," said Atwood. "MIP is a gateway offense to other crimes, and right now, the gate is wide open."

Sgt. Tito Rodriguez, a police officer working with DARE in the city's schools, believes the harm goes deeper than that. "If we don't provide a swift, sure, and severe deterrent, the child never knows the error of his or her way," Rodriguez said. "And if there's no consequence, we're enabling those juvenile offenders. We must let juvenile offenders know early on there are consequences for their actions before they turn eighteen and suddenly go to jail for what they have been doing," he said.

But lawmakers have softened the blow by reducing the fine for older drinkers.

Minors are fined $120 plus twenty hours of community service for a first MIP, $220 and forty hours for a second, and $300 to $500 plus sixty hours for a third, said Justice of the Peace Mike Smartt. But those older than eighteen years old are fined $70 for a first MIP, $120 for a second, and $220 for a third, Smartt said.

And judges are forbidden to look at an eighteen-year-old's juvenile record to see whether there has been a history of alcohol abuse. "We should be able to look at their juvenile records when we're sentencing those over eighteen or the whole message goes down the drain," said Smartt. "But we can't—it's a whole separate category. I don't write the laws," he added, "but this makes no sense to me."

When teenagers turn eighteen, the laws change suddenly. Instead of a fine and community service, those convicted of MIPs face the possibility of jail time. In Justice Court, Smartt was waiting to arraign nineteen-year-old Misty Brott, who had been charged with her eighth minor in possession of alcohol. "Is Misty Brott incarcerated, awaiting arraignment?" the judge asked a closed-circuit television monitor from the regional jail.

No answer. Then Brott's brother Dale, 21, clad in bright orange coveralls, told the judge that he thought she had been transferred out. "Is Misty Brott in this courtroom?" asked the judge. No answer again.

Later, Cascade County Attorney Brant Light said a warrant would be issued for Brott's arrest, but he also defended the justice system. "There are some towns around the state that don't do anything about kids who drink," said Light, "but we cite them, bring them in, fine them, require them to do community service, take their drivers' licenses away sometimes, and impose consequences on them.

"And we bring their parents in—sometimes I would send an officer out to bring in parents who failed to appear—and encourage them to take their own separate actions against their children. Most of those kids we only see once, so the system does work," he said. "Of course, there are some multiple offenders, but I don't see how we could do any more under the current statutes."

WHISTLE BLOWING

Later, I explored how the system should work.

I talked with two fifteen-year-old high school freshmen in Great Falls about a house party they hosted. I also heard from the parent who blew the whistle on the party. I discussed such parties with Sgt. Rodriguez. And I asked Candace Atwood about what parents should do.

Here's what each had to say:

Teens

This was the first time we'd hosted a party, and we really didn't intend it to turn out the way it did, said the high school freshmen.

There are a lot of parties. A lot of parents go out of town, and the kids use their houses for a party. And a lot of people just hear about it and come on in. Usually the alcohol just shows up. Someone brings it and nobody knows where it comes from, but no one asks any questions. Everyone feels more comfortable that way. That's the way it happened at our party. It just showed up.

It was the Monday of Easter weekend, and five of us went to a friend's house to watch movies. His parents were gone for the weekend and a lot of people knew that, so we kind of half expected something might show up. But none of us brought any alcohol or took anything from the liquor cabinet at our friend's house.

About 10:00 P.M., kids started showing up. Most of them were freshmen, but there were a few sophomores. One brought a bottle of sixteen-year-old whiskey, but no one really wanted to get into that. And there were probably two cases of beer for the twelve or fourteen of us.

We got some music going, but basically we just hung out. It was cold outside and no one wanted to go out. We just sat around talking. No one got seriously drunk and there weren't any fights or injuries. People started leaving around 11:00 P.M., and there was some beer left. There was a designated driver for the people who had been drinking. Several of us had gone to bed, but a couple of us were still up talking when the cops showed up.

We looked out the door, saw the cops standing there, said, "Oh oh, we're in trouble," and let them in. They gave us breathalyzer tests and we blew between a .037 and a .061 [0.1 is the legal limit for intoxication for adults]. They took the beer, and then we had to call our parents to come get us.

That was painful. Our parents pretty much understood and were happy that we were responsible about it, but they were mad. They grounded us for the next four weekends. What did we learn from that? Don't drink illegally. It's not as much fun as people say it is.

Mother

My daughter had made some plans, but I wasn't sure what they were, said the whistle-blowing parent. When she didn't come home, I checked the caller ID, found the phone book open with a number circled, and we finally found where she was.

My husband went out to pick her up. One of the kids answered the door, and he was quite intoxicated. My husband said he'd come to pick his daughter up. When she got in the car, he asked if she had been drinking, and she said "yes." But if I hadn't been checking, I doubt that we would ever have known.

While my husband was gone, I called the cops because I had always told my children that I wouldn't hesitate to report them if I found them doing anything illegal. When they got home, there was some yelling, and then my daughter went to bed.

The deputies didn't get to the house party until later and my daughter wasn't there, so some of the kids felt we had bailed our daughter out of trouble. She started to have trouble with her friends and I felt she needed to be held responsible for what she had done, so I told my daughter I was going to turn her in.

I called the sheriff's department again and asked them to cite my daughter. When we got to the school, the deputies were already there, so we had to walk across the commons area with our daughter and the deputies in front of about 400 of her fellow students.

She was horribly embarrassed, and I felt guilty, but it was something I had to do. My daughter was mad and humiliated, but I think she'll be OK with it. One of the kids approached me and asked if I knew how much what I had done was costing his parents. And I said, "That's too bad—what you kids did was wrong and illegal."

The sheriff's department was great; they did their job. But then when we went to court, I was told that the kids were being responsible, kids were going to do that sort of thing, and that the officers had been overzealous.

I felt like I'd been slapped in the face. I felt it was inappropriate for the judge to say that if kids are careful and don't get caught, it's OK for them to drink. What they were doing was illegal because they're still children. And I also have a real hard time with parents who bail their kids out of trouble.

I've told my kids I believe in tough love, but one of the kids asked me why I didn't let my daughter sit there and get arrested with the others. I told him I didn't want my daughter riding home with someone and not making it home.

When I was sixteen, my boyfriend was drinking and driving, and he was killed in a car wreck. These kids don't think it can happen to them, but it can.

I feel sort of like a pariah, but I guess I don't really care. One of my friends turned her back on me and I haven't spoken with her since, and several of the parents have told their children to have nothing to do with my daughter.

I feel bad that they've taken what I did out on my daughter, but I also have had a lot of support from others. One of the deputies told me that sometimes when you take a stand, you have to stand alone. So I don't care if others disagree with what I did. It was important for my daughter and for others. I don't want to see any of them get hurt.

Police Officer

When they drink, these kids are breaking the law, said Sgt. Rodriguez. Laws are inflexible. They don't change. And you don't get to abide by only the laws you happen to agree with. Are you loosening your own moral code when you break the law? Absolutely.

Parents need to know that kids under the age of twenty-one should not be present at a party at which alcohol is being consumed. That's where drunken people congregate, and it would be gigantically unfair if they were victimized by one of those drunks.

Legally, even if they aren't drinking and they are within arm's reach of alcohol, they are by statute in possession of alcohol and they can be charged.

If a person under the age of twenty-one reaches out and takes that drink, he or she shouldn't try to drive. A minor with a blood alcohol content of 0.02 can be convicted of driving under the influence. Kids can reach that BAC level with one beer, one shot, or one wine cooler. That tells you that the state is sending kids a clear message—if you have had anything to drink, don't get into that car.

There's a reason for these laws. Kids need to learn to deal with the stresses and stressors in life without needing a chemical substance to hide behind. If they resort to substances at that age, there's a strong likelihood they are going to develop a lifelong dependence on alcohol, and that's not good for our children or for our society.

When kids drink, they lose their inhibitions and they're more likely to take risks—sex, crimes, DUI, thefts, vandalism, and negligent vehicular homicide. Drunken kids can experience serious life-changing events, even life-ending events. Our laws are designed to give them a chance to grow up, become more mature, and gain some experience.

One thing people tend to overlook is that when people drink, they get drunk. Teens don't sit around and sip one glass of Chablis—if there's a bottle there, they drink it all. And drunken people make irresponsible choices.

When you get a bunch of drunken kids together and they all start making poor choices, parties take on a life of their own. Kids frequently make poor choices about sex, and they may get diseases, HIV, unwanted pregnancies, or date-raped. What starts out fairly innocently can become a life-changing experience very quickly.

The juvenile justice system, the courts, the schools, and law enforcement need to communicate and cooperate better to help raise children. But ultimately, the responsibility belongs with the parent.

Sometimes it seems like parents are afraid to parent, afraid that Big Brother is going to come and take their children if they discipline them. That's not true. But in some cases, kids have convinced their parents that they will turn them in if they get spanked, and the parents have bought into that logic. The kids are running the house, not the parents. And that's crazy.

I'm going to be a bit of a radical and suggest that parents need to parent their kids again. I think parents need to stop over-protecting their kids, and we all need to do a better job of supporting the agencies and individuals tasked with helping raise those children.

But do I want the government raising my son? No! If my son gets into trouble and is sentenced to do community service as a result, I would be derelict in my duty as a parent if I didn't make sure that he completes every phase of that sentence.

Teen Counselor

Kids have gotten smart enough to cut down on the size of their parties, but they frequently take a big party out of town and call it a camping trip, said counselor Candace Atwood. Parents ought to be alert to that.

Nowadays, many of the kids have police scanners to listen for trouble and beepers to alert each other or to make contact for drug buys. I'm amazed at the number of kids who have cell phones—and the number of parents who buy them for their kids.

These kids are all wired. There's a lot of electronic contact going on out there. I think parents should ask why their kids need to be in such close contact with their friends.

Some parents think that just because their kids have no money, they aren't using [chemicals]. But most kids are willing to share whatever they have. Or they're stealing and pawning things to support their habits.

I tell parents they will see changes in attitude before they can prove actual substance abuse. Look for changing grades, different friends, new attitudes, denial of responsibility, increasing belligerence—all are signs there may be a problem. Later, the kids may get sloppy and parents may find beer cans or a marijuana residue in baggies.

But that's the first line of parental denial—we haven't any proof so they can't be drinking or using. That lets them off the hook as well.

Parents are so afraid of their kids these days. They're afraid to walk into their kids' rooms because they're afraid their kids might get mad. What???

I encourage parents to network. Kids have a great network, and parents should get together and talk with each other too, checking stories and comparing notes. A lot of kids tell their parents they're going to someone's house, then they go out and party, but parents should be able to see right through that.

The best thing a parent can do is be consistent in setting boundaries and consequences. If you ground your kid for a week, follow through with it. Kids who know no consequences for their actions tell me that it feels like their parents don't care.

The toughest thing for parents is to turn their kids in. I just applaud parents who call the authorities on their drunken kids or call them in as runaways if they know the kids are out partying. If they don't do that, they're enabling that behavior. Kids hate it, but they get over it. Tough love is far harder on the parent than on the kids.

TEENS, ANGER, AND ALCOHOL

Kids who have no parental boundaries often feel there are no social boundaries, which is a sure recipe for trouble. I checked the Cascade County Juvenile Detention Center, where half a dozen teenagers were struggling to make sense of their lives. Alcohol, drugs, and anger—all were reasons they landed behind bars.

"Do we drink? Do we drug?" asked one wiry young man in institutional brown coveralls. "And does it get us in trouble? Of course! Drugs and alcohol—that's how we all got here," he said, as heads nodded around the room.

"So why do you drink?" asked Anne, a Great Falls grandmother sitting in with the teens. A member of Alcoholics Anonymous, she declined to provide her last name. "People piss me off," offered a muscular young man with a shaved head. "I drink a lot and smoke some pot so I can get rid of my anger. Otherwise I'd go out and beat the crap out of someone."

Many of these kids come from alcoholic families and repressed anger is common, said Kathy, who is involved with Al-Anon, the self-help organization for families of alcoholics. "These kids aren't allowed to show their rage," she said. "But they live with people who may come home in the middle of the night, smash every dish in the kitchen and then wake up the whole household and demand that everyone clean up the mess.

"But they don't dare show their anger because the retaliation would be so much more severe." Anne told the teens that one of the hallmarks of alcoholics is their latent anger. That comes from repressing their emotions, she said.

A young woman with thick, dark hair glanced up from a pamphlet she had been reading. "Yeah, I got provoked," she said with a nervous half-smile. "This bitch called me a slut, so I stabbed her. That's why I'm here."

"Did you use a big long knife or just a little short one?" asked a fifteen-year-old with the scrubby beginnings of a beard, who was sitting right beside me in a locked counseling room.

"Pretty short," the girl responded, measuring off about four inches with her hands. "I used a much bigger one when I stabbed a guy in a fight last time," he told her.

Anne stepped into the conversation again to tell the teens that fear is the root of many of their emotions. Fear turned inward becomes depression, she said, while fear turned outward becomes anger. "And you have a lot of be afraid of in this world," she told them.

"Hell, I'm afraid just to be sitting in a room full of people who go around stabbing each other," half-joked a slender young man with wavy blond hair. Personally, I couldn't have agreed more.

His only crime, the nervous young man told the gathering, was that marijuana happened to be illegal. "Nah, your crime was that you slammed your pickup into a police car while you were high," corrected his friend. "Yeah, that's right," the blond boy agreed. "And when it happened, it felt kind of good. It sure got my anger out."

But the whole episode was his probation officer's fault, he added. "He tricked me," said the boy. "He stopped giving me UAs (urine analyses) so I went out and smoked my brains out. I thought he was pretty stupid, but it was me that was stupid."

That story reminded another young man of the attempted car burglary that put him behind bars. The car happened to be across the street from a house being staked out by the police, he said, and he quickly attracted the attention of about a dozen officers. "We were pretty drunk," he said. "Otherwise, we would have seen them."

Anne stepped in again with a definition of insanity—continuing to do the same wrong thing in hopes that the results might somehow change for the better.

"So why did you drink?" she asked again.

"All of us learn from our mistakes," responded the bearding boy, thoughtfully. "But not all of us want to do what's right. I don't," he added. "Otherwise, I wouldn't be in here right now."

TEEN ABSTINENCE

But not all teens drink, either. Wearing a sash and a crown, seventeen-year-old Raylene Miller of Ulm visits schools with one simple message: Don't drink and don't do drugs. "I tell kids that I have had a problem with alcohol in my own family," said Miller, who is Miss Montana Teen USA, "and that I would never cause others in my family more pain."

Miller said she doesn't drink and she refuses to go to parties where alcohol might be served. "It isn't hard for me to refuse alcohol," said

Miller. "I'm a strong-willed individual, so what others think of me doesn't really matter. And I'm a Christian," she added. "Having God in my life means I don't need alcohol in it, and my church gives me extra support."

As a nondrinker, however, Miller is in a minority. A statewide poll of 15,455 teens shows that only 40.1 percent of eighth graders have never tried alcohol. That number drops to 22.5 percent of the tenth graders and 14.8 percent of high school seniors.

To change teen drinking behavior, the courts rely on the MIP school, which offers programs on alcohol use, drinking consequences, values, laws, and the progression of addictions. The school's recidivism rate has been 11 percent, but Candace Atwood, addictions therapist for ChemCare which runs the program, said that's a deceptive figure.

"They just take their parties further out of town, they get sneakier, or they just don't bother to show up in court at all," she said. Further, she has been troubled by the lack of responsibility that kids show. "This generation knows no consequences," said Atwood. "I ask my MIP classes what they intend to do to avoid coming here again, and it's rare to hear someone say they won't drink again. Instead, they say they'll run faster if they get busted."

Public attitudes must change, she said. "We tolerate alcohol abuse and think it's acceptable and we do a disservice to our children by passing those attitudes on to them."

It took a hard-nosed foster parent to get the attention of Allison Bayne, a sophomore at Great Falls High School.

She had been using alcohol and marijuana as an emotional escape from the foster homes she had been in since she was five, but one set of foster parents insisted she go to treatment at Benefis Healthcare. "They taught me how to take care of myself, not hurt other people, and not be so selfish," said Bayne. "It was hard to learn—it took me eleven months, and I didn't think I had a problem."

Her denial was strong, said Bayne. "I knew I was being stupid, but I didn't want to admit it. Then I finally began to realize that drugs and alcohol had really messed up my life." When she began treatment, Bayne said, she worried that she wouldn't have fun anymore without substance abuse.

"But that wasn't true," she said. "Alcohol just clouds things over, but now I can see things clearly, I'm having a great time, and I'm being accepted outside of the partying world—and they turn out to be some of the coolest people."

CHANGING FAMILIES AND COMMUNITIES

"Drinking starts in the home," said Tammera Nauts, the public school counselor for at-risk youth, "and parents need to assume an attitude of zero tolerance—under no circumstances should parents tolerate drug or alcohol use. And they have to be role models, too," she added. "If kids see their parents using alcohol for social pleasure or stress relief, they'll pick the same habit up for sure."

There's a big difference, though—kids are way more extreme. "Kids totally skip the social drinking phase," said Atwood. "They deliberately set out to get wasted, to get as hammered as they can."

Atwood also said teens have not been taught to entertain themselves. Instead, they turn to movies and video games, which portray extreme behavior. "The way we live now, everything is extreme," she said. "The bigger the risk, the better. Kids drink now to the limit."

Kids have created a mindset, she said, that says if they're bored, it's OK to get drunk. And a lot of parents have bought into that fiction. Families have to be more creative in doing family things. It's too easy just to do the chores, and then veg out in front of the TV. But that's no more responsible than hanging out in a bar. "Parents need to do more role-modeling things like outdoor activities or crafts or family home improvement projects," she said. "We need to model working and playing together."

That's exactly the direction in which the Gateway Recovery Center is moving, said its executive director, Rod Robinson. Programs are beginning to stress music and art, sounds and shapes, in addition to the cognitive aspects. Games teach problem solving and trust building.

"It's almost as much fun to teach adults how to play again as it is to teach kids," Robinson said. "I did a demonstration for our staff here," said counselor Janine Heib, "and I never saw so much laughter and giggling."

"I found myself in my big 'Playtool' hat and realized that I didn't have to be the big boss man today," Robinson added. "I gave myself permission to play."

Gateway is beginning to incorporate games like the 3-D Minefield, in which one player coaches a blindfolded player on how to walk through a make-believe mine field, while others provide verbal distractions. "It teaches people to communicate well, listen well, and trust in the guidance despite the distractions," Heib said.

Another game requires each player to think up a number, then get into sequential order without speaking. One group solved the problem with each player clapping out his or her number, for example. "These games teach problem solving, but they also develop trust and an understanding of what a support group is all about," said Robinson.

Banishing boredom is a big part of Gateway's approach. "We teach kids and families to challenge their beliefs, challenge themselves, and challenge the way they do things," said Heib. "When people lose challenges in their lives," added Robinson, "they pick up filler material, and it gets easier to pick up substances to replace the challenge."

Gateway also stresses the positive, not the negative. "Kids are so used to our pointing out their weaknesses, so we learn to focus on their strengths instead," said Robinson. "And they respond by brightening right up and improving their behavior.

"We're already getting much better outcomes with children and families," he said. "And I'm feeling our energy levels come up as our staff gets excited about this approach."

But it's not only individuals. Communities must also change, said Nauts. "We need to have parents watching out for all the kids in this village of ours," she said. "We need to have merchants who are sticklers for checking IDs, parents who don't make alcohol available, and a community that supports recreational activities that give kids something wholesome to do." Finally, she said we need to change our culture, including the mass media.

The White House Office of National Drug Control Policy recently released a study that showed 94 percent of the 200 most popular PG-13 movies depicted alcohol use. "Until we change our culture," said Atwood, "we're going to need a drinking age to make sure our kids are protected. Drinking is a form of risk taking, and we'll never change that behavior," she added. "But we need to help our kids make good decisions."

HARM REDUCTION

In a culture pervaded by alcohol, not everyone is convinced that abstinence is a realistic possibility. Instead, the focus at the Rocky Mountain Recovery Center is on harm reduction, which treats teenagers so dependent on alcohol that they require inpatient treatment.

"We know that some youngsters are not likely to be successful at complete abstinence, even though we don't tell them that," said Dr. Ron

Hughes, staff psychiatrist. "We promote abstinence, but we also raise their level of consciousness about the consequences of drinking."

After 30 days of sobriety and counseling, kids are in a better position to refuse to drink. Hughes knows that's a tough choice, however. "By law, kids are forbidden to drink, but they can get alcohol as easily as they get a carton of milk," he said. "Because it's illegal, though, they end up drinking in secret and binge drinking."

Hughes does not advocate making drinking legal for teens, but he said the law makes it hard to teach responsible drinking. "I can't sit these kids down and tell them it's OK to have one drink—but not to have six drinks—because it's not legal to have even one," he said. "And that presents a dilemma for me as an educator."

The teens at Rocky Mountain tend to have serious emotional problems, and it's not always easy to get their attention. Hughes gets it by having the kids tested for HIV, the virus that precedes AIDS. "When they have that needle in their arms, they suddenly realize they really could have HIV," he said. "Suddenly, they remember those tattoos, those shared needles, not using the condoms. Then they have to wait four or five days for the results and when the nurse finally shows up, they're as nervous as cats on a hot tin roof."

Realistically, however, Hughes sees little chance of changing teenaged drinking until there are similar reforms in the adult society on which teens model their behavior. Both are badly needed, he said.

"Alcohol is an enormous problem, simply enormous," he said. "Alcohol consumption is the most dangerous thing an adolescent can do. It's the single most important factor in teen suicides, auto accidents, fights, and domestic violence. If we were able to remove drinking from adolescents," he said, "we would solve a lot of problems."

COLLEGE CAMPUS ALCOHOL USE

But instead, teens carry that behavior into their college years, where it can become more extreme. Half of Montana's college students have downed five or more drinks in a single sitting within the past two weeks, according to a new state survey. That compares to 38 percent of the nation's college students who admitted the same drinking behavior.

Called "binge drinking," this lack of moderation creates serious consequences for the drinker, but it's also considered a danger sign of future alcohol abuse. The survey of 5,346 students on thirteen Montana university and college campuses also found that 75 percent of all students under twenty-one years old, the legal drinking age, had consumed alcohol within the previous thirty days.

"Three quarters of our students are breaking the law," said Jeff Linkenbach, an assistant professor at Montana State University-Bozeman who is in charge of the Montana Social Norms project. "We college administrators need to ask ourselves whether our goal is to bust these criminals or whether we need to adopt strategies to keep these people alive and reduce the harm from their alcohol use.

"We probably need to do both. We must support the law, increase its enforcement, and reduce the availability of alcohol to those underage, while showing concern for those who choose to break the law and to reduce the risks for them," said Linkenbach.

At the University of Montana, officials decided to crack down on fraternity drinking, which is often the most extreme on campus. "We were the first university in the country, as far as I know, to voluntarily ban alcohol at Greek functions," said UM Greek adviser Mike Esposito.

Students can still drink in their rooms, but only if they're older than twenty-one and there are no minors present. Missoula police officers contend, however, that the policy has only driven college drinkers downtown.

"We're hopping from bar to bar on the weekends to quell distur-bances," said police Lt. Mike Sunderland. "And at closing time, we may get 500, 600, 800 kids crowded out onto city streets. Some night when the conditions are right, we're going to have a major disturbance here," he predicted.

Montana State University at Bozeman hasn't been quite so tough. "We haven't done the mandated policy like UM," said Beverly Townsend, MSU's Greek adviser. "We haven't felt there's a need to yet."

But MSU has developed its own prevention programs, in conjunction with its students. "We enforce our alcohol policy in such a way that it is supported by students," said Jenny Haubenreiser, director of health promotion at MSU. "So we deal with behavior, rather than try to issue a blanket prohibition of alcohol," she said. "If you dramatically crack down on drinking, you're likely to provoke a revolt. Students need to have some ownership of the solution."

MSU has developed three programs in which student leaders serve as role models. *Expedition MSU* targets incoming freshmen. In the fall, about 200 students head out in canoeing, rafting, rock-climbing, or backpacking expeditions in groups of 10 or fewer students, along with student leaders and faculty members. For three to five days, the groups explore the mountains and streams around Bozeman and discuss campus life: academics, studying, drinking, drugs, and social norms. "These groups are led by students who don't use substances because they would affect their wilderness performances," said Haubenreiser.

Cat Cabs is a program in which student leaders volunteer to serve as designated drivers, ferrying students back to campus after big football games or other social events in which heavy drinking can be expected.

The *Zero Hero* program is a designated driver program in which bars agree to provide free soft drinks and coffee to designated student drivers.

The university also set up an *Insight* program to educate students about the dangers of drinking. "This is for students who have been referred to the program, generally because of alcohol violations," said Haubenreiser. "This way, we know we're talking to students who have been drinking when they should not have been."

PREVENTION ON COLLEGE CAMPUSES

While three-quarters of the state's college students used alcohol in the previous thirty days, a state health department survey of households found that only 58 percent of adults had used alcohol in the past month.

Why do students drink more than adults? About 70 percent of the students surveyed said it enhances social activity, 52 percent said it allows people to have more fun, and 46 percent said it facilitates sexual opportunity.

However, 42 percent of the students reported some form of public misconduct, ranging from fighting to DUIs, over the past year:

- 41 percent reported doing something they later regretted.
- 17 percent said they had been in trouble with college authorities.
- 15 percent were hurt or injured.
- 11 percent were taken advantage of sexually.
- 2.8 percent were cited for driving under the influence.

In fact, 66 students—about 1.2 percent of the sample—said they had been taken advantage of sexually ten times or more. "I think this survey provides good eye-opening information," said Darla Tyler-McSherry, president of Montana State University-Billings. "It stresses the importance of alcohol-abuse prevention programs on campuses."

One interesting finding was that students held an exaggerated view of student drinking. For example, 13 percent of the students said they do not drink at all. Only 43 percent said they had one drink or more in the previous week.

The student perception was quite different, however; 93 percent of the students thought the average student drank at least once a week, if not every day. "There's this perception that everyone else is doing it, so I guess I will too," said Linda Green, health educator at the University of Montana. "But when we really went out and surveyed it, for the most part, people weren't drinking irresponsibly," said Green.

The greatest number of students (29 percent) reported they began drinking at fourteen to fifteen years old; 13 percent said they started at twelve to thirteen, while 26 percent said at sixteen to seventeen.

One other interesting fact is that more than 62 percent of the students reported someone in their immediate family—grandparent, parent, aunts or uncles, spouses, or children—has a drinking or drug problem.

JUNE

Alcohol and poverty have been the two certainties in Bill Broderson's life, but now there's a third: liver failure. "I'm a dead duck," said Broderson, as he sipped a mid-morning beer at a downtown bar. "There's no cure for hepatitis C."

Hepatitis C can be treated, said Dr. Dan Nauts, medical director of the Addiction Medicine Center at Benefis Healthcare. But the treatment is complicated, expensive, and generally not available to patients who continue to drink.

"Anything that adds stress to the liver only aggravates the injury," added Dr. Julie Wood of the City-County Health Department.

Broderson has been drinking a lot, but eating little. At the health department, he weighed in at 134 pounds, nearly thirty pounds off his normal weight. Wood said he needed treatment at a detox center, but that she couldn't arrange it. "We could put you into detox now, but there's nowhere we can put you after that, so it's kind of like setting you up for failure," she told him.

She urged him to keep on fighting for Social Security disability benefits. "If we had a funding source, we might be able to open a few doors for you that we can't open now," she said, adding that he had been through the detox program at the Montana Chemical Dependency Center in Butte so often that he was no longer welcome there. She recommended he try to stay sober enough to be accepted at the Great Falls Rescue Mission.

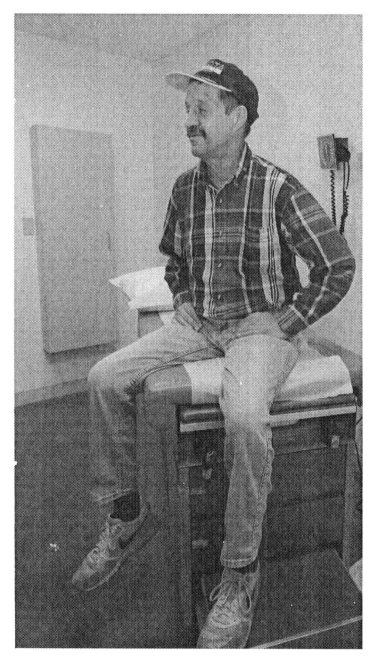

Bill Broderson discovered he had contracted hepatitis C.

Broderson moved out of the Rescue Mission a month ago and in with a friend, but he wore out his welcome there. Most nights, he's sleeping in a park. "Last week, Bill was looking real bad, real rough around the edges," said bartender Tara Fatz. "He had the DTs [delirium tremens] so bad he checked into the hospital twice, but they only kept him a day each time," she said.

Broderson confirmed the hospital stays and added that he also got a ride in a city police car. "I walked over to my daughter's house, but she wouldn't let me in," he said. "I was drunk and she has two little kids, so I can't blame her." Broderson remembers the cops putting him in the rear seat of the patrol car, but he can't remember where he was taken. It wasn't jail, he said, nor did they take him to a hospital.

Long pause. "My computer isn't working today," he said, tapping his forehead. It's a mystery where Broderson gets the money to keep drinking, and Broderson declined to clear it up.

"He had a $10 bill the other night and he wouldn't tell me where it came from," said Fatz. "I just grabbed it out of his hand and told him I was damned if he was going to drink himself to death in front of my eyes. Then I asked him the last time he had eaten, and he said four days ago. So I bought him a big bowl of soup."

These days, however, Broderson's digestive system is so shot he often can't keep even soup down. But stopping the booze brings on the DTs. "Sometimes the room spins around on me, and sometimes I see things like little mice running all over the floor," he admitted.

Detox is critical for Broderson now, said Rod Robinson, executive director of Gateway Recovery Center. "Giving up alcohol is a powerful fear for an alcoholic," he said. "To overcome that fear, we must provide some hope: employment or family reconciliation, for example. That lack of hope adds a tremendous barrier to treatment."

To me, that was a tremendous statement. I began to think about ways of introducing hope into Broderson's life. But first, Broderson needed one more session in the detox unit. I got a call from the hospital and went up to visit him. A few weeks before, he had been to Set Free Ministries, where he had been given a couple of bags of used, but clean clothing. Now, he asked earnestly, he needed me to do him a favor. So a few hours later, I found myself walking down a downtown alley, looking under the bushes for a box where he had stashed his clothing. Finally, I found it and retrieved it—feeling rather conspicuous in my navy blue sports coat and a tie—and tossed it in the back of my pickup.

Here are some facts about domestic abuse:
- Nationally, a woman is battered about every twelve seconds.
- Approximately four women a day are killed by their partners.
- Domestic violence causes more injuries than rapes, muggings, and car accidents combined.
- In half of spouse-abusing families, children are abused or neglected, as well.
- Children who grow up in violent homes are six times more likely to commit suicide, twenty-four times more likely to be sexually assaulted, sixty times more likely to be engaged in delinquent behavior as adults, and 1,000 times more likely to become abusers themselves.
- Domestic abuse costs Montana businesses more than $10 million a year in absenteeism and medical bills.
- Medical expenses from domestic violence total $3 billion to $5 billion annually. Businesses lose another $100 million in lost wages, absenteeism, sick leave, and non-productivity.

(Sources: YWCA Mercy Home, Mothers Against Drunk Driving)

THE ADDICTIVE CYCLE

Meanwhile, I stopped by to visit with Wava Goetz, a counselor and a member of our panel of experts, and found that she had begun to review the 700 cases she has handled over the past five years. When she did, she made a startling discovery—two-thirds of her cases were alcohol-related.

Many families were seeking help for problems fueled by alcohol abuse by one or both spouses, but others reported a history of alcoholism within the immediate family. "So without alcohol, I'd probably be out of business," she told me, "and that would be a happy day."

Alcohol can trigger a lot of fights, even in normal households. "Couples argue more when they drink," said Goetz. "We know that alcohol lessens inhibitions, so I speculate there's a greater likelihood of people speaking their minds without thinking much about it.

"And alcohol is a mood-altering substance, so they might also be more emotional about what they say—or what is said to them."

With inhibitions low and emotions high, it's easy for underlying anger to pop out, she said. Goetz added that she frequently counsels couples for marital problems, then runs into anger control issues that need to be addressed. If substance abuse is also an issue, it must be dealt with first.

"Sobriety is the first step," said Goetz. "Then we can do anger control. Then, finally, a couple can work on enhancing their relationship. But they can't do anything with these other problems going on." A submissive spouse can't learn to be more self-assertive if she knows she is going to be beaten up, explained Goetz, and an abuser can't comprehend the changes he needs to make in his life if he's drunk frequently.

"Some use alcohol as a temporary way of numbing their anger," she said, "but others use it as an excuse—I was drunk so it was OK to blow up and beat my wife." Abuse is the only way some people know to handle anger, she said, and so they'll always find something to be angry about.

"Over time, both the abuser and the abused come to believe that it's the victim's fault for provoking the abuser's anger," Goetz said. And that makes the whole cycle highly addictive. "After a while, normal life seems a little boring after all the tension and chaos."

Her long experience as a counselor had led Goetz to believe that anyone can reform. "Anyone can change if they are motivated to get better and if they have competent help to do it," she said. "So I don't write anyone off. But I'm also realistic enough to know that not many people will actually make radical life changes," she added. "Most people just do the minimum to comply with a court order or to get a spouse back."

ALCOHOLISM AND ABUSE

One place in Great Falls where there's help for the abused woman is the Mercy Home, which is run by the YWCA.

Last year, the Mercy Home provided shelter and emergency services for 175 women and children, said Lori Novak, executive director of the YWCA. That's down slightly from 190 the previous year, she said. "Now that the new [county] jail is open, women can get a twenty-four-hour period of protection in which they can apply for a court-ordered writ of protection," she said, "and we're also seeing an increase in the number of applications for protection. While I'm a little hesitant to praise the building of a new jail, this does seem to be making a difference."

Two years before, Great Falls opened a regional jail on Gore Hill to replace its century-old county jail downtown. In response to a lawsuit, a local judge had imposed a cap on the number of inmates. This meant, in effect, that the limited number of jail beds went to those committing the most serious crimes. People charged with public drunkenness, family

Abuse of alcohol and drugs by parents is the single biggest reason why families fall apart and children enter the welfare system, according to the Child Welfare League of America. It said that two-thirds of all welfare cases are caused by chemical dependency.

In Oregon, for example, 60 percent of all children placed in foster care come from families that have alcohol or drug problems. While child care professionals estimate that 67 percent of parents involved with the child welfare system need treatment for abuse of alcohol and other drugs, agencies can provide direct and indirect services to only 31 percent of those in need.

Source: (Child Welfare League of America)

disputes, or misdemeanors, were generally held for a few hours, and then released. So the new jail allowed the justice system to resume meting out punishment for all crimes.

In 1998, 370 incidents of domestic violence were reported in Great Falls, an eight percent increase over previous years, according to Mercy Home records. But neither Mercy Home nor the Great Falls Pre-release Center keep records of the percentage of domestic violence fueled by alcohol.

"I strive to promote accountability, that a person is responsible for a crime, not the substance," said Heidi Gibson, the center's domestic violence counselor. "Some try to blame the substance," she added, "but I don't let them do that."

TAKING BACK HER LIFE

In her fourteen years, Shauna has seen a lifetime of drunken abuse. This seventh grader has been beaten, yelled at, sexually abused, and introduced to alcohol and drugs—all by various family members.

"Now I know that the abuse wasn't my fault," Shauna told me, sitting on a couch in a motel room where she and her mom live. "And I know that alcohol and drugs will only make it worse, so I have to stay away from them."

Alcohol is one of the major contributors to abuse of children and spouses, according to experts. In the United States, a woman is beaten every twelve seconds, according to HHS's Center for Substance Abuse Treatment, and about half of the wife and child beaters also have substance abuse problems. An estimated 1,414 women were killed by intimate partners in 1992, it said, pegging the medical costs of injuries to women at more than $44 million annually.

But that's only part of the problem. Experts say three million children witness acts of violence against their mothers each year, leaving many of them primed to recreate similar abuse in their own adult lives. Many children—like Shauna—are also the victims of domestic abuse, which is one of the reasons the *Tribune* declined to print her last name.

Shauna remembers her stepfather as an abusive alcoholic who was particularly hard on her brothers. "Shauna was baby-sitting at five, cooking macaroni and cheese when she could barely see over the stove," said her mother, Doreen. "She had to grow up real fast."

Doreen said she divorced her husband because of his alcoholism and his abuse, but her oldest son, Fritz, grew into the same mold.

Shauna remembers a fight with Fritz that hurt her. "He hit me in the face," she said. "Everything went white, and I fell backward into a stairwell. He started kicking me in the ribs and wouldn't stop until someone pulled him off me." Bruised ribs kept her in bed for five days, she said.

It was Fritz who introduced her to methamphetamines, Shauna said, and her brother and his friends would buy her forty-ounce bottles of beer that they would drink behind closed doors in the bedroom. "When he abused me, it was usually no big deal because I was high," she said. "But later, I'd drink more to escape the pain."

Doreen remembers the Christmas of 1997 when her son—coming down off a high on drugs and alcohol—scarred her face. "He threw a garbage can at me, and my kids went after him," she said. "He almost threw Shauna through a window. He had me on the floor, pounding my head against it, and clawing my face with his fingernails," said Doreen. "My ten-year-old finally got through to the police, and they were there in about two minutes."

Now Fritz is in prison, she said. "I don't know if he even realizes what he has done to us," said Doreen. "I think he does," said Shauna, "but he doesn't know it's wrong."

Shauna also said she was sexually abused in an interstate truck for two months by her father. "All I ever wanted was to get to know my father," she said, "but he got me into his truck and raped me. He bought me all kinds of expensive things, but I'd rather live poor than live like that. Finally, my mom came out on a bus and got me out of there."

"That's when she really turned to alcohol and drugs," said her mother. "I got her back on a Friday night and by Sunday, I could see something was really wrong. I took one look at her, closed the door, and said, 'What did that son of a bitch do to you?'"

Doreen and Shauna filed a complaint with the Great Falls Police Department, said Detective Art Schalin, adding that he turned it over to the FBI because the alleged abuses took place over a five-state area. No charges were filed.

And Shauna went into treatment at Benefis Healthcare. At first, she was doing it only for her mom. Then she was caught with Dexedrine at school and charged with felony possession of dangerous drugs. At that point, she said, she knew she needed to turn her life around.

"I couldn't control anything that was happening in my life," said Shauna. "People were walking all over me. And I knew I had no future unless I regained control." Shauna said she has learned to be more self-assertive and to talk about her problems, particularly with her mother. "Treatment helped me see who I am, what good I am," she said. "It helped me enjoy life and accept myself.

"It's a whole lot better than waking up in the morning and wondering what I'd done last night," she added. "Now I wake up and say it's a brand new day and I'm Shauna—and it's an awesome feeling."

TREATING THE EMOTIONS BEHIND ALCOHOLISM

Bill Loy, executive director of the Anger Control Education (ACE) classes at the University of Great Falls, finds that alcohol and anger come in the same package, so he treats them together. "I would say that alcohol aggravates the situation for males in a good 85 percent of the cases and for women in at least 65 percent," said Loy.

Alcoholism is based in fear, he said. "Most alcoholics have an insecurity that doesn't allow them to communicate their emotions properly," he said. "They suppress their emotions until they ingest alcohol," said Loy. "Then those emotions come out improperly and fights are started, which lead to domestic violence."

Control is a big issue for most alcoholics, he said. "When they feel their lives are out of control, they're willing to use physical force to gain an illusion of control."

Military personnel, police officers, and firefighters—the people we trust to protect us—are the most susceptible to domestic abuse, said Loy. Part of the reason is job stress, but part is also control. "They get so accustomed to structure that they try to apply it to their own families," said Loy. "When they encounter resistance, it triggers the violence."

Shame, remorse, guilt, and anger build up to trigger a cycle of domestic violence that recurs regularly. The abuser denies he has a problem, blaming others for provoking his rages. And he denies that alcohol is a problem, protecting the substance that seems to numb him from a threatening world.

"We aren't a treatment center here, but the role of alcohol comes up nightly in our group discussions on anger control," Loy said. "It's an issue we address frequently." Alcoholics and abusers deny they have a problem, blame others for it, and minimize the impact of it. The ACE program works to improve honesty, accountability, and communication, said Loy.

About 200 clients a year come through the program, he said. Some are ordered by the court, others are referred by employers, and a number of individuals come to try to save marriages. "We have an extremely low recidivism rate," said Loy, "but every single person who has had to repeat this class had alcohol as a primary problem."

HARD TIME TO BE SOBER

After Broderson got out of the hospital, I gave him his clothes back and he began living with Jolena again, but it was a hard time for him. He simply had nothing to do but walk and try not to think about booze. He was still too sick to work. And his mind was pretty well shot so he couldn't read much, although he did find a great book for me in a pile of freebies, an environmental novel by Edward Abbey. Broderson told me I'd love the book, and he was right. In fact, I ended up going to a used book store and buying other works by Abbey, including *The Monkey Wrench Gang.*

Then Broderson found a fishing pole in a dumpster and talked about going fishing—but he needed a license. So photo editor Larry Beckner and I chipped in $5 apiece to buy him a fishing license. I took him out to the state office building, but it had closed for the day, so we agreed to meet in the morning.

Later that night, I got the cold chills as I remembered that I had left that money with him, and what a temptation that must be to an alcoholic striving desperately to hold onto a thin sobriety. I woke up a couple of times in the night worrying about him, then went on into work and called him at Jolena's house.

He was fine, he said, still sober and still had the $10. So I picked him up and drove him back to Fish, Wildlife, and Parks, where we bought the license.

ABUSE IS A SECONDARY PROBLEM

In Montana, a child is reported abused or neglected every thirty minutes, according to the Children's Defense Fund of Washington, DC. More than three million children nationally were reported to state agencies as suspected child abuse or neglect cases in 1996—an 18 percent increase since 1990. Of these children, 52 percent suffered neglect, 24 percent physical abuse, 12 percent sexual abuse, 6 percent emotional maltreatment, and 3 percent medical neglect, it said.

In its report last year, the National Committee to Prevent Child Abuse said most states listed alcohol and drug abuse as one of the main causes for neglect and abuse. Poverty and economic stress was the second most frequently cited cause. An estimated 520,000 children were living in foster homes as of March 31, 1998, a 30 percent increase from the beginning of the decade, said the Children's Defense Fund.

Federal, state, and local governments spent about $11.2 billion on child protection in 1995, according to the Center for the Future of Our Children, a foundation based in Los Altos, California. But that's only the tip of the iceberg because most kids will do almost anything to hold their families together.

SEXUAL ABUSE

Candy hid the sexual abuse in her childhood because she feared it would destroy her family.

She remembers a drunken brother beginning to sneak into her room at night when she was about ten. "But I never told my mother about it because I was afraid it would just upset things," she said.

Alcohol destroyed her family anyway. "My brother left home as soon as he could get away," Candy said. "My mother used to tell me she would leave as soon as I graduated from high school—and she did."

Candy's father was an angry drunk, and her brother became one, as well. "My brother was angry at my father never being around, angry about his drinking, and very protective of my mother," she said. "He would deny it today, but he became my father through and through."

Candy's turning point came when her mother came to wake her up one morning and found her brother asleep beside her in bed. "She just turned around and walked out," Candy said. "She wasn't getting any help dealing with her drunken husband or her drunken kid. And I knew then I would never get any help from her either, so I had to become more and more skillful at protecting myself."

It has taken twenty years of therapy for Candy to deal with the scars left over from her childhood. "I was chronically depressed from all the abuse at home," she said. "There never was a day when I didn't think about dying as a way to escape the pain. Mercifully, I never attempted it—I was a survivor. But it was an escape mechanism for me."

Unfortunately, such scars are increasingly common. "It's every-where," she said. "We're hearing about it now more than we did, but there's also more sexual abuse these days."

PHYSICAL ABUSE

In addition to the sexual abuse, physical abuse is also a big problem. In 1998, there were 370 reports of domestic abuse, with 295 arrests, said Great Falls Police Chief Bob Jones. In 1997, there were 342 domestic abuse reports and 287 arrests.

"Most of our domestic abuse cases involve alcohol, either by one or both parties," Jones said. "Alcohol plays a great part. People get angry, don't try to defuse the situation, and that leads to assaults."

Montana instituted a Domestic Violence Program last October with a statewide budget of $652,000 to assist human services agencies.

According to the Department of Public Health and Human Services, in 1996, those agencies provided these services:

- Tracked 3,000 cases of partner violence reported to law enforcement.
- Received 15,000 calls to various crisis lines.
- Gave 18,000 nights of shelter to families.
- Provided shelter to 900 men and 850 women.
- Served 170 battered men.

"Many don't come forward because of the embarrassment," said Loy. "Men are particularly embarrassed that their wives are beating them up, and they don't want to see their names in the paper."

But women are the most frequent victims. "The battered woman lives in a war zone," the HHS's Center on Substance Abuse Treatment reports. "She rarely knows what will trigger an abusive episode, and often there is little, if any, warning of its approach.

"She spends a great deal of time and energy trying to read subtle signs and cues in her partner's behavior and moods in order to avoid potential violence, but she is not always successful," it added. "Financial constraints and fear that the batterer will act on his threats to harm family members or continually harass, stalk, and possibly kill her often inhibit victims from leaving."

It's not an idle threat. Researchers have found that alcohol is involved in about half the incidents of domestic violence, and about 40 percent of male batterers are heavy or binge drinkers.

"A recent study found that more than half the defendants accused of murdering their spouses had been drinking alcohol at the time," it said. And a study of more than 2,000 American couples found rates of domestic violence were almost fifteen times higher in households where husbands were described as often drunk as opposed to never drunk.

There's been a renewed interest in domestic abuse in the years since O.J. Simpson's murder acquittal. Local police and prosecutors have been given extensive training and new tools to combat abuse, and the federal government has pitched in more than $1.6 billion to fund abuse prevention. However, it's a big job to change a generational lifestyle.

DIANE'S STORY

"My dad would sit down at the kitchen table and drink blackberry brandy all weekend. He and my mom were both the children of alcoholics, and it had been in their families for years," Diane told me, sitting in a restaurant a few blocks from her mobile home.

"I was the second oldest child, and I took the blame for almost everything. There were a lot of beatings. I never could figure out what I'd done so wrong to get beat so hard."

Diane's beatings suddenly stopped on her thirteenth birthday. "The day I became a teenager, they stopped. Maybe it was because I could run faster, maybe it was because I was a young lady."

At home, Diane was now allowed half a glass of beer—with no restriction on how many half glasses she consumed. It turned her into a wild child. "We'd find someone to buy beer for us—after all, we were vulnerable young women and men," she said. "They'd drop us off in the mountains, and frequently they'd come party with us. It was fun, but it was pretty destructive behavior."

She graduated from high school in central Montana at eighteen and left home the next day. She had her first child at nineteen, her first husband at twenty, and two more children before her first divorce at twenty-four. "My drinking was so bad that my parents had to take my children away and raise them," said Diane. "All I wanted to do was party."

At twenty-five, she entered into a marriage that lasted eighteen years and produced three more children. "We drank a lot, got into fights, and knocked each other around a lot throughout the entire marriage," she said. "I have to admit I brought a lot of it on myself just to get attention," she added, "and I could be abusive, too."

Only the anger remains after the marriage ended. "Even today, I'd like to tie him up to a telephone pole and beat the hell out of him with a baseball bat. He's one person I've not made my amends to yet."

As her marriage was ending, Diane went through treatment—but it backfired. Instead, she became addicted to poker. "The anger, fear, guilt, and shame all built up, and I stole my ex-husband's checkbook and wrote bad checks all up and down this town," said Diane. "Then I went on a three-day runner [drunk] and gambled all that money away."

Since her arrest January 4, 1997, she has been sober, she said. "Now I don't need a drink or a poker machine to have fun," she said. "And I have learned that I have an addictive personality. If I enjoy something, I want to do it over and over again, and I become addicted to it. I could be addicted to food, to gardening, to reading."

There are a lot of addicts in Great Falls, she said—but also a lot in every town because they deny their addictions. "Now that I understand these things about myself, I have a tremendous sense of peace," she said. "I feel better about myself now than I ever did in my life."

JULY

In July, Bill Broderson's life turned yet another corner.

He was drinking heavily, sleeping in the parks, and getting shakes and delirium tremens. Depressed, he swallowed a handful of the anti-depressant drug he had been prescribed. That put him back in the Benefis Healthcare detox unit for a weekend.

When released, he promised to try to stay sober enough to sleep in the Rescue Mission. "It would be nice to have a roof over my head again," he said. And food, too. In June, Broderson frequently didn't eat for days. One day when I bought him a bowl of soup, he couldn't keep it down.

"The Rescue Mission feeds you good," he said. "I get a half plate of their food, and I've gained two pounds." Sobriety stretched for a month, partially inspired by promises that brought Broderson some hope. One agency suggested he could get job training at the MSU College of Technology-Great Falls and that he might be eligible for a subsidized apartment temporarily.

"Bill's really looking good," said Tara Fatz of the Lobby Bar, where Broderson has done much of his drinking. "His clothes are clean and he's clean-shaven," she said. "I'm so proud of him."

Sipping an orange juice on the house, a clear-eyed Broderson beamed. It hasn't been easy. Sobriety has brought double vision at times and affected his balance, leaving him lurching when he's cold sober. But he talks about getting temporary work again as a painter, his profession for many years. And he got a job digging a hole for a homeowner trying to find a natural gas line.

"That paid me $15," he said. "It's nice to have a couple of dollars in your pocket. When I was drinking, it would have been gone in an afternoon, but now I can make it last for two weeks, mostly for cigarettes."

For Broderson, the critical test was the Fourth of July weekend, when a lot of his friends had time on their hands and government checks in their pockets. "Everybody was partying," said Broderson, "but I just stayed away. The way I figure it, if you stay out of the kitchen, you don't get burned."

CONSEQUENCES OF DRUNKEN DRIVING

On my checklist of stories to write was one on the perils of drinking and driving. I wanted to interview someone who could outline not only the personal tragedy, but also the financial hardships. So I began asking around, and folks at the Great Falls Pre-release Center suggested I talk with Scott Guess, who had been critically injured in a wreck that killed the other driver, a drunk coming home from a night of drinking.

It was dawn on August 25, 1990, and Guess of Great Falls remembered the sky as "blue but darker than sin" as he and his wife, Juli, drove through Nevada to visit his sister in Sacramento.

That's when he spotted the pickup truck heading straight toward him in the passing lane of Interstate 80. Guess slammed on his brakes, leaving 58 feet of skid marks, but the pickup driver never even slowed down.

Guess doesn't remember much of the head-on crash. "I heard the words, 'He's dead' and I thought it was me," Guess said. "My skull was fractured so badly that my eyes were offset by half an inch, and I was seeing four of everything."

But the paramedic was describing the condition of the pickup's driver. Later, police learned he had been drinking all night long.

Over the past decade, four times as many Americans died in drunken driving collisions than died in Vietnam, according to Mothers Against Drunk Driving. In 1997, there were 16,189 people killed in alcohol-related crashes—an average of one every 32 minutes or the equivalent of two jetliners crashing each week.

Drunken driving, however, actually appears to be on the decline. The National Highway Traffic Safety Administration says the proportion of highway deaths blamed on alcohol use has dropped from 57 percent in 1982 to 39 percent in 1997.

"I don't have anything against drinking," said Guess, "but drinking and driving is wrong. One person's choice can affect an entire community, and alcohol and gambling are on the top of my list of poor choices." The pickup driver, Burton D. Brown, 33, of McDermitt, Nevada, was killed in the wreck, leaving behind a widow and a grieving family. His blood alcohol concentration was .26, according to the police report of the accident.

After the wreck, Guess was conscious and in excruciating pain for an hour and 45 minutes that it took rescuers to cut him out of the wreckage of his small car. He was in surgery for 16 hours the first time. His sister, Tammy Donstad, drove to the hospital in Reno, but couldn't recognize him. "If the nurses hadn't pointed him out to me, I wouldn't have known he was my brother," she said.

"That particular weekend, there were three others in the intensive care unit who were victims of drunk drivers," she said, "and my first thought was that drivers convicted of DUI should be required to spend time in a hospital ICU."

Thirteen other surgeries followed for Guess, who spent most of the next two years in hospitals. "Scott has endured incredible pain since this tragic accident," wrote his attorney, Jim Regnier, in a letter to the Air Force seeking insurance benefits. "The multiple surgeries, the skull fractures, the migraine headaches have never left Scott without one day of pain."

Medical bills were more than a quarter-million dollars for him and Juli, who was hospitalized for three weeks with a severely broken leg, collapsed lung, and other injuries.

"That accident will affect the rest of my life," she said, "because I will always have to worry about having a rod in my leg."

Regnier estimated potential damages of the accident at $930,000.

"It ruined me financially," said Guess, adding that his $100,000 Air Force policy didn't come close to meeting even medical expenses.

The accident ended Guess's career as a telephone installer at Malmstrom Air Force Base. He now is retired on half pay. It ended the carefree days of hunting, skiing, and playing basketball or racquetball, although he does referee elementary school soccer games now. And, he says, it ended his marriage. "I don't blame my ex-wife," he said. "It was hard for her to hear the doctors say that I would never walk again."

But Juli Buchanan, who has since remarried, said she and Scott would probably have divorced anyway—the accident just hastened the process. "Right after the accident, I had to be away from Scott for so long because he was in the hospital," she said. "When he got out, he thought he had been given another life and he went another direction.

"But he was a lot closer to death than I was," she said, "so that's understandable."

For a long time, she said, she was unable even to talk about the accident without bursting into tears. Naturally, that affected her whole family. Her father, in particular, was angry about the accident and at the drunken driver. "It was my dad and my mom who were here with me when Scott was not," said Buchanan, "and it was my dad who saw me all cut up and hobbling around on crutches."

The Guess family was equally devastated. "It still upsets my mother because Scott can't do the physical things he used to do—even though he's doing things they never thought he would be able to do again," said Tammy Donstad. "And my father just won't talk about it."

She was on the phone daily with her parents, racking up a phone bill that exceeded $500 that first month alone. She said she took a two-month unpaid leave of absence to be with her brother in Reno, where her weekly motel bill exceeded her monthly apartment rent back in Sacramento. "It's amazing how people you don't even know can have such a dramatic impact on your life," said Donstad.

And it has affected the community of which Guess is a part. "He and I used to play a lot of basketball together, just one-on-one," remembered his friend Mike Allison. "He'd come over to my parents' place, we'd work a little bit, then frequently we'd play basketball until 1:00 or 2:00 in the morning."

The Guesses were not quite done painting their house in Great Falls when the accident occurred. Allison, numb, went over to finish the touchup. "It was like it happened to our family," added his wife, Wendy Allison. "We just had a sick-to-the-stomach heartache."

The next trauma was when Guess finally got out of the hospitals. "He looked like death warmed over," said Wendy Allison. "He was so skinny that his eyes were sunken back in his head." The Allisons sought counseling from Jeff Beazley, then pastor of the First Baptist Church in Great Falls. So did Guess.

"After the accident, his whole life caved in," said Beazley, now pastor of the Absarokee Evangelical Church. "Things had been going pretty good for him, but that accident took the air out of his tire."

For ministers and health care providers, that's a fairly common scenario. Vehicle crashes are the leading cause of death among people under thirty-four years old in the United States, according to the U.S. Department of Health and Human Services, and nearly half of them involve alcohol.

Alcohol interferes with psychomotor skills, such as brain-hand coordination, and with cognitive skills, such as information processing. A driver's risk of being involved in a fatal crash nearly doubles with each percentage increase in blood alcohol content.

BACs as low as 0.02 can impair a driver's ability to divide his or her attention between two or more tasks. BACs ranging from 0.03 to 0.05 interfere with voluntary eye movement and make it more difficult to track a moving object, such an oncoming car. BACs of more than 0.05 significantly diminish reaction time and information processing. A BAC of 0.1 is legally drunk in Montana and many other states, although there has been a push to drop that limit to 0.08. For a juvenile, the limit is 0.02.

The U.S. Justice Department says the number of drivers increased by 15 percent between 1986 and 1997, but the number of DUI arrests declined by almost 18 percent, from 1.8 million in 1986 to 1.5 million in 1997. As a result, it said, the arrest rate for drunken driving declined about 28 percent, from 1,124 arrests per 100,000 in 1986 to 809 per 100,000 in 1997.

But for the victims of a drunken driver, even one's too many. Guess has since remarried. He and his wife, Taya, have two children of their own, and he has adopted her two children from a previous marriage. Although he has built a new life, he feels his future was stolen. "I live with constant pain," he said. "And I know that life will bring me back to a wheelchair soon, as soon as the arthritis kicks in," he said. "So I'm living in the prime of my life right now. I have to make the most of it."

DUI LAWS

After talking with Guess, I knew I needed to talk with someone on the other side, someone who had been convicted several times of drunken driving. Again, I found a willing interviewee in the Great Falls Prerelease Center.

In all his years of drinking and driving, Curt Hiebert figured he's lucky he didn't do more damage. "Mainly, I just tore up cars, telephone poles, and guardrails," said Hiebert, now serving time in the Great Falls

Pre-release Center for his fifth DUI conviction. "I was really fortunate I didn't injure anyone else," he said.

Still, it has cost Hiebert dearly. "I've hit the bottom quite a few times—two failed marriages, numerous jobs, loss of driving privileges, and finally imprisonment," he said.

Since the Legislature made felonies of all DUI offenses after the third conviction, Montana spends more than $1 million annually locking up drunken drivers like Hiebert. In July, the Montana State Prison was holding forty-five drunken drivers at a daily cost of more than $2,500. Prerelease centers hold many more, including twenty-six in a special unit of the center in Butte at a cost of more than $1,000 a day. Nationally, more than half a million Americans were on probation or behind bars for drunken driving in 1997, almost twice the level of the mid-1980s, according to the U.S. Justice Department.

Looking back after his most recent treatment at Gateway Recovery Center, Hiebert can see the causes of his alcoholism more clearly. "I came from a dysfunctional family and used alcohol and drugs to hide the pain," he said. "I never learned to deal with my problems directly, and you don't mature when you're using chemicals to escape from pain."

His life has been a series of marriages, divorces, DUIs, and treatments. "One morning, I woke up and realized that I had to do something just for me," he said. "Finally, I was ready to listen. I'd run out of alibis." He figured if he stayed sober and kept going to Alcoholics Anonymous meetings, he wouldn't keep messing his life up and ending up in treatment or prison. Furthermore, AA was free.

"I've done a lot of harm to a lot of people, but I can't make up for the past," he said. "Yesterday is gone, but today is here and tomorrow is coming. All I can do is live responsibly today and tomorrow."

DUI standards are tougher today, and most experts agree that's making a difference. Montana Highway Patrol officers wrote 2,574 tickets for driving under the influence in 1998, down 6.5 percent from the year before.

About 29 percent of drivers in fatal crashes had been drinking last year, compared with almost 33 percent the year before. Col. Craig Reap, former Highway Patrol chief, recalled that half the drivers involved in fatal accidents in the 1980s had used alcohol. He attributed the change to tougher laws, more recognition of the drunken-driving problem, and greater use of designated drivers.

The tougher laws started in 1995, when legislators made the fourth or subsequent DUI a felony with mandatory jail time. The maximum penalty is 13 months. One requirement of the DUI laws is attending ACT (Assessment, Course, and referral to Treatment), which is an alcohol-counseling program.

Hiebert credits much of his personal growth to counselors at the Gateway Recovery Center, which offers ACT classes.

Last year, 225 people also took DUI classes at Benefis Healthcare, and that pace continues. Over the years, however, the number of people who repeat the class has dropped.

"In 1988, we had a 49 percent recidivism rate," said J.T. Lute, who runs the class. "Now we're down to 21 percent recidivism." He attributes that success to a low-key approach that stresses personal responsibility and education without blame.

"Blaming people doesn't work," he added. "It just makes them defensive." Public education has been increasingly effective, he said. "People are more conscious of DUI," said Lute, "but there will always be those people who are unable to stop after that first drink."

The problem with repeat offenders is a serious one because it's hard to change behavior with a law. The law now allows judges to order treatment earlier for a persistent offender and to suspend a sentence until treatment is completed, using jail as a threat to ensure compliance. The law also allows judges to order an interlock device placed on cars driven by repeat DUI offenders. That prevents a car from starting unless the driver passes a breathalyzer test in his own vehicle. "That may keep an honest person honest," said Al Recke, coordinator of the Cascade County DUI Task Force, "but a non-compliant individual will just go out and get another car."

Montana law allows law enforcement agencies to seize the cars from repeat offenders. "But usually those vehicles are not worth the money to seize, impound, and sell them," said Recke. His preference is to work with the wife or the girlfriend of the repeat offenders, encouraging them to take the keys away from the drunk.

"Frequently, you can't reach the drinker," said Recke. "The best you can hope for is that the significant other has enough courage to demand the car keys and not be intimidated."

Here's how DUI penalties stiffen:

- **First offense:** minimum of twenty-four hours in jail; maximum six months in jail and $500 fine.
- **Second offense:** minimum seven days in jail; maximum six months in jail and $500 fine.
- **Third offense:** thirty days in jail; maximum year in jail and $1,000 fine.
- **Fourth and subsequent offense:** a felony with imprisonment of not less than six months or more than thirteen months, which may not be suspended.

TROUBLE IS BREWING

By late July, Broderson was getting restive at the Rescue Mission. He knew he would be turned away if he showed up drunk, so it forced him to stay sober. But he was chafing under the requirement that he attend an evening worship service in return for his dinner.

And he felt the mission administrator was putting some pressure on him to become a part of its regular program, which would give him trusty status, but require that he spend the first month working inside the mission; if he needed to run an outside errand, an escort would be provided.

I was surprised one day to receive a letter at my home from Montana Sen. Conrad Burns. I was even more surprised to find that it was addressed to Broderson, care of my home address. So I took it down to the mission the next day and asked Broderson about it. "I'm not sure how long they're going to let me stay in the Rescue Mission," he replied, "and I don't have any other place where he could send me mail."

AUGUST

Two months of sobriety left Bill Broderson with a clear view of what he needs to survive. "My first job is to get a roof over my head, a base camp," he said. "After that, I can try to get a job and make a little money. But my health is shot," he added. "In the morning, I'm ready to run the miracle mile, but by about noon, I'm just depleted."

Broderson, who turned 50 in April on a birthday he can no longer remember, has been through more treatment programs than he can count during his decades as an alcoholic. He quit drinking shortly after being diagnosed with the liver disease hepatitis C. It's incurable, and drinking only hastens its progress.

But sobriety brought a whole new set of problems for someone who has nothing—no job, home, car, savings, insurance, or pension. For the past two months, Broderson has been living and eating at the Great Falls Rescue Mission.

Stays are usually limited to two weeks, but he has received several extensions, and Mission Director Eric Berger wants him to become part of the permanent staff, although Broderson refused because he would be confined to the mission for the first month.

"They do a lot of good there, but I really get cabin fever," he said. Broderson said he usually is awake by 5:30 A.M. and stares out a window or reads a magazine until the doors open at 7:00 A.M. "We're locked in again at 6:30 P.M. for our meal," he said. "Chapel starts at 7:30. Then I go upstairs, take a shower, and watch TV until the lights go out at 10:30."

Berger has been working with Pete Townsend, emergency services manager at Opportunities Inc., to get Broderson a subsidized apartment. In fact, Broderson's whole lifestyle is subsidized. He spent a weekend in the detox unit of Benefis Healthcare a couple of months ago, a bill that the hospital writes off as part of its community service program.

For more routine medical attention, he visits the City-County Health Department, which recently diagnosed the hepatitis C free of charge. Counseling for alcoholism is provided by the New Directions Center under a contract with Montana Community Partners, the state's mental health care provider. "There's a sliding scale for payments, but since I don't have any income, I don't pay," he said.

Broderson also has an MCP card that allows him to get medications, such as anti-depressants, for free. He has been told he is ineligible for Veterans Administration benefits because he went AWOL and left the Army with a dishonorable discharge.

He has applied for Social Security disability benefits and for Medicaid, but was told that a hearing date on his eligibility could be years away. "[Sen. Conrad] Burns and [Rep. Rick] Hill have some really good people who are working to get me a hearing date as soon as possible," he said. His one success, he added, has been getting his food stamps restored; he'll be receiving $125 worth of them each month.

A house painter for many years, Broderson has been looking for small painting jobs to make him a little money. "But I'm not going to be much good on ladders," he admitted. He recently visited the state Department of Public Health and Human Services in Great Falls to take some tests to determine if he would be eligible for vocational education training to learn a new trade.

Townsend, who has known Broderson professionally for years, watches his progress with optimism and apprehension. "He's looking real good right now, but I've seen Bill get back on his feet before," Townsend said. "My fear is that when he gets his own apartment, hangers-on will appear and he'll begin having problems again."

Townsend said he'll be more comfortable when Broderson gets a job. "The job program will be key," he said. "Sobriety can be temporary and housing can be temporary, but working a job program will be critical to his long-range success."

ALCOHOL SALES ON INDIAN RESERVATIONS

By some estimates, the unemployment rate on Montana's Indian reservations is about 80 percent, and drinking is a huge problem. But there was also a problem with racial sensitivity—I didn't want to come down on Native Americans too heavily in this series.

I had spent some time on the Fort Belknap Indian Reservation as we looked at fetal alcohol syndrome, but I had deliberately stayed away from using Native Americans in other stories because I knew we had to devote one major segment of the series to them. In my mind, that was August.

One of my reasons was that the Blackfeet tribe, on a reservation along the Canadian border just east of Glacier National Park, had just completed a major celebration, North American Indian Days. Over the years, the celebration had gotten drunker and more out of hand. No one had ever kept statistics on it, but the anecdotal information was all fairly bad—a lot of arrests for public intoxication and driving under the influence, a lot of fights and assaults, usually a fatal car wreck or two.

But this year, the tribe banned alcohol sales on the reservation for the entire weekend and found that the problems lessened. Since there were no good statistics from the preceding year, I decided to seek similar statistics from one weekend in August when booze flowed freely.

The differences between the two weekends were striking. During North American Indian Days July 8-11, there were ten traffic accidents, all relatively minor, all involving tourists; none alcohol-related. The weekend of August 5-8, there were six accidents, two with injuries, and half were alcohol-related. No DUIs were reported in July. There were five in August.

There were 98 arrests in July, but only 64 in August. That's because Browning was filled with tourists during North American Indian Days and because several of the Indian fire-fighting crews had been called out in August, said Liz Rutherford, tribal police statistician.

Police responded to 28 disturbances in July, 78 in August. And there were five reported assaults in July, nine in August. "Our assaults were way up, and I expect that half of them would be alcohol-related," Rutherford said. Two assault victims required medical treatment at Blackfeet Community Hospital in July, compared to five in August.

During the July four-day weekend, the hospital treated 54 patients in its emergency room. For the same period in August, there were 215.

Ten people came to the hospital seeking medical help for alcohol withdrawal when alcohol sales were banned in July; that number dropped to seven when alcohol was sold in August.

Eighteen people were arraigned in tribal court for open containers, disorderly conduct, and public intoxication in July. That number rose to 24 for the same weekend in August, plus there were seven DUIs and two minors charged with possession of alcohol.

ALCOHOL'S DESTRUCTIVE HOLD

But I went to Browning for more than statistics. I went to get a full picture of how alcohol has devastated the Indian culture. The Blackfeet tribe didn't use alcohol until white men introduced it in the mid-19th century and began, in their view, to use it as a weapon against them. Today there's a school of thought that holds that the death rate due to alcoholism demonstrates most clearly the theory of "survival of the fittest" when a new disease is introduced to a potentially vulnerable population.

I heard those stories through the day, and I saw them unfold around me as Beckner and I rode in a squad car with the tribal police. As the patrol car rounded the corner behind Ick's Bar, Lorinda Grant dropped the quart bottle of beer she had been swigging—but it was too late.

"Don't fool with my nerves, Jay," Grant told the officer as he put her in the police car. "I'm scared to go to jail. I've been hitting it hard for a month now, and I'm gonna go bananas without another drink. Why are you doing this to me?" she demanded, hands shaking and tears running down her cheeks.

"I'm keeping you safe tonight so you'll be alive tomorrow," Patrolman Jay Young Running Crane responded.

As Grant was being booked for public intoxication at the Blackfeet tribal jail that Friday night, three others also were being jailed for alcohol-related offenses—one for DUI, one for disorderly conduct, and one for trespassing.

"If we didn't have such easy access to alcohol, there wouldn't be such problems," Young Running Crane said. Native Americans in Montana—most of whom live on one of seven Indian reservations—account for about seven percent of the state's population. But they suffer from alcoholism in far greater numbers than others.

While specific data isn't recorded for Montana, national statistics show that Native Americans have alcohol dependence rates three times higher than the national average. Veterans Administration records show that 45 percent of the Indian vets were alcohol-dependent, twice the rate for non-Indian vets.

The Native American death rate for people ages fifteen to twenty-four is 11.4 times higher than for other Americans, according to HHS's Center for Substance Abuse Treatment. "The excess death of younger people is attributed to higher rates for homicide, suicide, accidents, and death attributable to alcoholism," said a report done in 1994 by CSAT.

The Indian Health Service (IHS) says that 17 to 19 percent of all Indian deaths are alcohol-related, compared with 4.7 percent for the general population. "Alcohol or other drug addiction is culminating in the destruction of Native American populations," the report concluded.

ALCOHOL'S IMPACT ON A COMMUNITY

Oddly, in Browning, the number of bars has actually diminished.

There's a motel bar on the east side of town and a state liquor store downtown. Two downtown bars lock their doors and admit only favored patrons, but sell beer and liquor to go.

Regulars buy booze from the three downtown outlets and drink in the alleys or "the jungle," a vacant lot with brush and trees beside one of the bars.

"I'm on the streets because I can't find a job and I'm an alcoholic," said Eula Kicking Woman, who said she is a University of Montana graduate and once worked for the Urban League and the Bureau of Indian Affairs.

With a population of 1,170, according to the 1990 Census, Browning proper has about 50 street people who live on the bottle, officials say. Statistically, if Great Falls had a problem that severe, it would have more than 2,300 alcoholics on the street.

While most people on reservations live far more typical, sober lives, many acknowledge that the effects of booze have undermined their communities. "Everyone on this reservation has been touched directly or indirectly by alcohol," said Herman Whitegrass, a chemical dependency counselor for the tribe. "In fact, most of us have relatives who are alcoholics, living on the street."

It's the alcoholics who provide most of the work for the reservation doctors, nurses, ambulance attendants, cops, and jailers. And it's their names that keep showing up on the police blotter.

"A lot of those people we've almost raised in this jail," Police Chief Fred Guardipee said. "Many of them spend the winter with us." Aldon Potts comes quickly to the chief's mind. "I don't believe Aldon has ever spent more than three consecutive days outside of our jail," Guardipee said. "And when he's here and sober, he just runs this place."

As it turned out, Potts had been released from jail just hours before with a 10-day sentence suspended on condition of good behavior. By suppertime, he was in "the jungle" trying to get a drink and in Ick's package store, where the clerk refused to sell him liquor. And a little before midnight, he was arrested again. After threatening to punch out the arresting officer and after pushing the jailer around, he was held overnight in the drunk tank.

"This jail is really just a revolving door for drunks," Young Running Crane said. "They get a bed and breakfast for a couple of days, then they either get a suspended sentence or they bond out for about $40."

Why is there so much drinking on the reservations?

Some doctors believe a predisposition to alcoholism is passed on genetically. One early study, for example, found that Indians have difficulty metabolizing alcohol.

However, that study was flawed, said Philip May, former chairman of the sociology department at the University of Montana and outgoing head of the University of New Mexico's Center on Alcoholism. "All of the remaining studies of alcohol metabolism among Indians found that Indians metabolize alcohol as rapidly, or more rapidly, than matched controls that were non-Indian," May said.

Furthermore, Indians are uncomfortable with the medical model because it suggests alcoholism may be inevitable, said Dr. Kathleen Masis, behavioral health officer for the IHS in Billings. "But being children of alcoholics predisposes people to alcoholism, whether or not it's inherited," she said. "Sons of alcoholics are four times more likely to become alcoholics themselves."

Like many tribes, the Blackfeet never used drugs or alcohol, even during religious ceremonies, until white men introduced it in the mid 1800s, Whitegrass said.

"The fur trappers who introduced alcohol to the Indians were either alcoholics themselves or they used alcohol abusively," Masis said. "So Native American people learned to use alcohol to get drunk."

That attitude was reinforced by the Indian Prohibition Action of 1832, which prohibited the sale of alcohol to Indians. It was repealed in 1953. Bootleggers abounded, and Indians learned to drink quickly, behavior that has been called the "gulping mechanism."

"They consumed alcohol quickly so that it would be in them, not in their possession where they could be caught with it," Masis said. Contributing to the problem was the loss of the Indian way of life. "Just look at the elimination of the buffalo, which destroyed their economic base—and that's only 100 years ago," Masis said. "Then look at their lost language, the boarding school experience, and the other abuses. Ask yourself what whites would have done."

The prevalence of alcohol abuse also explains why traditional treatment hasn't done much good, she said. "You can't just send everyone to treatment and expect them to come back and be sober when all their families, friends, and social support systems are still using alcohol," Masis said.

Darrell Norman, owner of the Lodgepole Gallery in Browning, said his father drank to get drunk, and he learned that behavior. "No one ever taught us to drink in moderation," he said. "We had no role models." One bad New Year's Eve convinced him he must change, so he quit drinking for seven years, Norman said. "Then my fiancée looked at me and asked what I was afraid of—the substance or myself? Now I can enjoy a good glass of wine or a microbrew. But I have also learned there's a limit beyond which I cannot go."

SPIRITUAL UNDERPINNINGS OF ALCOHOLISM

Loss of the traditional Indian religion has led to a spiritual gap that some fill with alcohol.

"There are more young people on the streets than there were ten or fifteen years ago," said Clifford Calf Tail, one of the street people of Browning. "But we need to be healed spiritually before we can be healed physically." Without a strong spiritual underpinning, Calf Tail said, Native Americans are powerless before the poverty, illness, premature death, and abuse so common in the community.

Earl Old Person, chief of the Blackfeet Nation, has worried about the increase in alcoholism during his years of tribal leadership. He was a member of the tribal business council for about four decades and has been chief since 1978. "Young people are seeking something," Old Person said. "A lot of them are doing traditional sweats to cleanse themselves and give themselves more strength. I think it's really helping our young people."

But the chief, who is seventy, said it has become harder for the elders to communicate with the young people.

"Some of our young people are afraid to talk to our elders, and some of our elders are afraid to talk to our young people because they are afraid they won't be accepted," he said. "But when we keep these things to ourselves, it only hurts us."

EMPLOYMENT AND SOBRIETY

High unemployment also has hurt Native Americans.

"There's no work around here," complained Garrett Many White Horses, a frequent resident of "the jungle." "If I had a job, I'd get my wife back. That's why families break up."

Native Americans make up about seven percent of the state's population, but Indian adults received 26 percent of the state's welfare checks two years ago when Montana began its push to get welfare recipients back onto the job. As the welfare rolls were cut in half in the past few years, Native Americans found it no easier to get jobs. Now they receive 42 percent of the adult welfare checks.

"We don't have jobs, and our people need work," Old Person said. "Fighting fires isn't pleasant, but our people do it to help their families. A lot of people think the Blackfeet Nation just wants handouts, but what we really want is jobs. Our people would work if it was there."

Masis of the IHS also links unemployment and alcoholism. "Someone who is employed, has a sober spouse, and is supported by a strong social support system stands a better chance of success," she said. "In fact, employment is one of the best predictors of success in sobriety."

Young Running Crane sees some hope in the DARE program, which is teaching students in Browning schools to avoid alcohol and drugs. And he keeps a strict eye on his own teenaged daughter, monitoring her activities and friends as he cruises the streets in his patrol car.

Masis has seen a growing sobriety movement on the reservations. "There's a lot of hope," she said. "I've heard that Native Americans are one of the fastest-growing segments of the American sobriety movement, which is one of the most powerful forces of our time." On the Blackfeet Reservation, Whitegrass teamed up with June Tatsey, the tribe's medical director, and Gerald Cooper, a security officer for the Blackfeet Tribal Hospital, to raise public awareness of the danger of alcohol by creating a series of sobriety marches.

At the first march several years ago, Whitegrass remembers stopping at each street corner and blowing sweetgrass smoke to the four compass points, called smudging, to purify the streets. "And I remember passing a big beer truck with the driver hiding his face in shame, so we smudged the beer truck, too," Cooper said.

Several hundred people joined them on that first march, and each march has grown a little bigger since. Out of the sobriety marches grew the idea of banning alcohol sales on the reservation during the North American Indian Days in mid-July.

"It was a gut-wrenching decision," said Tatsey, adding that she was terrified there would be a huge accident on the road to Cut Bank, a town off the reservation where the bars were still open. But earlier this year, it became obvious that something had to be done. "In seven weekends, we lost seven of our children, one each weekend," Cooper said.

Ultimately, the tribal council bought the notion and passed a resolution barring all sales of alcohol on the reservation July 8-12. Later, Tatsey, Whitegrass, and Cooper were relieved to find that crime and accident rates dropped dramatically during that period.

"We, as Indian people, have to solve our own problems," Tatsey said. "People have come to us with well-meaning solutions, but until we're willing to address our own problems, nothing will have changed."

Now, they're gearing up for a push to make the whole reservation dry—permanently. "We're all in the health care field, and we're looking at the future of our Blackfeet people," Tatsey said. "At one time, we were a strong, healthy people. Now we need a positive environment for our children, so the Blackfeet Nation can be healthy again."

Whitegrass noted that well-meaning efforts like welfare actually have made things worse. "Some people need the welfare system to get a step up, but other people get stuck in it," Whitegrass said. "I believe the welfare system has disabled us by enabling people to continue their destructive behaviors." Change must come quickly, Cooper said. "Are we going to walk into the new millennium with our heads held high, or are we going to stagger in drunk?" he asked. "It's our choice."

AN ADDICTION WITHOUT EXPLANATION

One noon Whitegrass took me down to the senior citizens' center to talk with some of the elders about their experiences with alcohol abuse. I was stunned at the prevalence and power of their stories, so I jotted down several of them. Here are some of those stories:

Connie Bremner, who runs the Blackfeet Senior Citizens Center, can testify to the damage alcohol does to reservation families by ticking off the deaths of her children and grandchildren.

"My daughter had twins," she said. "When they were fifteen, they were in an auto accident with a drunken driver, and one of them was killed. My forty-three-year-old daughter got a DUI just a block away from her house and was thrown in jail," she said. "She hung herself in the jail, was in a coma for days, and now she needs me to care for her. I've been doing that for 14 years.

"My youngest son got drunk and got into a fight with his half-brother and killed him. He's in prison now. And I have another son who got drunk, thrown in prison, and he hung himself, too. When I say that alcohol has affected all our lives on this reservation, I know what I'm talking about."

When Patrick After Buffalo was growing up, alcohol wasn't permitted on the reservation, although some bootleggers did bring it in. "My people were a peaceful people," he said, sitting at a table in the Blackfeet Senior Citizens Center. "The big event was prayer meetings."

Then After Buffalo joined the military and was a platoon leader in Korea. "I learned to drink and smoke there," he said. "When I came home, bars were open on the reservation and I became one of the biggest drunks here. I even sold my land to get drunk."

Alcohol originally was used as a weapon by white fur traders to steal land from the Indians, he said, adding that it still keeps the Indian people dependent and poor. He estimates that many people spend 60 percent of their incomes on alcohol. "I drank up my whole ranch before I repented, and I also had two uncles who drank so that their ranches came to nothing," After Buffalo said. "I've known people who lived at the bars and got into such debt that they lost their homes. It's an addiction without an explanation," he said.

Allen Redhead, who graduated from the University of Montana in 1985, is homeless, sleeping under the trees when the weather is good, crashing with friends when it's not.

"I wake up about 6:00 in the morning and start drinking my night beer," he said. In Browning, most alcoholics save one beer from the night before and drink it early the next morning to avoid getting the shakes, seizures, or hallucinations that can accompany temporary sobriety.

When Ick's Bar opens at 8:00 A.M., Redhead usually begins buying beer. He has some income—his elbow was crushed several years ago when he was run over by a train near Vancouver, Washington, and now he gets a disability check. "I was drunk," he said.

Whitegrass, the chemical dependency counselor for the tribe and head of the DUI Task Force, began his own drinking career at eleven or twelve. "Drunks like music, so I learned to play the guitar and started a band," he said. While the music was important, so was partying with the band. "Then I became a driver for my older brother and his friends," he said. "I'd drive them from bar to bar, and they'd get me a six-pack to drink while I waited."

Later, he began hitchhiking to Cut Bank, then riding the rails to Spokane and Seattle, where he lived in the hobo jungles and on the skid rows. "I learned how to drink Sterno and sell my blood to buy alcohol," he said. "I used to take my guitar and play music in the hobo jungles. I was deep into alcohol and drugs, and I had many thoughts of suicide. I used to dream of jumping off a railroad trestle as a way of escaping."

Finally, he ended up homeless. "I went on the streets for the comfort I didn't get at home," he said. "Street people take care of each other." Finally, he found fellowship in a treatment center and went on to preach sobriety to those around him.

"I guess I was just doing the research for my current career," he said. "But I'm one of the lucky ones who lived to tell about it." Some of the scars remain, however. "I used to do a lot of fighting in bars," Whitegrass said. "Now when I go into restaurants, I have trouble with people standing behind me because I'm so used to protecting my back. That's something I'll probably never lose."

Fred Makes Cold Weather is another of Browning's street people.

"I drank all my life," said Makes Cold Weather, a former truck and diesel mechanic who once had a home in the suburbs. "Alcohol has destroyed my life. I have ten children, but they're ashamed of me—they don't come around me no more."

Gene Ground remembers the day twenty-eight years ago that changed his life. It was a payday, and he had $165 tucked away in his wallet. "I told my wife I was going over to the store to get a few things, but I ran into two guys and we went over to the bar instead. They had two or three beers and they left, but I was there until 2:00 A.M. I could never have just one beer—when I went into a bar, I was there until it closed."

When he woke up the next morning, his last remaining $5 bill was beside his plate at the breakfast table. And his wife wasn't speaking to him. "All week long, never a word," he said. "Man, that was a long, cold, miserable, lonely week." The next weekend, his friends called him to come drinking, but Ground stayed home and watched a movie with his wife. She began talking to him a little.

The same thing happened the next weekend. Then the friends quit calling. "The weeks and months and years went by and I never took another drink," Ground said. "But for all the years that my wife lived, she never asked me if I had quit drinking."

Roger Rabbit, a certified Head Start teacher, is still drinking.

"Alcohol has ruined my life, and it ruined my family," he said, weaving a little in the morning sun as he stood out in front of "the jungle." He watched with interest the tribe's ban on alcohol sales during North American Indian Days, and he has heard it could lead to a permanent ban on alcohol. "If this reservation goes dry, I'd sober up, put myself in treatment and make another family," he said.

But some get lucky. One of those was Joyce Little Bull, who quit drinking after doctors told her the alcohol was killing her.

"When they told me that one more drink would be bad for me, I put my life in the hands of the Lord Jesus and stopped drinking," said Little Bull, a soft-spoken woman who has been working with the street people and volunteering at her church ever since.

Little Bull began drinking when she turned eighteen, "but it had gotten to the point about five years ago that I was drinking every day and living on the street." She remembers life on the streets as a desperate search for a drink. "I'd always be fighting for that next drink. And when I got it, I'd drink it fast so that I wouldn't miss out on the next one. Living on the street, there's no shame. The only thing we were concerned about was getting that next drink."

As dusk fell, the street people would watch to see who was buying alcohol, and then go party in a house where they knew the booze would be flowing. "But we knew we were going to be sick in the morning, so we'd save a beer—and then it would start all over again," she said.

For the past year, Little Bull has been sober and in a recovery program, but she has maintained her ties with those who continue to drink. Nearly fifty Browning residents are alcoholics living on the streets, she estimated.

Little Bull frequently works with the Rev. Mike McHugh, a Jesuit priest assigned to the Little Flower Parish in Browning the past fifteen years. "We've had some success in our treatment center, and we have more people in Alcoholics Anonymous," McHugh said. He and Little Bull preach a tough love on the streets.

"In the streets and alleys, I just love them whether they're drunk or sober," the priest said. "But it's a tough love—I never give them money or a ride somewhere. Sometimes I think I can only love them while they're alive and bury them when they're dead," he said. "That's a shameful thought, but I'm afraid it's a realistic one."

McHugh isn't sure whether prohibiting the sale of alcohol on the Blackfeet Reservation will do any good. "People must come to the point where they don't want to drink anymore, and I don't think they're at that point."

Earl Old Person, chief of the Blackfeet Nation, wants more federal funding for alcohol treatment centers, but he acknowledges that isn't the complete solution. "There are already a lot of programs to prevent it [alcoholism], but some of the young people on the streets of Browning have their own mindset," he said. "That's their life and they don't want to be bothered."

Alcoholism always remains a personal choice, Old Person said. "When you come right down to it, everyone has problems," he said. "I have problems that no one knows about, but that's no excuse to drink."

Little Bull no longer employs those excuses, either. "Many of the street people come up to me now and they tell me they want to be like me because I look so happy," she said.

FALLS OFF THE WAGON

We hadn't been back from Browning for long when I got an ominous phone call at an unusually early hour.

"I'm drunk," blurted Broderson.

Sobriety, pain, and the difficulty of trying to piece together a shattered life had apparently taken its toll. "I went out last night and got a beer," he said, and it was obvious he was back in the bar a little after 8:00 A.M. I really didn't know what to say. I could only hope that his money would run out.

DEBATING ALCOHOL SALES ON RESERVATIONS

Beckner and I also decided to visit the Fort Peck Indian Reservation, on which there was a move to ban alcohol altogether.

Visiting the reservation was not a decision we came to lightly. Fort Peck is in the northeastern corner of Montana, bordering Canada and North Dakota, and drive time is six hours in the daylight, longer at night when deer graze alongside the road and dance on the asphalt.

We met in the paper's parking lot at 5:00 A.M., were in Wolf Point late in the morning, interviewed and photographed until nearly dusk, got some supper and were back in Great Falls about 3:00 A.M.

A long day, but it was worth it because we spent several hours late in the day with Paula Firemoon. She told me that, every morning, she would get up and peek into her daughters' bedrooms to see if her nightmare was real.

"And every morning, their beds would be empty," said Firemoon, tears rolling down her cheeks as she sat at her kitchen table. "Then I would know again that they were really dead." Lorriane, fifteen, and Jessica, twelve, were killed by a drunken driver April 15, 1992. Since then, Firemoon has struggled to come to terms with her loss. Now the entire Fort Peck Indian Reservation is struggling with the question of whether alcohol sales should be banned within its borders.

Paula Firemoon decorates crosses on Highway 2 in Poplar where her daughters died when a drunk driver struck the car they were riding in.

Montana's Native Americans, most of whom live on one of seven reservations in the state, are struggling to find ways to staunch the pain caused by excessive alcohol use. According to national figures, Native Americans have alcohol dependency rates three times higher than the national average. That translates into higher accident rates, suicide rates, crime, and murder rates.

Some on the Fort Peck Reservation say banning the sale of booze might start turning things around. Opponents say it would only close some bars and restaurants, costing scarce jobs and tribal revenue. But Poplar, Montana, Police Chief Joe Leggett said 90 percent of the crime in his city is fueled by booze. "If it weren't for alcohol, we'd be out of business," Leggett said.

However, alcohol is readily available just off the reservation, and statistics from other reservations suggest that banning alcohol sales hasn't been very effective.

Alcohol was fueling Jon Louis Charbonneau on April 15, 1992. According to a police report, he had been to the local liquor store three times before noon that day to buy three half-gallons of vodka.

On his fourth visit in mid-afternoon, he was so drunk the manager refused to sell him more alcohol and called the police to report him. Charbonneau got in his car and roared out of town in the wrong lane of traffic on Highway 2, sending several vehicles into the ditch before slamming head-on into the car containing Firemoon's daughters and two other children.

"The perpetrator had been reported three times that day for being severely drunk, and was allowed to wander the streets until he hit the other car going 75 to 80 mph in a 55-mph speed zone," said Dr. James Melbourne, one of the first medical responders on the scene.

Charbonneau's blood alcohol content was 0.3, three times the legal limit for intoxication, according to the police report. "As a parent, one of our worst nightmares was to have your child run into a drunk driver," Firemoon said. "We adults know all the people who drink, but our kids don't know that, so they can't be defensive enough."

Funeral services for the two girls were held in the Poplar High School gym to accommodate the more than 700 mourners. Ron Luchau, alcohol and drug coordinator for the local schools, expressed the community's reaction in a guest column in the local newspaper, in which he wrote:

> We can stop the drunk driving, drunken public behavior, the buying and giving of alcohol and drugs to our children, the family violence, the intimidation of all of us. It is time for this community to get mad and stay mad. It is time for us to take back our yards and streets.

Some things changed. The speed limit has been lowered in the area where the girls were killed, and there's a new turning lane and pedestrian walkway with flashing yellow lights.

But despite greater public awareness, the problem remains.

"Right now, we have 150 calls for assistance a month, including twenty-one DUIs and a dozen domestic abuse calls—and we're only a four-man department," Leggett said. On this reservation with about 10,600 residents, it's rare to get a call that doesn't involve drunks.

"In fact, it scares me to go out on a call that isn't alcohol-related because I don't know what to expect," he said. Alcohol also takes a tremendous medical toll. "In the past three weeks, we have had three people die of direct alcohol abuse—and these were relatively young people," said Melbourne, the tribal health director.

Medical bills in those three cases alone came to $55,000, he said. "We have to treat people, but these are preventable illnesses. What happens when we spend all our health dollars on people who have elected to choose this destructive course of behavior?"

Melbourne's recommendation is prohibition. One possibility would be to ban the state liquor store and reservation bars from selling alcohol to Native Americans, an action that Melbourne acknowledges could be divisive and constitutionally flawed.

The other would be to ban all alcohol sales on the reservation, which tribal attorneys warn could lead to extensive litigation. "I would like to see a full prohibition, in part to exercise our sovereignty," Melbourne said. "But I'm not a politician, and I'm not sure they would want to face the resulting lawsuits."

The issue of prohibition has stirred up emotions on Fort Peck. "We've got a lot of money tied up in our liquor license and our gambling machines," said Mertice Marottek, owner of the Buckhorn Bar in Poplar. "And there's jobs to consider, too," she said. "We employ about twenty people here, including twelve who are Native Americans."

For fiscal 1999, state liquor stores in Poplar and Wolf Point bought about $480,000 in alcohol from the State Liquor Warehouse to resell to bars and private consumers. By banning alcohol, the tribe would lose the $55,000 to $58,000 it receives annually from its alcohol revenue-sharing agreement with the state.

Video machine gambling is a million-dollar business on the reservation, said Rick Ask of the state Gambling Control Division. Wolf Point and Poplar received about $100,000 as their share of gambling machine revenues in fiscal 1998. Because state law requires that gambling machines be placed in establishments that have liquor licenses, that revenue would be lost as well.

"That would be the end of the VFW, the American Legion, and the Elks Club," Marottek said. "Only the revenue from the sale of alcohol and gambling keeps them going."

Bootleggers would proliferate, she predicted. "Most people go out of town now to buy their groceries and their clothing, and I'm sure they'd be buying their liquor there as well," she said. "What are they going to do, put up roadblocks on every road out of the reservation?"

That could be a possibility, Melbourne said. "Enforcement is the key. We could cross-deputize the Montana Highway Patrol to help us enforce our tribal laws. It's really a matter of the tribe managing our own destiny."

Brad Tande, owner of Tande Grocery, operates the only liquor store in Poplar, which he said sells about $200,000 worth of alcohol to bars, restaurants, and individuals. "There's definitely a problem with alcohol here, but limiting sales is not the issue," Tande said. "Like everything else, too much is bad for you."

Instead, he said, society needs to treat the true causes of alcohol abuse. "People here have no jobs, no sense of self-worth, and they keep losing their sense of hope," he said. "They tell me, 'I wouldn't drink if I could get a job,' and I just tell them I'd be happy to go broke if they could get jobs."

Dr. Masis of the IHS office in Billings said prohibition hasn't worked on other dry reservations such as the Northern Cheyenne and the Crow, because she sees similar health problems on wet and dry reservations.

"It's a stupid idea—prohibition has never worked," said Rodney Standen, a local teacher, as he emerged from the state liquor store cradling a jug of wine. "When I was a kid growing up in South Africa, blacks weren't allowed to drink, so the bootleggers made a fortune."

But Masis said the process is more important than the end result. "From my training and experience, deciding to change things for the better is a good diagnostic sign," she said. "Even if what they decide isn't exactly perfect, it begins a process of improvement. And that's a very promising sign."

AN ARGUMENT AGAINST PROHIBITION

After talking with Masis and Melbourne, I was curious to know whether banning booze on an Indian Reservation does any good. The answer, I quickly learned, was no.

"Crime seems to be fairly constant, whether a reservation is wet or dry," said Mitch Pourier of the Bureau of Indian Affairs (BIA) in Billings. "With the proximity of liquor establishments right off the reservation, it doesn't seem to make much of a difference, except that the revenue generated remains off the reservation," added Pourier, an official with the BIA's law enforcement services.

To gauge the impact, I compiled statistics for two reservations where alcohol is sold—the Blackfeet and Fort Peck—and two others where alcohol is banned—the Crow and Northern Cheyenne.

On the Blackfeet Reservation, where alcohol is sold, thirty-two people were killed between 1991 and 1996 in twenty-five wrecks, twenty of which were alcohol-related.

On the Fort Peck Reservation, also wet, twenty-seven people were killed in twenty-one collisions, nine of which were alcohol-related.

On the Crow Reservation, where liquor is banned, forty people were killed in those six years in thirty-four crashes, twenty-two of which were alcohol-related.

And on the Northern Cheyenne, also dry, nineteen people were killed in fourteen wrecks, twelve of which were alcohol-related, according to the Montana Department of Transportation.

The Bureau of Indian Affairs keeps an eye on the number of child abuse and neglect cases that are alcohol-related on each reservation. The results were mixed. The Blackfeet Reservation had the best rate, with 38 percent of its fifty-one cases related to alcohol abuse.

Second was the Northern Cheyenne, where alcohol is banned. It reported 40 percent of its 314 child abuse and neglect cases were alcohol-related.

Third was the Crow, also dry, where 51 percent of 210 cases were related to alcohol.

Highest was the Fort Peck, reporting 55 percent of 544 child abuse cases were related to alcohol.

Indian Health Service records show that alcoholism is a medical problem on all four reservations. Of the eight reservations overseen by the Billings office, alcohol-induced psychosis is the seventh-leading illness and alcoholic dependence syndrome the twenty-first at IHS hospitals. But on the Northern Cheyenne Reservation, where selling or possessing alcohol is illegal, alcoholic liver disease is the second-leading diagnosis.

And the Crow Reservation, also dry, has its own fourteen-bed detox center to evaluate alcoholics and offer counseling. "It's illegal to have alcohol on this reservation," the center's assistant coordinator John Cummins Jr. said. "If they find it on you or in your car, you can be fined $50."

But Cummins noted that Billings, Hardin, and Sheridan, Wyoming, are all within a few miles—and all have bars and liquor stores.

"Our street people go there and sleep out in boxes near the bars and liquor stores," said Cummins, who estimated the reservation has about 100 alcoholic street people hanging out in the three cities.

Whiteclay, Nebraska, may be the nation's best-known example of the failure of prohibition. It's a tiny town of twenty-two residents that sells $3 million worth of beer a year, primarily to Native Americans with drinking problems. The town sits right outside South Dakota's Pine Ridge Indian Reservation, on which the sale of alcohol is banned.

Two decades ago, a University of Montana graduate student found that problems relating to alcoholism were more severe on dry reservations than they were on those that permitted alcohol sales.

In his 1976 study of seven reservations in Montana and Wyoming, Philip May found that reservations that legalized alcohol sales had:

- 28 percent lower mortality rate from cirrhosis of the liver
- 47 percent fewer suicides
- 18 percent fewer homicides
- 11 percent fewer motor vehicle accidents

"The overall alcohol-related death rate was 8.8 percent lower for wet tribes," reported May, now outgoing head of the University of New Mexico Center for Alcoholism.

He also noted that dry reservations that legalized alcohol sales experienced a short-term doubling of alcohol-related deaths, but that those rates declined steadily over a fifteen- to twenty-year period. "Legalization appears to be associated with fewer alcohol-related deaths and arrests," he concluded.

The reason is that prohibition, if not effectively enforced, changes drinking behavior. "On reservations that have legalized alcohol, new norms develop, norms of moderation and limitation," May said. "On dry reservations, however, you have norms of rapid, forced binge drinking that are encouraged by the law."

SEPTEMBER

Bill Broderson's binge lasted for about a week, but it took its toll.

With no money, he ate almost nothing, but he managed to cadge drinks from other drunks through those bleary, blurry days. He called me regularly from bar to bar, but I refused to buy him drinks. I would get him coffee, orange juice, or lunch, if he could handle it. Early one afternoon, Broderson called from the Red Door Lounge in downtown Great Falls. I needed to see him because I needed him to sign a release on his medical forms so I could ask the various hospital administrators to try to estimate what his illness had cost taxpayers and ratepayers over the years in which he needed treatment, but never could pay.

I picked him up in the bar and we walked to a small coffee shop on Central Avenue, where we got a couple of cups of coffee and sat outside in the warm sunlight. Suddenly, Broderson glanced down at the sidewalk and joked that when he got his shit together, he was going to buy me a new pair of boots. "I've been watching those, man, and they're disgraceful," he said.

I glanced over at him and saw him sitting there, dead serious but also dead drunk at noon, hands shaking, five day's of stubble on his chin. And I totally cracked up. I sat there laughing so hard the tears were rolling down my cheeks. After a moment's confusion, Broderson saw the absurdity of the situation and joined in the laughter.

Due to the drinking, he lost his bed at the Rescue Mission and began sleeping down in the bushes by the Missouri River. "One morning, I woke up and there were rats crawling all over me," he said. "I grabbed a rock and tried to smash them, but I couldn't hit any of them. That's when I knew they were all in my mind," he added. "It was the DTs again."

When he closed his eyes, he saw huge kaleidoscopes of radiant, flashing lights. They made him sick. "Then I started to get the chills, and I was really afraid that I could drown if I had a seizure and rolled into the river. That's when I knew I had to quit again."

But even after he was sober, he wasn't welcome at the Rescue Mission. He continued to sleep outside, watching the lightning at night and hoping it wouldn't rain. Food was still scarce. One day, he was given two doughnuts at Opportunities Inc. and an egg roll by an acquaintance.

Then, as the rains began descending on Great Falls, Broderson was allowed to move back in with Jolena Kipp Williams, whom he considers a daughter, sharing her two-bedroom house with her husband Reuben and their two small children.

One Thursday, with three weeks sobriety behind him, in laundered clothing and clean-shaven again, Broderson went before a judge in a hearing room at the Heritage Inn to determine whether he might receive Social Security disability benefits.

"I don't know who's more nervous, Bill or me," said Jolena Williams before the hearing, sitting on the edge of a stuffed chair in the lobby of the hotel. "He has been sick all morning."

Their lawyer came and took them to a hearing, from which I was barred. After the hearing, Broderson quickly adjourned to the men's room where he vomited up the apple juice and coffee that he had fortified himself for breakfast. "My stomach's been churning all morning," he admitted.

The issue, said Broderson's attorney, Cameron Ferguson, is that the law has been changed so that alcoholism is not a legitimate disability. But the permanent consequences of alcoholism are considered disabilities, he said: things like hepatitis C, cirrhosis, balance, and brain function.

"The judge wanted to know about my walking, lifting, and my energy level," said Broderson. "He wanted to know if I could carry a five-gallon paint can."

"Bill can't lift my baby," responded Williams, "and Brady doesn't weigh any more than twenty-five pounds."

Ferguson was given thirty days to submit a brief detailing Broderson's permanent disabilities, after which he said the judge could take two weeks to two months or more to render a decision. "What's the delay?" stormed Tara Fatz, manager of the Lobby Bar. "What's he supposed to do without any money to live on?" she asked.

But Williams had a longer-range worry. "I wonder what will happen to Bill if he doesn't get these benefits," she said. "He has such big plans, getting a trailer and turning his life around. What will he do if they don't give him anything?"

If Broderson is denied benefits, Ferguson will be out the time and money representing him because he is working on a contingency fee. Broderson said he agreed to pay Ferguson 25 percent of any retroactive back-pay settlement of the monthly $525 SSI disability payments.

There's no telling what that could amount to, but Broderson said he has been waiting for the hearing for more than two years. "I question a process that requires these people to jump through so many hoops that they need legal assistance that ultimately reduces the amount of help that they will receive," said Linda Godak, a state welfare department caseworker in Great Falls.

Furthermore, the process is notoriously slow. "I tell these people that they have to be like little bulldogs," Godak said. "Denial is almost automatic the first time, but they have to be persistent."

THE NATION'S POCKETBOOK

Half of Montana's welfare families may be disabled by alcoholism or drug addiction, social workers say. That was a stunning revelation to me as I began to turn the focus of my stories from how alcohol abuse takes a toll on human lives to how alcohol takes a toll on the nation's pocketbook.

This phase of my reporting was made more difficult because there are no exact figures. Many alcoholics and their families deny there's a problem, but caseworkers can make an educated guess by observing the symptoms.

Kim Brown of the Montana Department of Public Health and Human Services in Helena said she hears from social workers in the field that 40 percent to 60 percent of their cases involve alcohol abuse. "I suspect that alcohol is involved in at least 50 percent of the cases I see," agreed Linda Franz of the state public assistance office in Great Falls.

Three years ago, there was probably the same number of alcoholics on the welfare rolls, she said, but their percentage doubled as the caseload was halved under welfare reform. In fiscal 1999, an average of 5,344 Montana families received cash assistance totaling $2.07 million per month. By August 1999, that had dropped to 4,650 cases totaling $1.84 million. In some of the remaining cases, the alcoholism is obvious, admitted, and documented.

Carol Solis, another caseworker in Great Falls, remembers a woman who has been very open about her battle with the bottle over the past decade. "She's a single woman who couldn't cope, so she left her child with her parents to explore and find herself," Solis said. "She has done a lot of treatment: inpatient, outpatient, religious, whatever. But she constantly finds a job bartending, and she finds men who are abusive," said Solis. "She starts drinking again to mask the pain, then the babies have to go back to grandma and grandpa again."

By now, Solis said, this woman is at a point where there's no sense in putting her in treatment again because she knows it all. She just can't apply it to her own life.

"I see her begin to get herself together, get looking good, a glow in her cheeks, radiant hair," she said, "but then she leaves treatment and is back within six weeks, dull hair and eyes, sallow skin, saying 'It just didn't work again.' And this is a beautiful, intelligent woman who isn't even thirty yet," said Solis. "People have no idea the power of alcohol."

But most families aren't so open about their problems—and they're even harder to treat. "They must address their alcoholism before we can work on anything else to make them self-sufficient," said Franz.

She remembers a client—ironically, one who once worked with troubled kids—who denied being an alcoholic, but who couldn't keep the appointments for his own self-help programs. "Over and over again, he didn't follow through," said Franz. "He was facing his second sanction until he recently asked us to close his case because he planned to move. I suspect we were getting close to something he didn't want to admit, so he planned to go where people didn't know about him," she said, "but his case notes will follow him anywhere he goes in the state."

Not only does the alcoholic need help, but so does his or her family. "Some women just give up in these situations," said Solis, "and it's hard motivating them. It's hard for some women to believe that just because something bad happens to her, she's still worth something. Many of these women are isolated, afraid to tell people there's a drinking problem in their lives and that bad things are happening in her home."

Anger is a constant, fueled by frustration, denial, and guilt. "Alcohol is a big part of the reason our foster care caseloads are soaring," said Solis. "Parents are frustrated, can't cope, and turn to drink."

So caseworkers need to work on self-esteem, financial management, anger control, and probably the aftermath of domestic violence before they can do anything with job-training skills that can lead to employment. "We have to use a lot more community resources, and it takes much more of our time," said Franz. "Even though our caseloads are going down," she added, "we must work a lot harder with the people we have left."

HUGE COST OF ALCOHOL ABUSE

Montana usually has between 2,000 and 2,200 children in foster care on any given day, said Shirley Tiernan, chief of the family services bureau for the state human services department. "Alcohol use is a big factor in children being removed from their homes," she said. "Most of our foster care cases are related to alcohol abuse."

Nationally, Tiernan said, more than 50 percent of foster child placements result from excessive parental drinking. "That may not mean alcohol dependency. It may mean that the parents were drunk and there was no one to take care of the children. They may get them back in a couple of days when they sober up, then keep them for a couple of months until they get drunk again. There are an awful lot of binge drinkers."

The cost of foster care to Montanans was $13.4 million in fiscal 1998, increasing to $14.3 million last year.

Some single alcoholics get food stamps, but they aren't a majority of the caseload by any means, according to two local caseworkers. "There's not a lot we do for single people in Montana unless they're elderly, blind, or disabled," said Sharon Hansen, who supervises about 225 clients eligible for nursing home care, Medicaid, or food stamps.

Able-bodied adults without disabilities can only get three months worth of food stamps in a three-year period. "Many alcoholics and drug addicts fall under these rules, end up disqualified from receiving food stamp benefits, and move on to other areas or somehow survive on the street," said Godak. She believes the rule is too severe for people with severe disabilities, like alcoholism, because it doesn't give them enough time to deal with their problems. But alcoholism isn't always easy to spot, she said.

"I haven't had to turn many of them away because they show up drunk," she added. "They usually get themselves cleaned up before they come in to see me."

Godak can identify about thirty-five alcoholics among her 250 cases—about 14 percent of her workload. That may not be a complete number, "but it's all I can prove," she said.

State officials have difficulty tracking down the number of people in Montana who have been certified as disabled due to the results of alcoholism. Michelle Thibodeau of Helena, who runs the state program, said her office hasn't kept records on the disabled clients in Montana. "We just got computers in March and software in August," she explained. About 950 clients remain on the disability program in Region VIII, a six-state region that includes Montana, the Dakotas, Utah, Wyoming, and Colorado, said Thibodeau. That's about 31 percent of the people who had been certified disabled before the Social Security Administration changed its regulations and denied alcoholism alone as a disability.

"Changing the rules left a lot of people high and dry," said Hansen.

Godak wondered whether it made sense to delay paying benefits to an alcoholic until his or her illness had progressed to a point where serious medical consequences occurred. "You can pay now or pay later," she said. "If this country would address [alcoholism] right at the beginning, far less pain and duress would occur."

GENERATIONS OF WELFARE

Several years ago, America began to realize it was creating a class of people—more than three generations deep in many places—which knew no other lifestyle than welfare checks.

In fact, University of California-San Diego sociologist David P. Phillips analyzed nearly 32 million electronic death certificates over a fifteen-year period to conclude that the welfare lifestyle can be fatal. He found an average of 4,320 more deaths in the first week of every month than the last week of the preceding month, which he attributed to alcoholics and addicts overdosing after spending their first-of-the-month government checks on alcohol and other drugs.

The study "really highlights the extraordinary toll of substance abuse," said Lisa Najavits, a professor of psychology at Harvard Medical School. Partly as a result of this study, a Republican Congress forced welfare reform on Democratic President Bill Clinton.

In Montana, the focus for caseworkers changed from merely certifying eligibility to encouraging welfare recipients to develop job skills and find employment. "Five years ago, I wasn't in the middle of people's lives the way I am now," said caseworker Carol Solis. "It takes more time, it takes more effort, and it takes more of my heart."

In 1995, the National Center on Addiction and Substance Abuse at Columbia University estimated that the federal government spent $11.5 billion treating just the consequences of alcoholism in its entitlement programs such as Medicare, Social Security, Aid to Families with Dependent Children (AFDC), and food stamps. States spent another $1.4 billion, it estimated.

"In 1995, $60.3 billion, or nearly one in five dollars the federal government spends on all health care entitlements, will be spent to treat illness and conditions attributable to tobacco, alcohol, and other drugs," said the center. "This amount is three times as much as the federal government will spend on AFDC, and more than the combined total of AFDC and food stamps."

Now, Bill Clinton can boast about the success of "workfare." Welfare cases dropped from 14.1 million when he took office in 1993 to just 7.3 million in 1999. That worked out to 2.7 percent of the population receiving cash assistance, the smallest percentage since Lyndon B. Johnson was president. In 1967, the figure was 2.5 percent.

But America mirrors the problem in Montana: Those left on the welfare rolls are the least hireable, the ones with the greatest problems. Meanwhile, two ominous deadlines march on. The first is a three-year limit on the length of time a welfare recipient can continue receiving benefits. Many are approaching that deadline now. The second is a two-year extension of that time limit, provided the welfare recipient does at least twenty hours a week of community service.

After a total of five years, however, those people are no longer eligible for welfare unless they are in an area where there are extraordinarily few jobs, places like Indian reservations, for example. "I'd like to believe that at the end of that five years, our clients will be self-sufficient or those who are still in the system will have been determined to be disabled," said Solis. "But I know that's unrealistic, so I don't really want to think about it. But it means that I must find a way to make all my clients self-sufficient," Solis said, "before they hit the end of the road."

HOW'S BILL?

As these stories were running in the *Great Falls Tribune*, I began to get one common question: "How's Bill? Is he still sober?"

But for those who actually knew him, the question became more personal. Broderson is a mild-mannered guy who doesn't seem to have any malice or anger in him. As he drinks, he gets happy and increasingly sloppy until he quietly disappears and passes out.

In our office, Cathy Gretch frequently runs the front desk, screening visitors and fielding phone calls. So she became quite familiar with Broderson, drunk and sober. As he struggled with sobriety in the middle of September, she stopped by my desk with a present for Broderson. It was a shiny piece of sky-blue stone in a plastic baggie. I looked up at her with a question in my eyes. "It was a good luck charm for my son, Stevie," she said. "On the bad days, this stone always made him happy because it reminded him of the sky. I want Bill to have this in hopes he has better days ahead."

All of a sudden, I was almost in tears. Stevie Gretch was four years old when he died a few years before, and it had taken a terrible toll on Cathy and her husband, Jim. I couldn't begin to imagine the importance of that stone in remembering her lost little boy and the strength it must take to give it away.

A day or two later, I took the little piece of polished stone out to Broderson at his daughter's house and told him about it. He seemed to appreciate its significance and promised that he would personally thank Cathy the next time he stopped by the office (which he did). "I'll always treasure this," he told me, "and that little pair of Leatherman knife/pliers you bought me; they're the only two gifts I have from true friends."

ALCOHOLISM AND WORKPLACE PRODUCTIVITY

Another place where alcohol abuse takes its toll is in the workplace. The U.S. Department of Labor reports that substance abuse costs American businesses more than $100 billion a year. It said that 500 million workdays are lost each year to alcoholism. More than 14 percent of American workers reported heavy drinking, defined as five or more drinks on five or more days in the past month, it said. The Montana Department of Labor doesn't keep track of statistics on alcoholism.

According to the Governor's Budget Office, however, the local problem doesn't appear to be as severe as it is nationally. It said Montana's 11,138 state employees have an employee assistance provider, VRI, but only 4 percent of those who use it confess to a substance abuse problem.

VRI's employee assistance program is available to about 250,000 government and private employees. In 1998, it counseled about 5,000 workers, of whom about 5 percent admitted problem drinking. "But I would guess that the true figure is closer to 20 or 25 percent," said Mary Sarff, VRI's behavioral health coordinator in Billings.

The typical complaint involves a worker who can't get along with his or her supervisor. "The complaint is frequently that the supervisor is on his case about performance and he just can't get along with that person," said Sarff. "But the employee may also know that, due to his hangovers or the fact that he leaves early on Fridays, he's hindered from doing the job his supervisor expects," she added.

Another common scenario is the wife who comes in to discuss her husband. "She says that he has a problem at work, but that the reality is that he's just not up to snuff," said Sarff. "He's drinking too much, not doing his job, and having problems at home."

Meanwhile, a new national study shows that workplace absenteeism has reached its highest level in seven years. A survey of 400 human-resource officials found that dollars lost to absenteeism jumped 32 percent from last year in those companies. The average cost of absenteeism ranged from $572 to $757 per employee, according to a survey by CCH, a provider of human resource and employment information.

But one researcher argues those costs are abnormally low because they don't take into account the moderate drinker. "These are the people who have a couple of drinks at lunch, and the behavioral manifestations are so minimal that their co-workers don't know they're impaired," said Jonathan Howland, a professor at the Boston University School of Public Health. A couple of drinks may give people a 0.03 or 0.04 blood alcohol content level, Howland told me in a telephone interview from Boston. They tend to have more accidents and create more problems, he said.

Howland and five other researchers recently ran tests at the Maine Maritime Academy, giving some desk officer cadets enough alcohol to bring their BAC levels to between 0.04 and 0.05, but giving others a placebo.

"Participants were randomized to one of four bridge simulator scenarios, each representing passage of a fully loaded container vessel through a channel with commercial traffic," said the study. "Performance was significantly impaired by this low dose of alcohol," it concluded. The unpublished study noted that aircraft pilots, commercial ship operators, air traffic controllers, and nuclear power plant operators aren't barred from working until their BAC levels hit 0.04.

Performance can also be impaired by heavy drinking the night before. "On the day following high exposure to alcohol, people don't function as well as they normally do," said Howland. "We call that the hangover effect."

Twenty percent of the average workforce is chemically dependent, and they create about 40 percent of the problems, said Howland. And a co-worker with a blood alcohol content level only halfway to the point of legal intoxication can slow productivity, create a dangerous situation, and impose additional burdens on co-workers. "Fully 21 percent of the workers in our study report being injured or put in danger, having to redo work or cover for a co-worker, or having to work longer and harder due to the drinking of others," Howland said.

The maritime study concluded that "Alcohol's true contribution to workplace productivity problems, occupational injury, and injury in general may be greatly underestimated because low-dose alcohol exposure is frequently unobserved or assumed to be benign." Howland is hesitant even to guess the true cost of alcohol impairment on the job. "I just know that the estimates are way low," he said, "and whatever the true figure is, it's huge."

EXCUSE FOR A BINGE

Not long after I spoke with Howland, Broderson stopped by to tell me that he was heading on down to Helena because a friend wanted him to work on a porch. I asked how he planned to travel 90 miles southwest of Great Falls. He just winked and held up one thumb.

That afternoon after work, I dropped by the Lobby Bar to tell Tara Fatz—who had been helping keep an eye on Broderson for me—that he was heading down to Helena to work. "The hell he is," she snapped. "That's his old stomping ground. He's heading down there to get drunk."

She quickly went to a phone, called three saloon owners along Last Chance Gulch, told them Broderson was back in Helena, and asked them to shut him off. Several days later, Broderson returned, sober but a little more haggard than usual. "Mamma Hen tried to cut off my supply," he reported. "I went to a couple of places, but they wouldn't serve me so I finally just went out, got a twelve-pack, and drank it by myself."

After one drunken night, he said, he woke up sober and came back home. I never did learn whether there was really a porch in need of work, or whether it had been repaired.

ALCOHOL AND MEDICAL COSTS

In addition to pumping up our welfare rolls and draining our workplace productivity, alcohol abuse also eats up a substantial chunk of our medical dollar. How much? "Thirty to 50 percent of all hospital admissions nationally are related to alcohol," said Dr. Dan Nauts, medical director of the Benefis Healthcare Addiction Treatment Center.

Although alcohol isn't generally perceived to be so dangerous, abusing booze can harm every organ in the body. However it's a hidden factor because alcohol abuse usually doesn't show up on hospital charts.

Rod Snyder, chemical dependency counselor at Benefis Healthcare, can tell you all about this disease. A quarter-century of drinking left him with pancreatitis and liver damage, ailments that are most often diagnosed independently—not for the alcohol abuse that caused them. "I should have died a lot of times," he said. "I went into treatment once with a BAC of 0.5, and that alone should have killed me."

That BAC level is five times the legal limit for intoxication. "My last treatment was with the Salvation Army, which had a long-term program for chronics like me who had been through numerous treatments," he said. "I was there for 104 days. There were about twenty-five of us in the program six years ago, but I only know of two or three of us who are still living."

One or two drinks a day may actually be healthy. Recent studies have found moderate drinking can halve the risk of an ischemic stroke, caused by a blood clot in the brain. But heavier drinking negates the benefit. Seven drinks a day triples the threat of having a stroke.

The first part of the brain that's affected causes the disappearance of inhibitions, said Snyder. "That makes it impossible for people to give rational consideration to their impulses," he explained, "but it's those inhibitions that frequently keep them alive."

Alcoholics are much more injury-prone than nondrinkers. "It's estimated that 20 percent of all outpatient visits are related to substance abuse," said Nauts, "and that's primarily alcohol."

At the Benefis emergency room one recent Friday, eight of seventy visits were clearly alcohol-related, a hospital spokesperson said. "I'd guess our percentage averages somewhere between 10 percent and 20 percent," said Dr. Kevin McCafferty, an emergency room doctor. But the toll is much higher elsewhere. Some national statistics indicate that alcohol is involved in 66 percent of fatal accidents, 70 percent of homicides, and 37 percent of suicides.

"Each year, more than 100,000 deaths in the United States result from alcohol-related causes," the HHS secretary reported to Congress in 1997.

Another symptom of alcohol abuse may be a general fatigue. "When you go to bed drunk, you're not really sleeping," said Snyder. "You're just passed out. So you don't get the deep REM sleep that you need, and you wake up tired."

Fatigue can also come from the improper nourishment that afflicts most alcoholics. "Beer has a lot of calories, but they're empty calories," said Snyder. "There's no nutrition in them. They just turn to fat. That's why you see a lot of alcoholics with skinny arms, skinny legs, and a gut they must haul around in a wheelbarrow," he added. "They're starving themselves to death."

Often, heavy drinkers can't remember what they did under the influence of alcohol. "Blackouts often come in the latter stages of drinking," said Snyder, "but people prone to alcoholism, especially females, are prone to have earlier blackouts. Alcohol overwhelms the brain, leaving people with little memory of what they have done," he said. "Once they start, blackouts become more frequent and last longer."

Short-term memory loss can also be a warning sign. "I have a patient, sixty-seven years old, who can tell me what he had for breakfast the morning of his high school graduation, but who can't tell me what he had for breakfast this morning," he said. "That's called cognitive impairment."

In the early stages of alcoholism, drinkers build up a tolerance for alcohol, needing progressively more of it to achieve the same high. When the tolerance to alcohol disappears, that's usually a sign of liver damage. "The liver can't filter the alcohol out of the bloodstream, so it spills alcohol directly into the blood," said Snyder. "You see a guy who's used to drinking a case of beer a day suddenly being knocked on his butt by a beer and a shot. That's a sign of serious liver damage."

A lot of Snyder's clients have problems with the liver or pancreas, but a number also have heart problems. "Alcohol is hard on the heart," he said, "but it's also hard on the skin. It ages people prematurely."

In the latter stages of alcoholism, the entire body depends on booze. Stopping drinking can be fatal. That's why many alcoholics keep a morning bottle beside them in bed—to guard against a sudden onslaught of involuntary sobriety that could send them into delirium tremens or convulsions.

"A lot of alcoholics have fatal diseases," said Snyder, "but most of them share one other fatal ailment that I call terminal uniqueness." Simply put, that means no one believes that the problems of alcohol can happen to him or her. "They can look at mountains of medical data, then look up and tell me that it won't happen to them," said Snyder. "It's classic denial, and if we can't break it down, it could very well be terminal."

TREATING SYMPTOMS, RATHER THAN CAUSES

But the consequences of alcohol abuse aren't that well known because we're all too accustomed to treating the medical illnesses, rather than their causes.

Dr. Dan Nauts noted that hospitals and doctors still are unlikely to list alcoholism as the primary cause of a disease because that used to be a category that wasn't reimbursable by insurance carriers. At Benefis Healthcare, the admissions office reported that alcohol is mentioned as a cause of illness in only about two percent of the admissions in August.

At Johns Hopkins University, however, doctors reviewing patient charts estimated that 25 percent of all admissions were as a result of alcoholism. Their report said 15 to 30 percent of all hospital admissions nationally have that same cause.

A report by the Dartmouth Medical School said 25 percent to 50 percent of hospital admissions are alcohol-related.

The Medical College of Virginia Hospitals found that up to 69 percent of its accident victims had been using alcohol and that alcoholics were seven times more likely to become trauma victims than nonalcoholics.

To get beyond the symptoms, the U.S. Department of Health and Human Services a few years ago looked at the true causes of death and found that about half were caused by the following factors:

- tobacco (19 percent)
- diet and activity patterns (14 percent)
- alcohol (5 percent)
- infections (4 percent)
- toxic agents and pollution (3 percent)
- firearms (2 percent)
- sexual behavior (1 percent)
- motor vehicles (1 percent)
- illicit drugs (1 percent)

But alcohol spreads across the entire list. For example, it can weaken the immune system and leave the human body more vulnerable to infections.

At the University of Texas Medical School in Houston, 50 percent of the trauma victims admitted after car wrecks were intoxicated. About the same percentage of pedestrian auto victims were drunk, as were other trauma patients. But 80 to 90 percent of the stabbing victims were intoxicated, it said.

The Center for Substance Abuse Treatment (CSAT) in Washington, DC, reported that alcohol plays a role in half the nation's homicides, 50 percent of the burns, 48 percent of the frostbite and hypothermia cases, and 40 percent of the falls. "Alcohol has been detected in the majority of adults who drown while swimming or boating," it added.

Alcoholics are frequently malnourished, convinced that booze contains sufficient nourishment. "More than half of all people who incur traumatic brain injuries have been drinking; the percentage can range up to 72 percent," said CSAT. "Patients with traumatic brain injuries are often dependent on their families or are wards of the state," it reported. "Even patients with mild head injuries sometimes experience permanent changes in cognition and behavior. The cost of caring for patients with traumatic brain injuries exceeds $25 billion annually."

And by reducing inhibitions, alcohol becomes a leading cause of risky sexual behavior. "Untreated alcohol and drug users are among the highest cost users of health care in this country," said the Center of Alcohol Studies at Rutgers University. "They currently fill 10 to 50 percent of hospital beds, contribute a large share of admissions to emergency rooms, and consume overall up to 15 cents of each American health care dollar."

The family of an alcoholic requires two to three times as much health care as the family of a non-alcoholic, according to the National Council on Alcoholism and Drug Dependence (NCADD). While the alcoholic requires most care, nonalcoholic family members are also above average health care consumers. Alcoholics die young, an estimated nine to twenty-two years prematurely for those with liver diseases. *The Journal of the American Medical Association* estimated that the total cost of alcohol-related deaths in the United States exceeds $75 billion a year. "If you want to solve the cost of medical care in America," said Dr. Nauts, "it's by solving the problem of alcoholism."

OCTOBER

Still sober and still seeking a place to live, Bill Broderson sought help from the Cascade County Indigent Shelter Program. No luck. "They told me this program wasn't really set up for indigents," Broderson said. "They said that if that were the case, people like me would flood them and they'd be out of money in no time."

Later, Cascade County Commissioner Peggy Beltrone agreed the Indigent Shelter Assistance Program didn't really live up to its name. "That program was primarily a rental assistance program so that people don't get kicked out of their apartments as winter approaches," she said. Commissioners didn't feel a need to duplicate assistance offered indigents by the Great Falls Rescue Mission, she said.

Since Broderson was homeless much of the time, he figured he was an indigent. However, the indigent program's residency requirement was a little confusing for him. "You must reside in an apartment for a month before you qualify for help," Broderson said, "and in Cascade County, they asked for proof of residency for another sixty days." He couldn't provide either, he said. "If you have a home, I guess they're poised to help you, but what about guys like me who sleep in boxes?"

Furthermore, he said he was told that women with children have higher priority than single males for the program's limited funding. "I was pretty well told that single guys can forget this program."

As part of my effort to pin down the social costs of alcoholism, I knew I needed to spend time in our jails and our prisons because those become the home of drunken drivers, wife beaters, those who steal to buy alcohol and drugs, and those who harm or kill others while drunk or high. I was stunned to discover that the vast majority of our inmates have substance abuse problems, primarily with alcohol. "I've lost three years of my life in prison because of alcohol," said Jay Gilder, an inmate at the regional jail on Gore Hill, just outside the city limits of Great Falls.

He's not alone. Gateway Recovery Center has evaluated 115 prisoners at the regional prison, but only found five or six inmates who didn't require chemical dependency treatment. The state has 135 inmates housed in the facility, but only seven in treatment and another six in aftercare. Fifty-eight inmates are currently waiting for treatment.

Does the counseling make a difference? Listen to some of the voices from the regional prison and make up your own mind:

Morgan Cochran is serving five years in prison on two alcohol-related domestic abuse cases out of Hill and Blaine counties. He has completed three treatment programs, been kicked out of three other programs, and is on the waiting list at the jail. But he doesn't think he has a problem. "Nothing I've learned so far has made me want to stay sober," he said, sitting in a cement-block classroom in the new jail. "Those other treatments didn't work because I didn't want them to work. They say people must hit rock bottom (to quit), but my rock bottom may be death. Prison isn't my rock bottom."

Cochran said his cellmate's release the day before got him to thinking about drinking. "I know the day I leave this place, I'm going to go up to that store on the corner, buy a 40-ounce beer and drink it," he said. "That's how I know I'm not ready to leave this place yet."

Cochran said he has been sober for his two years behind bars and he's willing to try treatment again. "But I don't honestly know how treatment is going to help me," he said. "I figure I've got until 2003, and then they've got to let me go." The answer, he knows, is abstinence—and that means a reversal of his lifestyle. "My way to control anger is to drink," he said. "My way to show emotion is to drink. My way to love someone is to drink. My way to work is to drink. Every aspect of my life involves drinking," said Cochran. "Now I need to learn to function without alcohol." If he can do that, said Cochran, his goal is to be an alcoholism counselor.

Chauncy Brown, serving three years on a criminal mischief charge in Cascade County, has been taught to accept personal responsibility, but it's hard when alcohol is such a convenient scapegoat. "Every time I did a crime, I was drunk," he said.

Brown added that his uncles used to get him drunk at six or seven years old to watch him behave stupidly, and that he has been an alcoholic ever since. "There are a lot of people in here who have been screwed up on alcohol and drugs," said Brown. "In fact, I don't know anyone in here who didn't commit their crimes on alcohol and drugs."

Brown had also been in two alcohol-treatment programs that did little good. "I like to kick back and have a beer with my older friends who are responsible," he said, "but I also like to drink with my younger friends—and that's when things start to get rowdy." This treatment program has taught him he has little choice but to reform. "If I don't change, I'll be in prison for a long time," he concluded.

In 1990, Bruce Jorgenson was released from the Montana State Prison near Deer Lodge after serving three years for a strong-arm robbery in Missoula that he says he committed while drunk. But he couldn't quit drinking, even after four different stints in three separate treatment centers.

"The day I got out [of the Thunder Child Treatment Center in Sheridan, Wyoming], I got drunk," said Jorgenson. "I got on the bus to Billings, but there was a layover and I went to a casino. I drank about ten beers, came back to Great Falls, and began drinking again." Finally his probation officers sent him back to prison to serve a ten-year sentence that had been suspended on condition of good behavior. "Nothing is worth losing your freedom over," said Jorgenson. "But I was drinking every day, so I guess I'm addicted."

Now Jorgenson is participating in the regional prison's substance abuse program, which forces him to think of the consequences of his actions. "I'm real tired of being locked up," he said, "and even having one beer could put me back in here. I'm real scared of drinking again."

Jorgenson said he might return to his home on the Fort Berthold Indian Reservation in North Dakota, where there could be less pressure from his peers to join them over a few beers. But he remembered that the reservation now has a huge gambling casino, which would provide a constant temptation for him. "I've had a lot of good chances in my life," he said, shaking his head. "I can't understand why I have walked away from all of them for something that's no good for me."

Paul Parpart had been drinking but says he wasn't legally drunk the night in 1993 that he killed a teenager in Yellowstone County. "I was heading back to a party," said Parpart. "I went through a stop sign, hit a car in the intersection, and killed a fifteen-year-old kid."

At the end of 1997, he finished serving a four-year term for negligent homicide, including another alcoholism treatment program, his third. But a relapse sent him back to prison to serve a suspended ten-year sentence. "I guess I wasn't ready to quit," he said. "I was willing to risk the consequences for a 'thrilling' lifestyle. Now I've got mixed emotions," said Parpart. "I don't care that much about drinking or drugging, but there's always a nag in the back of my mind that I'd like to have one last drink."

Jay Gilder is trying to learn a lesson from his problems with alcohol.

First, there were three DUIs in his teens, followed by a couple of quiet decades in which his offenses didn't come to official attention. "Then I got drunk and belligerent in a bar and they found cocaine in my pocket," he said, "so I did time in prison." When he got out, he got another DUI—and it became a felony, combined with his earlier offenses.

"I did thirteen months, got out, reoffended by drinking again, and came back," he said. He received no alcoholism treatment during his previous prison stays, but he thrived on the Gateway program at the regional jail. "Here, you look at thinking behaviors and why you drink," Gilder said. "Now I know that I'm an alcoholic and that partying only hides my character defects."

And although treatment programs haven't done much good for some fellow prisoners, he thinks it's a crime to lock people away without offering them a chance at rehabilitation. "I see a lot of people come in here because of their drinking," he said, "but they only get bitter and go back to drinking when they get out. Throwing someone in prison without treatment doesn't do a damn thing. It only leads to repeat offenders."

LEFT IN LIMBO

Meanwhile, Bill Broderson was in limbo. He was still awaiting word from a Social Security Administration judge over whether he can qualify for disability benefits. Although alcoholism is considered a disease, that's not enough to qualify for a monthly disability check. But a subsidy is available for those who have abused alcohol so badly that there is chronic, irreversible physical damage.

Dr. Julie Wood of the City-County Health Department examined Broderson last September and made the following conclusions: "I feel his ongoing medical problems include (1) his hepatitis C; (2) his degenerative joint disease, particularly of the spine; (3) his depression; and (4) alcoholic dementia.

"His problems have certainly been exacerbated by his alcohol abuse," she added. "However, all of these, with the exception of the depression, are irreversible and will continue to give him chronic problems."

There's no indication how long it could take the administrative judge to rule. "Right now, I'm just sitting around, waiting to hear," Broderson said. About the middle of October, the strain got to him. Broderson went back down to Helena and got drunk for a solid week. When he returned, he was sober, but he looked like hell. His skin was yellow, his hands shook, he was having trouble with his balance, and his thoughts were muddled and confused.

ALCOHOL-RELATED INCARCERATION

While Broderson was in Helena, I went down to Deer Lodge because I had heard that substance abuse treatment there was minimal. Instead, I was excited to find that it had turned around. And I found the same pattern of alcohol and drug abuse that I had seen on Gore Hill.

Eighty-five percent of the inmates at Montana State Prison are locked up for crimes fueled by alcohol or drugs. In 1998, the state spent $46.8 million locking away its adult criminals and another $1.5 million on pre-release centers and parole officers. Those figures don't include expenses for county or city jails. Nearly 60 percent of the state's inmates need immediate chemical dependency treatment, said counselor Ken Ingle, who was responsible for turning the chemical dependency program around.

"I know a few people in here who say they don't have a drug or alcohol problem," said inmate Marty Quick, "but I don't believe I know any that I actually believe." Scott Rule, who heads the prison's inmate advisory council, agreed that inmates commonly use alcohol to bolster their addictive personalities. "We're all addicts, whether it's booze, drugs, gambling, or sex," he said.

Montana's substance abuse figures are a little higher than the national average. Eighty percent of all prison inmates are locked up for crimes related to alcohol or drugs, according to a recent study conducted at Columbia University. America spends about $40 billion a year to lock its citizens away.

"Drug and alcohol abuse and addiction are implicated in the crimes and incarceration of 80 percent—some 1.4 million—of the 1.7 million men and women behind bars in America," said Joseph A. Califano Jr., chairman of the National Center on Addiction and Substance Abuse at Columbia University. "Contrary to conventional wisdom and popular myth," Califano added, "alcohol is more tightly linked with violent crime than crack, cocaine, heroin, or any illegal drug."

Prisons contain a population about equal to that of Houston, the nation's fourth largest city. Twelve of America's fifty states have populations smaller than the number of American prisoners.

TREATMENT IN PRISON

Booze is why Clive Kinlock is serving a seventy-year sentence at Montana State Prison. A native of Jamaica, Kinlock came to Malmstrom Air Force Base, but got kicked out of the service because of his violent behavior. "I was blasted, and a couple of guys got in my face," he said quietly in an interview in the high-security side of the prison. "I dealt with it the best way that I could, which was physical violence."

As his military career was ending, Kinlock was increasingly unable to deal with the responsibilities of marriage and fatherhood. "Marriage drove me to drink," he said. "Baby after baby caused me to run from responsibility. Drink caused me not to be the husband I could have been or the father I should have been. That was a simple lack of responsibility on my part."

In November 1991, as the bank was foreclosing on his house in Great Falls, Kinlock spent the night drinking, then abducted the barmaid, raped her several times, and slit her throat. "When I woke up the next morning and realized what I had done, I wanted to turn myself in," he said. "Then the police took matters out of my hands and arrested me. I sobered up real quick then."

Crimes such as Kinlock's are not unusual these days.

"From 1980 to 1996, the number of people in prison has tripled due overwhelmingly to criminal activity spawned by drug and alcohol abuse," according to the National Center on Addiction and Substance Abuse at Columbia University.

"Thanks largely to alcohol and drug abuse, the rate of incarceration for American adults was 868 per 100,000 adults in 1996, compared to fewer than 100 per 100,000 for most European countries and 47 per 100,000 for Japan," it said.

Meanwhile, many American inmates sought help in vain, it said. "From 1993 to 1996, as the number of inmates needing substance abuse treatment climbed from 688,000 to 840,000, the number of inmates in treatment hovered around 150,000," said the report, "and much of the treatment they are receiving is inadequate."

Recognizing the need for treatment, the 1995 Montana Legislature expanded the prison's chemical dependency program and funded six counseling positions. But even that wasn't enough. Waiting lists contained the names of 500 or 600 inmates seeking help, and Ingle was forced to concentrate on treating the convicts closest to release.

With a seventy-year sentence, Kinlock wasn't eligible for a treatment program—but he wasn't about to be stopped by mere policy. "Clive was one of the meanest pricks in this institution," said Bill Martin, head counselor on the prison's high-security side. "He did a lot of fighting in the yard, and he hurt a lot of people."

Kinlock's perspective changed, though, when his wife came to visit him in prison and he wasn't allowed to hold his newborn son. "I realized then that I would never have a significant role in my son's life," said Kinlock. "So I decided to connect with my Higher Power to become a better person." That wasn't easy to do, however.

"Clive was in communication with me for six months, persuading me to get him into the program," said Martin. "He was so persuasive that I finally let him in. I figured he'd probably break in about a month, but he took off and now he's a real leader, a positive force in my groups." The program is designed to help chemically dependent offenders by breaking down their denial and leading them to voluntary self-change.

ERRORS IN THINKING

At a recent group meeting that I sat in on, inmates talked about their problems. One convict discussed his anger over beatings from an alcoholic father, while his younger brothers got toys and new clothing.

"One day, my brother got a new jacket, and I was jealous," he said, "so I poured gasoline on it and set it on fire and told him to go jump in a mud puddle."

"You've had an awful childhood, and you've done some awful things yourself," responded counselor Dan Oberweiser, "but you can't go on being a victim and using that as an excuse to keep going down the same path."

Similarly, he intimated that many inmates use their drinking as an excuse to continue criminal behavior. "We usually committed our crimes sober and then partied later," agreed another inmate. "But when I got caught, I'd tell them I was drunk and plead diminished capacity."

The groups spend a lot of time looking at a chart called *Errors in Thinking*, a list of excuses for continuing criminal behavior. Below are the ten things the group was working on:

1. Closed Thinking
Some people are not receptive to change, don't think critically, and make no disclosures. They are good at pointing out and giving feedback on the faults of others, and they lie by omission.

2. Victimstance
People view themselves as victims, but not as victimizers. They blame others (their family, childhood, social conditions, the past, and so on.)

3. Viewing Self as Good People
These individuals focus only on their own positive attributes, fail to acknowledge their own destructive behavior, and build themselves up at the expense of others.

4. Lack of Effort
Some are unwilling to do anything that appears boring or disagreeable; they use "I can't" which really means "I won't."

5. Lack of Responsible Performance
Responsible living is perceived to be unrewarding and unsatisfying, particularly if there's no immediate payoff. There is also no sense of obligation.

6. Lack of Time Perspective

The past is not perceived as a learning tool, and others are expected to act immediately upon demand. Decisions are based on assumptions, not facts.

7. Fear of Fear

People have irrational fears but refuse to admit them. They have a fundamental fear of injury or death and a profound fear of putdowns. They also feel worthless when held accountable.

8. Power Thrust

There's a compelling need to be in control of every situation, even if it means manipulation and deceit. People refuse to be dependent unless someone can be taken advantage of.

9. Uniqueness

People see themselves as different and better than others, but they expect others to do things they fail to do. They cope with fear of failure by being super-optimistic, but quit at the first sign of failure.

10. Ownership Attitude

All people, places, and things are perceived as objects to possess, and there's no concept of the ownership rights of others. Sex is used for power and control, not intimacy.

"Once, we simply freed clean and sober criminals," said Oberweiser. "Now we have found that we need to change their thinking. Many of them don't like themselves, and that's why they self-medicate."

For Kinlock, sobriety and treatment meant coming to terms with the consequences of the crimes he committed. "I began thinking about the pain I caused my family, and the pain I caused my victim and her family," he said. "That's when I knew I needed help."

Kinlock said he can make between $20 and $25 a month working for the prison's chemical dependency program, and that he has begun sending $10 a month to a battered women's shelter. "That's my way of making amends," he said. "Before everything happened to me, I battered my spouse. I'm not proud of it, but I feel I'm one of the reasons those places exist, so I want to help. It's a way of healing and learning to live with myself."

Kinlock is still legally married, but his wife and family now live in Calgary, Alberta, and he sees them only about once a year. He also expects to be deported back to Jamaica when he finishes his prison sentence.

For now, however, he works as an inmate counselor with the chemical dependency program on the high-security side, which provides a huge challenge—even behind bars. "It's still about choice," said Kinlock. "It would still be real easy to go back into the unit and smoke a joint or drink some pruno," a fermented liquor made in prison of fruit and sugar water. Virtually everyone is prone to such temptations.

"In this institution, I don't believe I've run into five people who didn't use alcohol or drugs prior to the commission of their crimes—or right afterward," Kinlock said. The prison's chemical dependency program has been successful because it is primarily run by inmates who help other inmates. Kinlock works for the program as an inmate counselor; a half a dozen others form an inmate advisory group to brief Ingle on their concerns and suggestions.

OWNERSHIP AND SOBRIETY

As the inmate advisors sat around a table on a recent afternoon, their enthusiasm was contagious. To an outsider like me, it was obvious that they had been given some degree of ownership of their lives—and that they were excited about the prospect.

"It was the first time anyone had asked my opinion about anything," said Rule, who is serving a twenty-year sentence, with five years suspended, on a 1990 incest conviction. "It got inmates talking to other inmates. It allowed us to take responsibility for our own treatment."

That's not an easy process for anyone. "You must be committed to turning your life around," said Ed Cowan, serving a thirty-year sentence, with twenty years suspended, for molesting a child. "I've committed to changing my behavior, my feelings, and some of my bad thoughts."

Rule said he came to prison the first time with a drinking problem, but he returned the second time with a sobriety problem. "I couldn't live life sober," he explained. "But now I'm learning to live my life sober. I'm doing the [sweat lodges] and working with a priest who's a Zen Buddhist and encourages meditation."

To supplement the counseling, inmates have formed several Alcoholics Anonymous groups at which attendance is voluntary. "It's the one thing I do for myself," said Quick, who is serving a fifteen-year sentence for intimidating a witness in an earlier drug case, "and when I miss it, I feel like I've been cheated."

With those attitudes, the treatment programs have been successful. Three years ago, the prison offered two recovery groups, attended by about eight inmates each. Today, there are about 150 inmates enrolled in the chemical dependency programs. Three years ago, there were two Alcoholics Anonymous groups attended by three or four inmates, said Ingle. Today, there are five, attended voluntarily by about 100 inmates.

"Now I'm glad I'm in prison," said Derek Montoya, serving a twenty-year sentence, with ten years suspended, for sexual assault. "It has taught me that I don't ever want to be back here again. I'd be lying if I told you I'm never going to have a drink again, but as long as I hold on to the spirituality I learned here, I'll be OK."

Although there has been some improvement, there's still a substantial waiting list for alcohol and drug treatment at MSP. Three years ago, as many as 600 inmates awaited treatment, and Ingle estimated he could only treat about 25 percent of the convicts who needed it before their release. Last month, the waiting list was down to 345 inmates. Ingle also did a follow-up check on inmates who had been through his program. One year after release, only nine percent had been re-arrested and one percent had violated their parole.

By comparison, 48 percent of all prison inmates violate their parole or probation or commit a new crime within three years after their release, said Department of Corrections spokesman Mike Cronin. It costs more than $20,700 to lock up one prisoner for a year, so it doesn't take long for the chemical dependency program to justify its $280,000 budget.

"If this program keeps eighteen inmates out of prison for a year, it more than pays for itself," said Ingle. While the program makes an impact, said Ingle, so does prison itself. "You won't find an eighty-acre patch of land anywhere in Montana that contains more human suffering than there is here," he said. "So, if it's pain that turns people's lives around, it lives right here in MSP."

EMBRACING NATIVE PRACTICES

Randy Pretty Weasel has known much of that pain, but after a lifetime behind bars, he has finally found the help he needs to turn his life around. It combines alcoholism treatment with traditional Native American religious practices, since most of the Indian inmates are addicted to alcohol and drugs.

"I know a few people here who are not addicted to alcohol and drugs, but they are very rare cases," said Pretty Weasel, a member of the Crow tribe whom I met on the prison's high-security side. "They're a very small percentage of our prison inmates."

Pretty Weasel is no exception. He was first jailed at age five when he tried to run away from home to avoid the drunken beatings and has pretty much been behind bars ever since. He was drinking by the age of seven or eight, he said, and also picked up the anger. He's been in prison five times on charges ranging from negligent homicide to rape to assaulting police officers. He is currently serving a ten-year assault sentence.

"I'm a violent person," Pretty Weasel said. "When violence raises its head, I deal with it violently. That's been the case since I first came here at eighteen, right out of high school." Finally, Pretty Weasel learned how desensitized he had become in prison.

"I saw people get their brains splattered in here, and it didn't affect me at all," he said. "Finally, I knew there was something wrong with me, and I began to pray." At the same time, he began to realize what a poor role model he was for his three children, aged four, six, and eight. "I always said I didn't want to be like my father, and look at me now," said Pretty Weasel. "Now I need to change so I can show my kids they don't have to grow up and be like me."

So, like Kinlock, he sought to get into the prison's chemical dependency program. That was a formidable obstacle, however, since it already had a waiting list of about 500 inmates and the first slots went to inmates nearing their release date. "I'm a very determined person," said Pretty Weasel. "I kept telling them I needed help with my chemical dependency, but also with my violence. Then I'd wait a month and tell them again."

"He wore us down with his persistence," agreed Martin, the chemical dependency counselor. "It finally became apparent that the only way to shut him up was let him in," said Martin, who is also Native American— Cherokee on his father's side, Creek on his mother's.

So Pretty Weasel began a treatment program called the "Medicine Wheel and the 12 Steps" that combines traditional Indian practices with the Alcoholics Anonymous program. "They gave me things I could understand," said Pretty Weasel.

"They brought in people who had gone through the program to talk about the problems I have and offer solutions to chemical dependency and violence," he said. Inmates use sweat lodges regularly to cleanse themselves, physically and spiritually. They do most of their group sessions in circles where each person has a right to be present, each has a right to express himself or his feelings, and each has an assurance that what is said in the circle will not be repeated outside the circle.

The medicine wheel is a circle with four spokes that represent the compass points, the seasons, and the cycles of life. Above is the Creator and below is Mother Earth. There's also a seventh direction—the center. "To feel and participate in this system, we must live in a harmonious and balanced way," reads the literature distributed to inmates. "We find the balance within ourselves.

"We don't see large numbers of Indian people in AA because it's so hard to understand and relate to," the Medicine Wheel literature reads. "AA was designed by two white males who eventually, along with the first 100 members, wrote the Big Book and started a very successful movement, which to date has not expanded into the Indian community where the problems of alcohol are rampant."

For Pretty Weasel, that struck a chord. "This [Medicine Wheel] program is run by Indians for Indians," he said. "It hit the nail right on the head. It lets me know my place in this world and helps me do what I need to do." Counselors said Pretty Weasel used to be one of the most vicious inmates on the high-security side. Now he's trusted to sit talking alone in a prison classroom with me and photo editor Larry Beckner. I was a little nervous about the opportunity, but Pretty Weasel's manner was respectful, his voice was quiet, and his eyes were gentle. Sobriety is one of the keys. "When people abuse alcohol and drugs like I did, it can ruin a life," he said. It can also take a life. "I have (taken a life)," he said, "and I'm not right with that."

NOVEMBER

On Monday, November 1, I was serving as the *Tribune's* night editor, reading rough copy for our copy desk from mid-afternoon until about 10:00 P.M., an assignment I've been asked to take on every week. We had been through an abnormally dry summer. The prairie grass of our northern plains was tinderbox dry, and on this particular wind-whipped evening, much of it was on fire. At about suppertime, I was handed a message: "Bill will be at the Red Door until his $$$ runs out." I ignored it.

But about two hours later, Broderson called again to tell me that he was still at the bar, his money had run out, he needed a beer, and he had the papers I had been seeking, a financial breakdown of the costs of his medical treatment over the past five or ten years. I had requested the financial breakdown with Broderson's signed authorization, but health officials insisted on sending the figures to Broderson to give to me, rather than sending them directly to me.

That did change things somewhat, so I hurried to the bar, trying to figure out how I could accept these papers from him without buying him a beer. By the time I hit the Red Door, I still wasn't sure. Once inside, though, I was relieved to find that Broderson had changed his mind. He was pretty thoroughly sloshed and was happy to give me the documents. He did, however, ask me for a ride home. I was relieved to be able to take him to the home of his "daughter," Jolena Kipp Williams.

We were a study in contrasts, I in a terrible hurry lest northern Montana burn in my absence and Broderson in the slowest of slow moods. He wanted to talk, and every time he thought of something new to say, he stopped dead in his tracks to say it.

Just as we got to the door of my pickup truck, he stopped, pulled out the Leatherman (a small gadget for fishermen and recreationists with a knife, file, screwdrivers, and a pair of pliers) that I had bought him and said, "I've still got your knife, and I'm never going to lose it. This is very precious to me." Then he dropped it, retrieved it, and slowly clambered into the truck. As gently and swiftly as I could, I drove him to Jolena's home, worried that if I shook him up he might explode like a sun-warmed can of beer.

I was on edge the night I took Broderson home, but that wasn't unusual. I spent most of that year running scared. Writing stories both so emotionally draining and so technically overwhelming is hard all by itself. Writing twelve of them in a row without a break is a hundred times worse. And being committed in advance (and publicly, no less) to achieve that feat was terrifying.

November was the worst. It was the story that I knew would make or break the series, an attempt to detail the hidden costs of alcoholism. I had broached the whole subject with Dave Lewis, the governor's budget director, and Lewis did me an enormous favor by volunteering to call together for an afternoon all the budget directors of the state agencies affected by alcoholism.

So a group of us met in a big conference room in Helena, where I began by asking about the known costs of alcoholism. These were fairly obvious, things like the Montana Chemical Dependency Center, DUI classes, DARE funding, and the like.

Then I asked about the hidden costs of alcoholism. What proportion of the Department of Corrections budget was caused by alcohol abuse? How much of the Human Services budget was devoured by welfare recipients unable to work because of their alcoholism? How much of the foster care budget goes to raise kids whose parents are incapacitated by booze? Their response made a dead silence seem noisy.

I came away from the meeting thoroughly depressed. Walking out of the state office building with Roland Mena, who heads the state's chemical dependency program, I complained that I felt as though I had been trying to force square pegs through round holes all afternoon.

Mena grabbed my shoulder and swung me around. "What you have done this afternoon is tremendously important," he said. "This is something that state government has never tried to determine. Your articles [in the *Tribune*] have served as a catalyst to force us to look at this problem in a new way. We may not have answers today, but we will next year. And the year after that, we'll get better statistics. That's why it's so important to force us to look at the root causes of the problems we treat."

I was heartened by that. But the payoff came sooner than Mena or I expected. I began making calls in about a week and found that the budget directors had begun talking with some of their key staff members, and they were now willing to address the problem.

The budget directors began telling me that alcohol costs state government—and Montana taxpayers—dearly.

Montana spends nearly $19 million a year in known costs to regulate the sale of booze and treat some of the obvious alcohol-related problems. That's greater than the annual budget for the Montana Highway Patrol, which is about $16.6 million. Most alcoholics deny they have a problem, however, so the hidden costs drive the state's spending up significantly.

The budget directors estimated that Montana spends between $150 and $200 million in treating the hidden costs of alcoholism, a figure that made *Tribune* Executive Editor Jim Strauss nervous. He insisted that we use the low range of the estimate, and he arbitrarily cut even the low range on numbers that seemed unreasonably high to us.

We concluded that hidden costs may total an additional $135 million. That's more than the state spends on the university system, about $120 million a year. "I can't quarrel with your numbers," said Lewis, director of the governor's budget office. "It's certainly eye-opening to see the amount of money that alcohol costs the state."

There is revenue incoming. In 1999, Montana expected to receive $21.8 million through liquor sales, selling liquor licenses, and taxing liquor, wine, and beer. After subtracting the administrative costs of issuing liquor licenses and collecting the taxes, that left the state roughly $21 million in profit. Here's how we spend it—and much more.

SUBSTANCE ABUSE TREATMENT

State health officials spend millions of dollars treating substance abuse, primarily alcohol, but also other drug abuse. Some of those programs use federal funds that are administered by the state. Montana spends $5.5 million on substance abuse treatment programs, said Dan Anderson, administrator of the state health department's Addictive and Mental Disorders Division. It also spends $2.5 million to operate the Montana Chemical Dependency Center in Butte, plus an additional $1 million on regional and county centers.

Anderson said $3 million is spent on a federal alcohol-prevention program, and another $163,000 on an indigent youth treatment program. In addition, the division spends about $850,000 on dealing with high-risk pregnancies and caring for the young children of high-risk mothers. The program served 1,400 women across the state, of whom 25 percent reported alcohol abuse and 9 percent illicit drug use, so one-fourth of the funding for high-risk pregnancies could be considered a hidden cost.

Known costs: $12.2 million
Hidden costs: $212,500

FOSTER CARE COSTS

Montana spends about $40 million on adoption assistance, foster care, and assisted independent living programs.

Montana has 2,000 to 2,200 children in foster care on any given day, said Shirley Tiernan, chief of the health department's family services bureau. "Alcohol use is a big factor in children being removed from their homes," said Tiernan. "Most of our foster care cases are related to alcohol."

Roughly three-quarters of the cases have underlying chemical dependency issues, estimated Chuck Hunter, head of the health department's Division of Child and Family Services. That's a hidden cost of about $30 million, Tiernan said. But that was one of the costs that made *Tribune* editors nervous, so we cut it again to $15 million.

Known costs: none
Hidden costs: $15 million

FAMILY VIOLENCE

The state spends $703,000 to counsel children on domestic violence.

How much of that can be attributed to alcohol abuse? "Most of our domestic abuse cases involve alcohol, either by one or both parties," said Great Falls Police Chief Bob Jones. "Alcohol plays a great part. People get angry, they don't try to defuse the situation, and that leads to assaults."

Last year, Montana instituted a Domestic Violence Program with a statewide budget of $652,000. According to figures provided by the YWCA Mercy Home, domestic abuse costs Montana businesses more than $10 million a year in absenteeism and medical bills.

Again, Hunter estimated that about three-quarters of the domestic abuse cases have underlying chemical dependency causes. If half the cost of domestic abuse can be attributed to alcohol, that would be $8.5 million. But we decided to be conservative again and halve that figure to $4.25 million.

Known costs: none
Hidden costs: $4.25 million

COUNSELING COSTS

Montana spends $260,000 a year on its Employee Assistance Program (EAP), which says that only four percent of the state workers report substance abuse problems. That seems low in light of the fact that the health department estimates that nine percent of the adults in the state need substance abuse treatment.

And Great Falls counselor Wava Goetz recently reviewed the 700 cases she has handled over the past five years and came to a startling discovery. Two-thirds of her cases were alcohol-related.

Known costs: $260,000
Hidden costs: none

WELFARE COSTS

There's also the welfare world. The state spends $89 million in federal Medicaid funds, $52.4 million on food stamps, and $26.7 million on the FAIM (Families Achieving Independence in Montana) program.

It spends an additional $16 million on child-care funds to cushion the transition from welfare to entry-level job wages, plus $185,000 to stock the state food bank network. State health department officials estimate that 25 percent to 50 percent of their clients are unable to hold jobs because of their alcohol abuse. The low end of that estimate would be $46 million.

Known costs: none
Hidden costs: $46 million

MENTAL ILLNESS

The state spends $84.4 million on treating mental illness. Much is not related to alcohol, but some is. "There are clearly some people suffering from mental illness due to alcohol or drug use, either by themselves or by their parents," said Anderson. "And it's often impossible to determine which is the primary problem."

Anderson noted that 26 percent of the patients admitted to state mental hospitals have a dual diagnosis with a mental illness and chemical dependency. That percentage of the mental health budget would be $21.9 million. Again, we halved that cost to $11 million to be conservative.

Known costs: unknown
Hidden costs: $11 million

DEVELOPMENTAL DISABILITIES

The state spends about $38 million to fund developmental disability centers in each county, as well as the Montana Developmental Center (Eastmont) in Glendive, Montana, but alcohol and drug abuse aren't a significant problem, said Joe Mathews, who heads the health department's Disabilities Services Division. "FAS/FAE patients are present, but not in a significant number," Mathews said.

Known costs: none
Hidden costs: low

VOCATIONAL REHAB

Vocational rehabilitation serves about 7,000 Montanans a year, but only 150 of them last year had alcoholism as a primary diagnosis, said Mathews. The department doesn't track those who have alcoholism as a contributing problem, he said.

"My guess is that a fairly substantial number of people we serve have a secondary diagnosis of alcoholism," he said. "But that's strictly a professional guess. We don't track that and I don't have the data to back that up." The vocational rehab program is budgeted to spend $14.9 million this year, and Mathews estimated that 25 percent to 30 percent of that could be attributed to alcohol abuse.

Known costs: none
Hidden costs: $3.7 million

SPECIAL EDUCATION

The state Office of Public Instruction spends $1.9 million a year on an alcohol- and drug-free educational program for students.

And it spends $33 million educating children with various disabilities, including fetal alcohol syndrome and fetal alcohol effect—both of which are caused by mothers who drink while they are pregnant. Only a small percentage of the students have FAS/FAE, but educators note that attention deficit disorder (ADD) has the same symptoms as FAE, except that there's no proven cause.

Proving FAE "requires mothers to admit that they've been drinking during pregnancy," said Gail Cleveland, who was in charge of the Great Falls school district special education program. "So they deny it, and the physicians don't press the issue." Education officials can't estimate what percentage of the special education budget may be attributable to alcohol abuse, but a conservative 10 percent would be $3 million.

Known costs: $1.9 million
Hidden costs: $3 million

JUSTICE DEPARTMENT

The state Department of Justice spends about $3 million each year on substance abuse programs, including the cost of the DARE programs in public schools. And it underwrites a DUI Task Force to the tune of about $250,000 a year.

In fiscal 1999, Montana Highway Patrol officers wrote 3,300 tickets for driving under the influence of alcohol, about 6.5 percent of the 50,400 tickets written that year.

And about 29 percent of the drivers involved in fatal auto collisions had been drinking, down from about 50 percent a decade ago, according to Col. Craig Reap, former head of the highway patrol. The highway patrol budget is about $16.6 million a year, so 6.5 percent of its budget—$1.1 million—could be considered a hidden cost.

Known costs: $3.25 million
Hidden costs: $1.1 million

COURTS

State district courts cost taxpayers $3.4 million a year. It's impossible to break out what percentage of this is alcohol-related.

Known costs: none
Hidden costs: unknown

CORRECTIONS

Since the Legislature made felonies of all DUI offenses after the third conviction, Montana spends more than $1 million a year locking away drunken drivers.

And a number of prisoners were released on probation or parole, but were imprisoned again because their continued drinking violated the terms of their release. The Department of Corrections could not give a specific number because it does not track the reasons for parole or probation revocations.

The state spends $34,000 for a substance abuse program at Pine Hills, plus $265,000 more on a similar program at the Montana State Prison. But that's only a drop in the bucket for the juvenile and adult justice programs, which total $64 million.

A health department study several years ago found that 60 percent of all prison inmates had a lifetime alcohol disorder, compared to about nine percent of all Montanans. But a prison study showed that 85 percent of its inmates had substance abuse problems, were imprisoned for crimes committed while they were drunk or high, or committed crimes to get the money to buy alcohol or drugs.

"I know a few people here who are not addicted to alcohol and drugs, but they are very rare cases," said inmate Randy Pretty Weasel, an alcoholic who is serving a ten-year assault sentence. "They're a very small percentage of our prison inmates." Taking the lower of the estimates, 60 percent of the Corrections Department's $89 million budget could mean a hidden cost of $53 million.

Known costs: $1.3 million
Hidden costs: $53 million

When we finally agreed upon the *Tribune's* estimate of the hidden costs of alcoholism, I was both pleased and relieved. I had never seen a comprehensive estimate of those costs before, so I thought we had really

Montana Highway Department traffic safety chief Al Goke estimated that alcohol-related traffic deaths cost state residents $83 million a year. That's based on last year's 85 fatalities and an average loss of $980,000 per life estimated by the National Safety Council.

Goke estimated injuries in alcohol-related crashes cost Montanans $62 million, with 1,829 wrecks each averaging a medical bill of $34,100, according to the National Safety Council.

And property damages came to about $4 million a year, with 2,142 crashes causing an average of $1,700 in damage.

The total statewide bill for drinking and driving in Montana comes to about $150 million a year, Goke said.

added something to the public dialogue surrounding alcohol. And I was glad that our editors had the courage to put the *Tribune's* name and reputation behind the estimate.

HELP FOR BRODERSON

Finally, there came an end to Broderson's wait. The verdict: Heavy drinking has finally left him so disabled that he's eligible for help from the federal government.

"The claimant is unable to perform even sedentary work on a sustained basis, even if he stopped drinking," wrote Administrative Law Judge Henry M. Paro in a decision for the Social Security Administration. That means that Broderson will get a government check for $525 a month.

It was a difficult call because a 1996 reform of Social Security denied that alcoholism is an illness sufficient to grant federal benefits. However, if a drinker has done permanent, irreversible harm to his body, then he or she can win assistance. "Claimant has an impairment of continuous alcohol abuse," Paro wrote. "He has an extensive history of uncontrolled drinking, and he has failed numerous detox attempts and treatment episodes. His alcohol abuse is continuous, and he has maintained no significant period of sobriety, in spite of numerous negative consequences."

Paro took note of a doctor's finding that Broderson suffered from hepatitis C, degenerative joint disease, liver function abnormalities, and mild alcoholic dementia.

"Although the claimant's health problems have clearly been exacerbated by his continual alcohol abuse, Dr. [Julie] Wood concluded that the claimant is unable to maintain employment, given his multiple medical conditions which are irreversible," said Paro.

The judge agreed, noting that Broderson hasn't worked in 15 years and has no job skills. "The medical evidence supports a finding that even if claimant stopped drinking, the combined effect of his multiple medically determinable physical and mental impairments would remain and would prevent him from performing even sedentary work on a sustained basis. For this reason, the claimant's alcohol abuse is not a contributing factor material to the determination of the claimant's disability," the judge concluded.

So, after waiting for more than two years, Broderson won Social Security disability benefits from the federal government. That's a normal delay for the government, but Broderson was unusual in being successful the first time around. The judge also found that Broderson was incapable of handling his own finances and ordered that payments be made through a trustee who would monitor how the money was spent.

With retroactive benefits to the time he filed his disability claim, Broderson spent $2,500 to buy a small house trailer. "I was locked up in the [Rescue] Mission one night, staring out the window, and I saw one of those trailers go by," he said. "And I said to myself, 'I'm going to get one of those if it's the last thing I do.'" Now Broderson is looking for a place in the country to park it and a black Labrador retriever to share it with.

He also spent several days doing vocational rehabilitation testing to determine whether he might be employable with some additional job training, an unusual development since he had already been designated as disabled. But even as he struggled to put a new life together, his past came back to haunt him. "I was out walking last weekend when two cops stopped to talk to me and asked for some identification," he said. "When I showed them, they told me there was an outstanding warrant for my arrest, so I spent the night in jail."

The warrant was a DUI citation from about four years ago, said Broderson, so he made a preliminary court appearance and bonded out for $125. "I've already spent about 37 days in jail for that ticket," he added, "so I've probably got enough time that I won't have to serve any more. But I still have to show up in court again."

PAYING THE COSTS

While I struggled to get information about the hidden costs of alcohol in Montana, I found there was more information about the cumulative costs of alcohol abuse on the national scene. And that got me to thinking.

In every saloon, I thought, there should be a costs jar. For every dollar you push across the bar, put another two bucks into the jar to pay for the damages. That would cover the cost of the city cops arresting and jailing a drunken driver—or repairing the damages in a DUI accident. For every $10 spent on a bottle of wine in a grocery store, put $20 in another costs jar. That would pay teachers to baby-sit kids with brains addled by second-hand booze while they were in the womb.

For every six-pack of beer you buy in a convenience store, slip another $15 in the jar. That would treat victims of domestic abuse, jail the abusers, or reimburse businesses for those too hung over to go to work the next morning. For every $10 bottle of whiskey at the state store, stick $20 in the jar. It would be used to pay the medical bills for those whose livers are shot or whose brains have been fried by booze.

The National Institute of Alcohol Abuse and Alcoholism has estimated that excessive drinking costs Americans more than $175 billion each year:

Health care $22.6 billion
- treatment $15.9 billion
- detox and rehab $6.7 billion

Premature deaths $36.7 billion

Impaired productivity $81.2 billion

Crime $23.6 billion
- cost to victims $9.6 billion
- corrections $7.5 billion
- lost economic potential $6.5 billion

Social welfare $13.3 billion
- payments $12.5 billion
- administration $820 million

TOTAL: $177.4 billion

HUGE SOCIAL COST

Alcohol is a $100 billion business in America, but it costs much more than that to repair the damages of alcohol abuse. Some experts estimate that cost at more than $175 billion, but that's a conservative guess—and it doesn't include a lot of hidden costs:

- It includes the cost of imprisoning those who commit crimes under the influence of alcohol, for example, but not the cost of police departments to catch them or the justice system to weigh their guilt and sentence them.
- It includes the cost of lost productivity to individuals, but doesn't attempt to estimate how much that might cost employers or businesses. The U.S. Department of Labor estimates businesses lose $100 billion a year due to substance abuse.
- It includes the cost of educating children with fetal alcohol syndrome/effect, but not the children with identical symptoms whose mothers wouldn't admit to drinking while pregnant.

"In terms of impact on our society, there's no question that alcohol abuse does the most significant and pervasive damage," Joseph Califano, chairman of the Center on Addiction and Substance Abuse at Columbia University, told me.

Here's how those costs break out:

HEALTH CARE

The National Institute on Alcohol Abuse and Alcoholism (NIAAA) has estimated that medical expenses attributable to alcohol abuse were $22.6 billion in 1999. The bulk of that money, $15.9 billion, went to treat such ailments as cirrhosis of the liver, HIV infection, and trauma. Another

$6.7 billion was spent on specialized alcohol services, including detoxification, rehabilitation, prevention, training, and research, it said.

But Mothers Against Drunk Driving estimated alcohol-related medical costs this year at $34.2 billion, adding, "That's 48 cents per ounce of alcohol consumed." Dr. Dan Nauts, medical director of the Addiction Medicine Center at Benefis Healthcare, said national studies have shown that 30 to 50 percent of all hospital admissions are related in one way or another to alcohol.

A study by the Center of Alcohol Studies at Rutgers University also suggests a greater medical cost than NIAAA. "Untreated alcohol and drug users are among the highest cost users of health care in this country," it said. "They currently fill 10 to 50 percent of hospital beds, contribute a large share of admissions to emergency rooms, and consume overall up to 15 cents of each American health care dollar."

"Those are low estimates," said Califano. "Most estimates measure only the cost to alcoholics, things like heart disease, cirrhosis, or accidents, but not the costs to children of alcoholics, the spouses of alcoholics, their siblings, families, and friends. And most of them have significant medical problems, both physical and emotional," said Califano, former secretary of the U.S. Department of Health, Education, and Welfare. Americans spent $1.1 trillion on health care in 1997, according to the National Coalition on Health Care in Washington, DC.

PREMATURE DEATH

Nearly 115,000 people die prematurely of alcohol abuse each year, said the NIAAA.

Many of the deaths are due to auto crashes, homicides, suicides, accidents, and HIV infections. And many of the victims are between twenty and forty years old.

The NIAAA estimated their reduction in lifetime earnings at $3.7 billion.

The loss is particularly great on Indian reservations, where the Indian Health Service says 17 to 19 percent of all deaths are alcohol-related, compared with 4.7 percent for the general population. "Alcohol or other drug addiction is culminating in the destruction of Native American populations," said a recent IHS report.

IMPAIRED PRODUCTIVITY

Roughly 26 million American workers have a chemical dependency problem, said the NIAAA—including 24.6 million with a history of alcohol dependence. It estimated their lost productivity at $81.2 billion this year. This measure was primarily for lost earnings, but also included household productivity. "This study has not attempted to estimate the burden of drug and alcohol problems on work sites or employers," it added.

The U.S. Department of Labor, however, has estimated that substance abuse costs American businesses more than $100 billion a year.

Even that estimate is low, argued Jonathan Howland, a professor at the Boston University School of Public Health, who has done extensive studies on the economic consequences of drinking on the job. "Alcohol's true contribution to workplace productivity problems, occupational injury, and injury in general, may be greatly underestimated because low-dose alcohol exposure is frequently unobserved or assumed to be benign," said Howland.

He hesitates, however, to guess the true cost of alcoholic impairment on the job. "I just know that the estimates are way too low," he told me, "and whatever the true figure is, it's huge."

FETAL ALCOHOL SYNDROME/EFFECT

As part of its impaired productivity estimate, the NIAAA included $1.2 billion to treat the effects of fetal alcohol syndrome/effect. That's the medical term for people whose brains were damaged before they were born because their mothers drank while pregnant. Health experts say each child will require medical care and supervision costing $1.4 million over the patient's lifetime.

But Ann Streissguth of the University of Washington fetal alcohol syndrome unit, estimated annual costs of FAS/FAE at $2.5 billion a year, double that of the NIAAA. Other experts argue that's only the tip of the iceberg because it doesn't take into account many of the kids diagnosed with attention deficit disorder.

Robin A. LaDue, the clinical psychologist in Seattle who works with the fetal alcohol syndrome unit at the University of Washington, told me in a phone interview that the symptoms of FAE and ADD are identical except that physicians can't prove the cause.

"Many physicians don't want to stigmatize these children by labeling them," said Carole Kenner, professor of nursing at the University of Cincinnati, "and others do not want to anger affluent clients whose alcohol consumption is considered legal and socially acceptable." The federal government spends $5.4 billion on its special education program to educate children with disabilities.

CRIME

Estimating that alcohol abuse contributes to 25 or 30 percent of violent crime, the NIAAA pegged its cost at $23.6 billion. That figure included $9.6 billion lost to the victims of crime, $7.5 billion for the cost of prisons, and $6.5 billion in lost productivity for those locked away. The study concluded that drug addiction caused three times more economic loss than alcoholism. But another study by the Center on Addiction and Substance Abuse at Columbia University disagreed sharply.

"Alcohol is a bigger culprit in connection with murder, rape, assault, and child and spouse abuse than any illegal drug," said its chairman, Califano. Eighty percent of prison inmates are alcoholics or drug abusers, he estimated.

"Of the $38 billion spent on prisons in 1996, more than $30 billion were paid out for the incarceration of individuals who had a history of drug or alcohol abuse, were convicted of drug or alcohol convictions, were high on drugs or alcohol at the time of their crimes, or committed their crimes to get money to buy drugs," said Califano.

MOTOR VEHICLE CRASHES

The study, conducted by the Lewin Group in Washington, DC, estimated the cost of alcohol-related car wrecks at $29.6 billion. About half of these costs, however, are included in other categories, such as premature death and health care. The remaining costs for damaged or destroyed property are included in the crime category.

By comparison, Mothers Against Drunken Drivers (MADD) has pegged the costs of alcohol-related crashes at $45 billion a year. And MADD estimated that survivors of such crashes suffer an additional loss of $40.5 billion a year in quality of life. "Alcohol-related crashes cost society 95 cents per drink, or $1.90 per ounce of alcohol consumed," said a report by MADD.

SOCIAL WELFARE

The NIAAA estimated that alcohol abuse resulted in impairments for which federal and state governments paid $12.5 billion in benefits. It estimated that alcoholism also resulted in $820 million in extra administrative overhead.

"While it would appear that 30 to 40 percent of the beneficiaries do use illicit drugs and/or abuse alcohol, it would appear that for most of these individuals their use of alcohol and psychoactive drugs is not of such a severity to have impaired their ability to gain employment," it concluded. Again, other experts suggest these figures are low.

"Substance abuse-related costs to solely the nation's public child welfare system are $10 billion a year, or more than 70 percent of such spending," said a report this year by Columbia University's National Center on Addiction and Substance Abuse.

"This $10 billion does not include the costs of providing health care to abused or neglected children, operating law enforcement and judicial systems consumed with this problem, treating developmental problems these children might suffer, providing special education for them, or lost productivity," it added. "Nor does it include the costs attributable to child abuse and neglect that are privately incurred."

HHS's Center for Substance Abuse Treatment (CSAT) estimates that half of wife and child beaters have substance abuse problems, and it puts medical costs of abused women at $44 million a year. But that's only part of the problem. Experts say three million children a year witness acts of domestic violence against their mothers or fathers, leaving them primed for similar abuse later in their lives.

UNCALCULATED COSTS

The NIAAA estimate doesn't take into account the cost of counseling and therapy.

CSAT spends about $1.2 billion a year on alcoholism and addiction research. And Americans spend about $5 billion a year on alcoholism treatment, according to the Substance Abuse and Mental Health Services Administration.

TEEN DRINKING

The Office of Juvenile Justice and Mothers Against Drunk Driving have estimated that teenaged drinking costs Americans $58 billion annually. Underage drinking is the nation's largest youth drug problem, it said, killing 6.5 times more young people than all illicit drugs combined.

"Alcohol is the number one drug of choice among our nation's youth," said Karolyn Nunnallee, who was national president of MADD, "and it is costing our society an average of $577.91 per year for every household in the United States."

SELF-INFLICTED DAMAGES

Columbia's Center on Addiction and Substance Abuse released a report in 1995 lumping together the effects of alcohol, drugs, and tobacco. It said:

"In 1995, $60.3 billion, or nearly one in five dollars the federal government spends on all health care entitlements, will be spent to treat illness and conditions attributable to tobacco, alcohol, and other drugs." That's a needless cost, it noted, because all three are used voluntarily.

RAY OF HOPE FOR BRODERSON

Days after the story of Broderson and his trailer ran in the *Tribune*, I got a call from a reader who lived in a small trailer park in Dupuyer, a town northwest of Great Falls on the edge of the Rocky Mountain Front.

Himself a recovering alcoholic, the caller thought he knew Broderson and understood his problem. He described Dupuyer as an accepting small community—the kids in the nearby school had asked him to be the Santa Claus in their upcoming Christmas pageant, he said, and he was clearly excited about the prospect.

The lot he offered Broderson was inexpensive—just $100 a month; deer and elk grazed right behind the trailer. But best of all, he had two black Labrador dogs, a breed that Broderson had once owned and still loved. I told Broderson about the call the next day, and he was excited. "That sounds perfect," he said with conviction in his voice. "I'm going to make that work."

The reader drove down from Dupuyer a day or two later and met Broderson for coffee. They seemed to hit it off, and I was beginning to think I was seeing light at the end of the tunnel. Instead, it was the locomotive.

I began to hear rumors that Broderson was on a bender, so I checked with Tara Fatz at the Lobby Bar. She hadn't seen him, but she'd heard the same. So I made a lunch-hour tour of the downtown bars to see if I could find him. I finally saw him sitting in a bar I'd never seen him in, hunched over a half-full beer glass and looking miserable.

Over half an hour, he was at various times defiant, nonchalant, and penitent. Finally he acknowledged that he had let his friends down. "You're a big-handed son-of-a-bitch," he told me. "Why don't you just slug me and be done with it?" But I wasn't angry, just terribly disappointed, and I told him so. I finished my coffee, turned, and walked out.

A week or so later, I heard that Broderson was back in the detox unit at Benefis Healthcare, so I went up to visit him. He looked awful, a scrawny little thing in a flannel nightshirt and a scruffy robe. As we talked, he blurted out his confession: He had hocked his trailer, the one he had paid $2,500 for, to a guy in a bar for $200 with a promise to redeem the trailer in a week for $250. His time was up the next day and he didn't have the money. What could he do?

Not much, I said, but I promised to call his payee, Pete Townsend of Opportunities Inc., to tell him that Broderson was back in the hospital and also that the trailer was gone. Finally, I left, just shaking my head. How could anyone piss away such promise?

WHAT CAN GOVERNMENT DO?

I was in Helena over Thanksgiving and dropped by the governor's office the following morning to visit. I wanted to know whether, after having read most of this series of stories on alcoholism, Gov. Marc Racicot had any good ideas on ways the state could help promote reform.

First, it's legal to drink, noted the governor, a former attorney general. "There's a hope for a balance and appropriate restraint, but that's always a problem," Racicot said. "I know of few families who haven't been harmed in one or another way by alcohol abuse." The state has tried alcohol prevention programs, said Racicot, but it's difficult to prove what didn't happen.

Legislators toughened the penalties for driving under the influence of alcohol, and there has been a decline in the number of alcohol-related crashes. Montana has also made a major push to educate youth about the dangers of alcohol abuse.

"But it's very difficult in a free society to compel people who are not in violation of the law to conform to stricter social norms," he added. So how would the governor reform the state's alcohol abuse policies?

"I don't know how to do things differently," he admitted. "If I did, we'd do it." That was a sad admission, but it clearly told me that if anyone was going to come up with solutions for reform, it would have to be a part of these newspaper articles.

DECEMBER

After leaving detox, Broderson had burned most of his bridges. When the trailer was taken away, the couple who had been housing Broderson asked him to leave. "I love Bill like a father, but we can't handle this," said Jolena Kipp Williams. "He's drunk all the time. He's not even trying to meet us halfway anymore."

Tara Fatz, manager of the Lobby Bar downtown, felt betrayed by Broderson's relapse. "He came in here so drunk he could barely talk and I threw him out, told him not to let me see his face again until he was sober," she said. "I told him I was damned if I was going to watch him kill himself."

Unfortunately, that looks to be the next step for Broderson, who was diagnosed earlier this year with incurable hepatitis C, liver damage, and mild alcoholic dementia. He found a series of friends on whose couches or floors he could crash for an evening, and then he woke in the morning to drink again. I thought that by pawning his trailer, he had sold his dream. He seemed without hope.

Some months earlier, I had talked with a guy named Mike Misener, whose story had chilled me because it seemed stranger than fiction. But he had survived the ravages of alcohol. I kept wondering why Broderson hadn't. Misener told me that life is like an elevator for many alcoholics. They have to hit the bottom before they get off—and some don't survive the crash. "When you're in the throes of alcohol or drug addiction, nagging and threats do no good," said Misener. "Even intervention doesn't work."

Misener's experience demonstrates the challenge of treating alcoholics. "What works is consequences," said Misener. "When you get so sick and miserable that you can't take it anymore, you'll change. Unfortunately, I had a high threshold for pain."

In fact, Misener narrowly escaped death a number of times. "I've crashed a car at 120 mph, gone into DTs [delirium tremens] on an operating room table, and nearly burned to death in a house fire when I fell asleep in a chair with a cigarette in my hand," he admitted. "This disease will kill you if you don't get into treatment."

At nineteen, Misener married and kept his drinking under control for about five years. "I was drinking heavily, but not at work," he says. "Then I began drinking twenty-four hours a day.

"My wife asked me to slow down—not stop, just slow down—but I wouldn't let anything come between me and my drinking," he says. "Not even my wife and two children." So he left them and began drinking more. At the urging of friends, Misener eventually checked into the Galen Treatment Center. He managed to stay sober for six months.

After another year of heavy drinking, Misener was given another chance. "One of my friends took me out and got me so drunk I passed out," he says. "Then he took me back to Galen and turned me in for more treatment." But Misener hadn't hit the bottom yet. "On the bus on the way home from Galen, I was drinking again," he said.

Finally, Misener ended up once more in the hospital. He says he was way beyond seeing snakes and spiders. Now he had full-blown hallucinations—he would see a real office populated by Halloween monsters. Doctors at the Montana Chemical Dependency Center didn't expect him to live more than two weeks, he said, and that's when he knew he had to change his lifestyle. "I had always thought that someone was a worse drunk than I was," he said, "but I found that I had turned into that person."

Changing his life required him to change some ways of thinking.

- It required him to be honest. "I used to be a really accomplished liar and manipulator," he admitted. "In fact, I was really proud of the way I could con people."
- It required him to be patient. "Drinking was an instant fix," he says. "I had to learn to live life without instant gratification. I had to learn to live life at its own pace, not always trying to push it or improve on it."
- He had to admit mistakes. "Perfectionism is one of our biggest stumbling blocks," he said. "I'm not doing my program or my job perfectly, so I may as well give up and take a drink. I had to learn that I'm only human, I make mistakes, and I can live with them."
- Most important, it required him to admit that he can never take another drink. "The only power I have over alcohol is not to take that first drink," Misener said, "because if I do, I'm powerless. I must have more, no matter what the cost."

MOTIVATION TO CHANGE

To get a better understanding of treatment, the *Tribune* sent me to Center City, Minnesota, to visit the Hazelden Foundation.

"Hazelden is one of the nation's foremost treatment centers," said Rod Robinson, executive director of Gateway Recovery Center in Great Falls. Alcoholism experts in New York City and Washington, DC, also recommended I visit Hazelden, a facility with a $57 million operating budget that treats about 5,000 patients a year on its main campus. It also has satellite centers in Florida, New York, and Chicago.

About 60 percent of its patients remain sober for at least a year, said Jerry Spicer, its former president and CEO. That compares with an average success rate of 35-40 percent for the industry as a whole, which usually provides thirty days of treatment, followed by group meetings.

Why is Hazelden so successful? I wanted to know how they did it. At Hazelden, one of the ground rules was that I stay away from the patients, who were in a vulnerable emotional state and who had been promised their privacy. But foundation officials gave me a tour of the grounds, then set me up in a conference room and paraded alcoholism experts past me on about an hourly rotation.

One was Bob Ferguson, their alumni director. After two failed treatments, Ferguson originally found himself at the Hazelden Foundation to cure his addictions to alcohol and cocaine. "When something went wrong in my life, I wanted a quick fix from outside," said Ferguson, a fast-talking New Yorker. "I didn't want to change *me*. I wanted to change the world around me with a chemical."

Although he knew he needed help, Ferguson really didn't want to recover either. "In my mind, addiction was exciting and recovery was boring," he said. "I had it backward in my thinking, but Hazelden helped me invert it."

Over the past half century, more than 50,000 people like Ferguson have found help at the Hazelden Foundation, which is about forty miles north of Minneapolis. There's no magic cure. It's all about motivating people to stay sober, and then giving them the tools to do it.

"I could look around me and see people just like myself," said Ferguson, "so I felt connected. And the alumni were incredible. They were back on the units during the day and speaking to us at night. They became role models for me because I could see they were so happy in their lives. They provided me something I'd never had before— motivation to change," he said.

Ferguson spent twenty-eight days at the treatment facility, receiving help from an inter-disciplinary mix of medical doctors, chemical dependency counselors, psychologists, and chaplains.

Then he spent four months in an aftercare unit on the rolling hills of Hazelden, where hiking and biking trails wend around a string of small lakes.

That was followed by four months in a halfway house. With the help of an active 12-step program, Ferguson has remained clean and sober since 1992. But he doesn't count his first two unsuccessful treatments as failures. "I needed to fall flat on my face before I could get it through my thick skull that I needed to take all the advice I was being given," he said.

Addiction is a terrible disease, and it's hard to cure.

The reason, said Spicer, is that an alcoholic's brain functions differently than that of most people. "New research on the brain is showing that drugs and alcohol stimulate a deep-seated reward center for some people," he said. "Then continued usage actually changes the way the brain works. People start drinking because they enjoy it," he said, "but end up drinking because it feels awful when they stop."

When they enter treatment at Hazelden, patients undergo a thorough physical examination, and then are monitored carefully as they undergo detoxification. Then they're assigned rooms in the foundation's six residential treatment centers, which look like college dorms. The cost of the average inpatient treatment is about $15,000.

Here, they'll spend a month learning about alcoholism, receiving counseling for the personality problems underlying it, and learning how to live without a drink. Since the disease affects every area of an alcoholic's life, the cure must be interdisciplinary, said Spicer, involving doctors, chemical dependency counselors, psychiatrists, and chaplains.

Hazelden has about 1,050 employees, including 110 chemical dependency counselors, a dozen chaplains, eight psychiatrists or psychiatric therapists, and a number of doctors on contract as needed. This holistic approach has become known as the Minnesota Model.

One of Hazelden's founders, Daniel J. Anderson, described how he and others came up with that approach in the early 1950s: "There's been a bunch of physicians trying to help alcoholics get well physically, and it's not working too well. There's a bunch of clergy people who've been trying to sober them up, save them, and give them ethics; that ain't working too well either. Then we have a bunch of social workers trying to pick up alcoholics' home lives and blaming their condition on the wives, and there's a bunch of psychiatrists trying to shrink their heads. Nothing's working.

"So I said, maybe we would do it all. We'd put it all together. Maybe we'd fix them up physically and try to help them with social problems. If they're mentally ill, we'll shrink their heads a little bit. And we'll also include AA members and the clergy. In short, we decided that we've got to have an interdisciplinary staff, and we'll create a total learning environment for alcoholics," said Anderson.

John MacDougall, supervisor of spiritual care at Hazelden, describes alcoholism as a foundation of genetic predisposition, overlaid by environmental provocations such as job stress, failing relationships, low self-esteem, anger management, or boredom. The greater the genetic predisposition, he said, the fewer environmental provocations are needed to trigger alcoholism.

Addictions such as alcoholism, said MacDougall, are a disease in which the mind works against the best interest of the body. Arresting the disease requires a person to live by certain rules, rather than doing what he wants or what he thinks would be right. One of those rules is never take the first drink.

"Think of addiction as a used car salesman," MacDougall tells his clients. "Everything he says to you—sports, the weather, women—is for one purpose and one purpose only: to get you to buy a car.

"It's the same with alcoholism. Everything is to sell you a drink, and the facts could matter less. Feel bad? You need a drink. Feel good?

Celebrate with a drink. Another rule is to quit lying to yourself and others.

"Honesty and accountability are desirable traits in someone else, but they are a matter of life and death for me," said Ferguson. "If I don't keep on employing them, I'll fall back into addictive behavior that will be destructive to me." Another is that an addict alone is powerless to change his or her own life. It takes help from a Higher Power. Some look to God, while others believe they find a greater source of collective wisdom in their Alcoholics Anonymous groups.

Mike Schiks, executive vice president of recovery services for Hazelden, recalls an addict who wrestled with the concept of a Higher Power for three years, then came to a group therapy session convinced that he had finally found an answer upon which everyone could agree. Skeptical group members awaited his explanation. "All I know," said the fellow, "is that it ain't me."

A good diet and exercise are also important to recovery. Since the root of the problem seems to be an imbalance in neurochemicals, a lot of research is being focused on drugs. Naltrexone has been effective in reducing a craving for alcohol, and it is sometimes prescribed at Hazelden.

"But we also use other techniques for controlling craving, things like meditation," said Spicer. "And we're experimenting with biofeedback and acupuncture." Ultimately, the key is finding a balance to life that doesn't revolve around alcohol.

"Our mission is not just to get people to stop drinking," said Spicer. "It's all about living a better quality of life." Some never achieve that. They remain in an arrested stage of development.

"It took me about a year before I realized I was no longer obsessed with alcohol," said Ferguson. "I was passing a bar one day when I realized I wasn't thinking about drinking and I wasn't thinking about not drinking; I was actually thinking about where I was going."

But recovery doesn't happen alone. Ongoing treatment is a critical component at Hazelden. That's why the facility keeps some patients on campus in an aftercare program for up to three months at a cost of $240 a day. Others may be encouraged to join a halfway house in Minneapolis, where recovering alcoholics can work during the day and return home to a safe environment. That costs $101 a day.

"This is a chronic illness," said Spicer, "and we've learned that people need a continuum of aftercare services. We don't send people home cured. We empower them to understand their addiction and make changes in their lives."

More than 55,000 people are active members of the Hazelden Foundation Alumni Association, and one of the alumni is assigned to sponsor each outgoing patient, getting that person into Alcoholics Anonymous groups and helping him or her stay straight.

According to AA, there are more than two million recovering alcoholics, and they take care of each other. MacDougall tells of a stressful layover in the Atlanta airport a few years ago. He had an operator page "friends of Bill W," the co-founder of AA, and a small crowd of airport employees and passengers quickly convened to help him. Several sat with him until his next plane took off, he said.

"Regular meetings and working the 12-steps have been critical to my recovery," said MacDougall, now sober for 10 years. "I'll always be an addict, but if you just practice what AA teaches, you can stay straight, one day at a time, for the rest of your life."

Of course, that advice applies practically across the board. "If people would just follow health care recommendations, there would be a tremendous savings," said Schiks. "Imagine what would happen if we all quit smoking, drank moderately, exercised, and ate a healthy diet. It could be revolutionary."

LOSS OF HIS DREAM

Broderson drank heavily in other downtown bars for the next two weeks, then checked back into the Benefis Healthcare detox unit, unable to work out a way of redeeming his trailer.

But substance abuse treatment has never worked for Broderson either. Over the past decade, he has been in and out of treatment twenty-eight times at five different hospitals, according to an analysis supplied by the state Department of Public Health and Human Services.

He went through the program at Benefis sixteen times, the Montana Chemical Dependency Center in Butte seven times, the Gateway Recovery Center program three times, and the Boyd Andrew Chemical Dependency Center and Northern Montana in Havre once each. His outstanding bills over the past decade were:

- Benefis—$19,550
- MCDC—$6,930
- Northern Montana—$3,080
- Gateway—$1,020
- Boyd Andrew—$180

Since 1990, Broderson has rolled up bills of $30,760, which taxpayers or ratepayers have footed. That's an all-too-common scenario.

A team of economists in Madison, Wisconsin, recently looked at the expenses racked up by nineteen drunks on State Street near the University of Wisconsin campus. It found that they had been jailed in 1998 for a combined 1,077 days at a cost of $54,000. And from 1996 to 1998, they had received detoxification and alcoholism treatment costing $342,000, which had barely interrupted their chronic drinking.

So why didn't treatment work for them, or for Broderson? First, Broderson liked his lifestyle. Although he was staying with his surrogate daughter and her family this fall, he found himself talking about how enjoyable it had been living under a bridge alongside the Missouri River. In addition, he didn't seek the treatment. It sought him.

"When the judge looks at you and says, 'Treatment or six months in jail,' I'd say, 'Right! I'll beat you to the [treatment] center.' But my heart was never in it." He doesn't know many people who aren't drunks, and his behavior quickly even alienates *them*. "The people I hang out with are always drinking," he said recently, "so I'm always drinking too."

Alcohol is legal, and it's everywhere. "I was in a treatment center once, and there was a beer sign that was blinking on and off right outside my window," said Broderson. "I watched it for about a week and then I said to my cellmate, 'Let's get out of here and go get a beer.' So we did."

Finally, he hasn't held a steady job in fifteen years, leaving a huge fear about how to survive without alcohol. Broderson said he has tried to commit suicide several times.

"I'm no good to anyone," he said. "So why should I be hanging around here, just taking up space?" With alcohol, he's in the process of killing himself slowly but surely.

Finally, Pete Townsend found Broderson an efficiency apartment in an old downtown building right across the street from my Lutheran church. It had a bed and a couch and a chair, but there was no bedding and the kitchen was bare.

Townsend also paid off the loan against the trailer, but they still had nowhere to put it. So I took Broderson out to Sun Prairie Village on a chilly morning to get his worldly possessions out of the trailer. They fit in two cardboard boxes and two grocery sacks, mostly dirty clothing that he had received second-hand from Set Free Ministries, some eating utensils and half a dozen coffee cups that I had given him which were souvenirs of newspapers on which I once worked.

It broke my heart as he fumbled through a drawer in which he knew he would find the polished little blue stone that the late Stevie Gretch had so loved. "It has to be around here somewhere," he kept mumbling, but it never showed up.

One thing that did show up was the sheath that once held the Leatherman knife/pliers. But he never did find that little implement either. I guess the fishing dream had floated down the river of alcohol as well.

ARRESTING THE DISEASE

As I watched Broderson and his drinking buddies struggle with booze, I had to conclude that alcoholism *is* an illness—and there's no real cure. You can arrest the disease by quitting drinking, but that's not easy. Most treatment centers fail more than half the time.

The National Institute on Alcohol Abuse and Alcoholism (NIAAA) studied about 1,700 patients a few years ago to determine what it called "post-treatment drinking outcomes." Of the patients institutionalized for treatment and receiving aftercare, only 44 percent managed to stay sober for three months. And only 26 percent of the patients receiving outpatient treatment were able to manage three months of uninterrupted sobriety.

"We can expect a good outcome in about 35 to 40 percent of the cases," said Dr. Richard K. Fuller, director of the NIAAA's division of clinical and prevention research. "Alcoholism treatment helps a lot of people," Fuller told me in a telephone interview, "but there's still lots of room for improvement."

NIAAA's mission is to develop and test new alcoholism treatment to allow addicts a better chance of recovery. "We'd like to improve our outcomes from 35 percent to 50 percent—or even better," said Fuller.

In Montana, state officials believe their abstinence success rate is a little better than the national average because the state hospital is constantly adopting new treatment strategies. The Montana Chemical Dependency Center institutionalizes and treats about 900 patients a year, said Roland Mena of Helena, who heads the state's substance abuse program. "MCDC provides residential, free-standing treatment," said Mena. "That's a medically monitored program in which patients receive medical care, detoxification, and treatment."

There are some drugs, like Naltrexone, that seem to reduce the craving for alcohol, but MCDC generally doesn't use them. "It's fairly expensive to use them," Mena explained, "and there's some controversy over their effectiveness."

Instead, patients are encouraged to eat better, sleep better, talk with other patients, and work out their problems with counselors before they go into an outpatient program. Outpatient clinics focus on helping alcoholics lead normal lives. Doctors know there's a biological predisposition to alcoholism, but abusive drinking can also be driven by psychological, social, or spiritual problems.

"If we approach alcoholism solely as a medical illness, we'll fail," said Rod Robinson, executive director of Gateway Recovery Center, which operates an outpatient program in Great Falls. "But if you recognize that this is a multi-faceted problem," he added, "then the probability of recovery is phenomenal." Gateway hasn't the resources to keep an up-to-date success rate, he said.

Counselors recognize that many of the brain chemicals that are out of balance in alcoholics are the same chemicals underlying mental illness. For example, alcoholism is accompanied by mental depression about 40 percent of the time.

"They look for something to lift them out of their depression, and alcohol provides an instant euphoria," said Robinson, himself a recovering alcoholic. "But there's a tremendous letdown later," he added. "It's enormously ironic that they choose a central nervous system depressant to lift them out of their depression."

Disregarding biology, just living in an alcoholic family predisposes a person toward alcoholism. "There's a learned pattern of behavior in families where this illness is active," said Robinson. "Every aspect of their lives trains those children to become alcoholics."

A number of social stressors can also drive people to drink. Patients regularly tell counselors they began drinking heavily in response to failing relationships, financial problems, boredom, anger, loneliness, and depression. Another major stressor is the job: problems with the boss or with co-workers, with making deadlines, with excessive mistakes, or with tardiness and absenteeism.

Finally, advertising itself creates a social pressure to drink. "Advertising contributes to alcoholism, especially in young people who watch a lot of sporting events or the champagne-moonlight romances," said Judy McGovern, who was a Gateway counselor.

She suggested that the Budweiser talking frogs are the liquor industry's equivalent of Joe Camel, the ad campaign that got the tobacco industry in trouble. As drinking increases and people try to hide their dependence on booze, alcoholism almost invariably leads to lies and deceptions. "Value systems in alcoholic families are lost or skewed," said McGovern. "People who come from dysfunctional families may not know what they value or trust in life, while others with a set of moral values may be violating them every day due to their usage."

Those lies and deceptions only worsen the problem, said Robinson. "Those people pack a tremendous amount of guilt and shame that they can't get rid of," he said.

Once counselors see the encouraging signs of reform, they send their clients to Alcoholics Anonymous meetings, where groups of people with the same problems offer mutual help and support. The 12-step programs such as Alcoholics Anonymous teach addicts that they must turn their lives over to a Higher Power because alone, they are powerless to deal with alcohol.

"AA has a tremendous track record," said Robinson. There are more than 89,000 AA groups meeting around the world, including 64 meetings per week in Great Falls alone.

A national membership survey a few years ago found that the average member had been sober for five years. But that doesn't reflect the number of AA members who fell off the wagon and resumed drinking.

One reason, said Dirk Gibson, supervisor of the Addiction Treatment Center at Benefis Healthcare, is that court-ordered treatment generally doesn't work. "That turns AA into a form of punishment," he said. "Why should seeking help be punishment?" Furthermore, not everyone fits into the AA mold.

Gibson noted that 65 percent of AA members were men and the average age is 42. Less than two percent of the members are under the age of 21. "We used to require all our patients to attend AA, but now we only make those go who fit the AA profile," Gibson said. He said counselors will work to find alternative social support systems for teenagers, Native Americans, and women.

At Benefis, the emphasis is now on motivation. "Without motivation, it doesn't matter what other resources you have," said Gibson. "Without motivation, you have nothing." One way to do that is by stressing the pleasure that an alcoholic can find by changing a lifestyle. Another is by stressing the pain he or she can avoid by quitting drinking.

Many realize that on their own, said Dr. Dan Nauts, medical director of the Benefis Addiction Treatment Center. "A majority of the people who quit abusing substances do it on their own without treatment. Fifty percent of heroin addicts who stop using do so without treatment. Motivation is really the key."

One critical aspect is an intensive assessment in which counselors carefully listen to a patient in order to understand his or her individual concerns. "Once you figure out what's important to people, you must keep reminding them that they can achieve it," said Gibson, "and you must give them the confidence to believe that they can change. When those two things bisect, change occurs."

He cited the case of a retired military officer, intelligent and well read, who kept drinking himself into the hospital's detox center. They worked to find a reason to keep the man from drinking, but couldn't. Even death wasn't a threat. But when they told the patient that he was likely to die in a nursing home, unable to control his movements or his bowels, that struck a nerve. "He called me a month later and said, 'I'm ready to make a change,'" said Gibson. "And he did."

Benefis doesn't keep track of its success rate, said Gibson, partly because it can't decide what to measure. "We do ourselves a disservice if our only goal is abstinence," said Nauts. "We need to look at outcomes including health, healthy relationships, staying out of trouble, keeping a job." Gibson is convinced that motivational therapy, a relatively new concept practiced by fewer than 100 counselors in America today, will make a tremendous improvement in treatment. "Treatment isn't failing," he said. "We're just getting smarter about a tremendously complex issue."

NOT JUST A PUBLIC HEALTH CONCERN

I looked around to find out what some of our neighbors are doing and found that the Division of Alcohol and Substance Abuse in Washington State says treating alcoholism saves tax dollars.

A study estimated the total economic costs of alcohol and illegal drugs at $2.54 billion. But it found that treatment cut medical costs from an average of $9,000 over a five-year period to $3,500. For a group of 493 mentally ill clients, treatment cut medical costs from among $5 million a year to $2.8 million.

And infants of drinking mothers averaged $5,447 in medical expenses for their first two years of life, compared with $3,694 for those whose mothers had been through treatment. Finally, the state found that untreated clients earned an average of $153 a month, but those who had been treated averaged $288 a month and those who had also received further vocational training made $421 a month.

"Not only are these people no longer draining the system, but they're contributing to it with their earnings," Antoinette Krupski, the division's research administrator, told me in a telephone interview.

"Our data show that substance abuse is not just a public health problem, it's a problem for criminal justice, child welfare, public welfare, and mental health," Krupski said. "Everyone has a piece of this problem, whether they like it or not. But the cost to public systems decreases dramatically for those who participate in treatment," she added. "It's very cost-effective. The savings to public institutions far exceeds the cost of treatment, even for those who are deemed hopeless."

The federal government also knows it must put greater emphasis on treating alcoholism and drug abuse, particularly in rural areas and on Indian reservations.

"Rural areas have unique needs," said Dr. H. Westley Clark, director of the federal Center for Substance Abuse Treatment, in a telephone interview from Rockville, Maryland. "Alcohol and [crystal methamphetamine] have reared their ugly heads in rural areas which don't have the resources to meet those needs." Clark said the federal government would team up with local caregivers to improve substance abuse treatment. Closing the treatment gap is one of five goals of the federal agency, said Clark. Others include:

- Reducing the stigma of alcoholism
- Improving the treatment system

- Providing better research to local caregivers
- Addressing medical workforce issues

"We have scheduled a series of public meetings that will allow us to go to Congress and present our plans based on public input, not just a bunch of bureaucrats coming up with these things on our own," Clark said. But none of the four meetings are to be held in rural areas or on Indian reservations. They were scheduled for Hartford, Connecticut; Chicago, Illinois; Portland, Oregon; and Tampa, Florida.

"I have personally already been to New Mexico to look at Native American issues, and I will be going out into rural areas to talk with them about their problems," said Clark. "While it's not on our written schedule, it's on my personal agenda."

But one member of the national advisory board for the Center for Substance Abuse Treatment said that progress had been slow. "I try to bring treatment in rural areas and Indian reservations to the table and get something going," said Rod Robinson, executive director of Gateway Recovery Center and an enrolled member of the Crow tribe. "And they have moved on some of those issues, although I believe that movement has been fairly minimal in relation to the rest of the country. The treatment dollars tend to flow to where the people and research institutions are."

REDUCING DOMESTIC VIOLENCE

Harvard University has a highly effective program for alcoholics who abuse their spouses and children. Called behavioral couples therapy (BCT), it provides counseling for husband and wife together.

"We're enlisting the spouse as an ally to help reward and support abstinence, but we're in no way seeking to make the spouse responsible for the recovery of the patient," said Timothy J. O'Farrell, chief of the

Harvard Families and Addiction Program (HFAP). Beyond that, the patient is more likely to come to counseling if his spouse is there, and the odds of success increase with each session.

The patient and the spouse agree to promise each other every day that they will remain sober that day, and they are given a calendar to record that day's events. Both parties agree not to discuss past drinking problems or future drinking fears since they can cause conflict. And they agree to undertake a series of special assignments:

- "Catch your spouse doing something nice" requires each person to notice and comment on one pleasing behavior each day.
- "Caring day" is a day in which each spouse does one special thing for his or her partner.
- "Shared rewarding activities" is important because many couples have quit going to ball games or dances, or picnics, the things that brought them together in the first place and that can improve the odds of positive recovery.

"Things have often been pretty negative, and it's difficult not to stay stuck in the past, even as you try to move forward into a different future," O'Farrell told me. "After we deal with the addiction itself, we try to focus on joint positive activities."

Nearly two-thirds of HFAP's alcoholics had been violent toward their wives in the year before counseling, O'Farrell said, but that rate was cut in half in the two years after the program. And violence was nearly eliminated when the husband quit drinking completely, O'Farrell added.

"Taken together, the data from two studies show that reduced hospital and jail days after BCT [counseling] save more than five times the cost of delivering BCT [services] for alcoholism," he said.

INCENTIVE FOR PILOTS

The Hazelden Foundation has developed a highly successful program to work with professionals, in this case airline pilots. That's a natural, given the volume of air traffic in and out of the Minneapolis airport each day. More than 90 percent of the participants in the program, called the Human Intervention and Motivation System (HIMS), remain sober two years after treatment, said John MacDougall, the foundation's spiritual care supervisor.

One key is the motivation of keeping lucrative careers and retirement benefits, he noted. But another is the emphasis placed on aftercare. Pilots receive relapse prevention education and two years of ongoing therapy and supervision, including random drug and alcohol testing. Those who relapse may be subject to intense monitoring for the remainder of their careers.

Barton Pakull, chief psychiatrist for the Federal Aviation Administration, makes a decision on whether the pilots may resume flying based primarily on their attitude, whether the pilot is angry about his disease or grateful at the opportunity to arrest it. "I worry about the white-knuckle dry drunk going back to flying because he's eventually going to be tempted to try drinking again out of anger or self-pity when things go wrong," Pakull told Hazelden. Since 1975, more than 2,000 pilots have completed the program and returned successfully to their careers.

TREAT WELFARE RECIPIENTS

"If I were the governor of Montana, I'd impose a users' tax on liquor sales to fund alcohol treatment," MacDougall told me when I was at Hazelden. He suggested using Minnesota's "rule 25" of the state welfare code as a model for such treatment. That earmarks a percentage of the welfare funding to be used for substance abuse treatment on the theory that treating the illness is a lot cheaper than the costs of welfare, increased medical bills, and likely criminal costs.

He cited the case of a fifty-year-old Minneapolis woman with a history of seven unsuccessful treatments behind her. The state paid for twenty-eight days of treatment, followed by four months of extended care and three months in a halfway house, he said, and she has been sober ever since. "Some of the greater success stories are those with less motivation than airline pilots," said MacDougall. "And it's still cheaper to treat addicts than it is to bear the costs of untreated addicts."

IDENTIFY ALCOHOLIC MOTHERS

Alaska is launching a $30 million, five-year program to identify children with fetal alcohol syndrome and get treatment for their mothers.

Researchers believe there's a 70 percent chance that mothers who have damaged one child by drinking during pregnancy will deliver another FAS child. The Centers for Disease Control say up to seven children per 10,000 births are afflicted with FAS nationally, but estimated it affects fifty children per 10,000 in Alaska.

Treatment can cost $1.4 million over the lifetime of the child in Alaska. Congress has also provided funding for diagnostic screening of the mothers of FAS children in Montana, the Dakotas, and Minnesota.

MAKE IT HARDER FOR KIDS TO DRINK

The University of Minnesota School of Public Health has put together a series of policy solutions for cutting underage drinking, including regular compliance checks to make sure alcohol isn't sold to minors and increasingly severe administrative penalties for those who do sell it. One of the more controversial recommendations is licensing each keg of beer that is sold.

"Let's say someone buys some teenagers a keg of beer or two," said Kay Provine, prevention specialist for the Hazelden Foundation. "They head out to the woods, get drunk, and scatter when the cops come. All that's left is the keg. Now, if those kegs were registered, the cops could go back to the individual who bought them and hold him responsible," she told me. "Or if the shopkeeper sold to the underaged kids, he could be held responsible, too."

It's particularly important to keep teens from drinking, she noted, because binge drinking can damage late brain development. Between the ages of seventeen and twenty, teens undergo significant brain development, including maturation of the fronto-temporal region. That's the area squarely behind the forehead, which scientists have identified as the brain's ethical decision-making center.

EXTEND INSURANCE COVERAGE

Insurance regulations need to be changed to provide better protection for youth between eighteen and twenty-five years old, said Mike Schiks, vice president for recovery services at Hazelden.

"It's a great black hole of coverage," said Schiks, adding that most teens are beginning to experiment with alcohol before they are thirteen. "Most therapists will never admit it," he said, "but there's really not very much reason to take on a patient at seventeen, knowing that he won't be covered at eighteen and he'll likely drop out of treatment."

Schiks said Hazelden gave away $3.5 million in patient aid, much of it to teens "and it still wasn't enough. If the insurance doesn't pay, the illness doesn't go away," he told me, "so we scramble to find a way to provide it. A large number of people in this country go without help, and frequently, that means our kids," said Schiks. "For me, that's the biggest heartbreaker."

NEUROFEEDBACK

Helena author Jim Robbins wrote in a recent issue of *Psychology Today* about recent advances in neurofeedback that might affect alcoholics. Neurofeedback is the technique of altering the frequency of a person's brain waves. Using monitors and a video screen, people can be trained to decrease the frequency of their brain waves to relax without taking a drink or to increase the frequency of their brain waves to fight weariness.

Eugene Peniston, a researcher at the Sam Rayburn Memorial Veterans' Center in Bonham, Texas, treated a group of twenty alcoholics using neurofeedback techniques and claimed an 80 percent success rate. "The cure rate seems improbably high," he said. "We won't know the actual impact of this therapy until larger samples are studied."

HELP FOR NATIVE AMERICANS

Ray Daw, director of the Nanizhoozhi Center Inc. (NCI), in Gallup, New Mexico, believes that a holistic approach—from prevention to intervention—can clean up a problem. "We've been able to reduce public intoxication in Gallup by 49 percent," said Daw in a telephone interview. The center is funded by the Indian Health Center and is operated by two tribal governments, the Navajo Nation and the Pueblo of Zuni.

As a high-volume, low-cost facility, NCI serves an average 20,000 intoxicated clients per year by utilizing a five-day detox program and a twenty-eight-day treatment program that includes traditional Native American practices. "Generally against their wishes, the majority of the clients are picked up by local law enforcement officials and brought to

NCI under a New Mexico state 'protective custody' statute based on dangerous behavior to one's self or others," said an NCI outcomes report.

Before the protective custody law was implemented, an average of thirteen people died of substance abuse problems each month during the winters. Currently, the mortality rate is down to four a month, said the report. NCI said 43 percent of its clients remain sober, 15 percent drink moderately, 15 percent report periodic binge drinking, and nearly 28 percent remain alcohol dependent. But Daw noted that most outpatients return to a hostile environment fraught with high unemployment and family problems.

In addition to the interventions, NCI has done a lot of work on preventing alcohol abuse, said Daw. It has also worked to reduce the availability of alcohol and cracked down on the problem bars. From 1975 to 1995, the results have been stunning:

- Premature death rates for McKinley County were roughly three times the state rate, but dropped by 54 percent.
- The county's accident mortality rate has declined 59 percent.
- The county's homicide rate dropped 50 percent, the suicide rate was down 52 percent, and alcohol-induced mortality rates as a whole declined 42 percent.

"Unlike three decades ago, McKinley County's mortality rates for homicide, suicide, and drug-induced mortality now approach or are below both the New Mexico and national levels," said NCI.

TREATING ADDICTS IN JAIL

Expand the substance abuse treatment programs in the nation's prisons, said Joseph Califano, chairman of the National Center on Addiction and Substance Abuse at Columbia University.

"To me, the most insane part of this system is that we don't take advantage of treating the nation's captive population," said Califano, former secretary of the U.S. Department of Health, Education, and Welfare. "It's cost-effective because we know it will reduce subsequent problems, and almost all of those people will be getting out of prisons someday."

In Montana, corrections officials estimate that 85 percent of the state's prisoners are alcohol- or drug-addicted, committed their crimes under the influence of alcohol or drugs, or committed their crimes to buy alcohol or drugs. However, 500 to 600 inmates at Deer Lodge are on the waiting lists for substance abuse treatment, and many of them will be released without it.

TREATMENT RATHER THAN JAIL

Jailing alcoholics or drug addicts is a "failed social policy," the Clinton administration's drug policy director said in 1999. Barry McCaffrey, director of the White House Office of Drug Control Policy, advocated treatment rather than incarceration in the nation's correctional system. One of his suggestions was a greater use of drug courts.

In Oregon, for example, Portland has the STOP program for drug addicts and alcoholics. It's a voluntary choice for treatment, but addicts agree that if they drop out of the program, they'll appear before a judge for sentencing with no defense or excuses—which provides for a swift and sure sanction.

In an outcomes analysis, researcher Michael Finigan of the Northwest Professional Consortium found that those who graduated from the program had 76 percent fewer arrests than a similar comparison group. "Our drug/alcohol court is effective because it marries good treatment with judicial oversight, which provides the hammer to keep people in treatment," Finigan told me.

"In a treatment center, people can wander in and out without consequence," he explained. "With judicial oversight, that's no longer the case. Now they have a judge, who is a godlike figure to many of them, who seems to take a personal interest in them," said Finigan. "That really motivates them."

His analysis found that treatment saved residents of Multnomah County $2.50 for each dollar spent on the program. For residents of Oregon itself, adding in welfare and corrections costs, the savings were even greater—$10 saved for each dollar spent, he concluded.

In mid-December, Broderson was back in detox, just where we'd first met him. Larry Beckner and I went up to visit him one evening in the wardroom that had become so familiar. The nurses smiled and waved us through, clicking open the locked door from their control station. Broderson was gaunt, bored, dispirited (literally and figuratively), and craving nicotine. After long experience, the nurses wouldn't let him out of their sight—they knew he'd walk downtown to cadge cigarettes and beer.

I told Broderson I would be leaving in a few days to head back East so that my wife Susie and I could spend Christmas with our children, three-fourths of whom were in the West Virginia general area. He said good-bye, but he seemed unusually somber so I asked why. "I won't see you again," he said. "I'm not going to make it into the new year."

The last picture of Broderson that Beckner took still haunts me. Sitting on the edge of his bed, Broderson had finished as much of a hospital meal as his stomach could handle. Then he rolled sideways, told us goodbye, and asked us to turn out the lights. Before I did, Beckner took the picture of a fifty-year-old man who looked to be in his mid-seventies with sallow cheeks and black stubble, lying curled up in a hospital bed in a fetal position.

I was startled by his conviction that death was near. Over the next few days, I carefully wrote up his obituary and tucked it away in an advance story queue, labeling it "hold until Broderson's death." Mercifully, we didn't need it that year.

POSTSCRIPT

Our series had ended, but my relationship with Broderson didn't. I couldn't turn my back on him and say, "Sorry, but so long."

I made a point of checking in with him once or twice a week or he would stop by my office, chat for a while, then head out the back door and collect all the cigarette butts left by employees not allowed to smoke in our office.

I quickly ran into one major conflict of interest, though. Broderson's payee, Pete Townsend, wanted badly to get rid of the trailer. It now had a book value of $2,500, because that's how much Broderson paid for it. Having that kind of an asset jeopardized his monthly SSI disability payments, as well as the rent on his little apartment.

Furthermore, Townsend couldn't find a place in town where Broderson could economically park and live in the trailer. So Townsend wanted to sell it, but didn't even have a place where he could advertise and show it. And the trailer dealers wouldn't touch it, either.

Townsend asked me if I would buy it for $500, just to get it off Broderson's hands. I was tempted, although I told Townsend that I didn't want to take advantage of the situation—that if Broderson ever wanted the trailer back, I'd sell it back to him for the price that I had bought it.

In retrospect, that was a copout. Broderson would never be able to use that trailer again, and I knew that. My wife Susie put her foot down and said she didn't want to buy the trailer, even at that price. And a friend, Jack Gannon, urged me not to buy the trailer because of the appearance of impropriety.

Finally, I went to Executive Editor Jim Strauss and explained the whole situation. Nope, he said, I couldn't buy it because that would be a conflict of interest. How about writing another story, he suggested, that explained the situation, said the trailer was for sale, and listed Townsend's name and phone number?

Gratefully, I did that, and Townsend called the next day to say that the trailer had been sold for $1,000. I told him it was the best free advertising he would likely ever see.

That left Broderson with a roof over his head, but not much more. He received food stamps and $25 in walking-around money, which he usually received on Monday morning and drank by Wednesday night.

He asked for a television set to occupy his time, and Townsend bought him one, a huge old clunker that Broderson couldn't possibly haul down to the pawnshop to finance a week's drunk.

One Monday early in February 2000, Broderson called from the Red Door Lounge, drunk at noon. "I can't go home," he said. "My fair weather friends are waiting for me to come home with my weekly allowance, and I don't want them to get it."

Townsend had previously spoken of the vultures who would take advantage of Broderson when they learned he had money. Now he had three of them sitting in his apartment. "They're waiting for me there," he said. "They don't have a key so they won't leave because they can't get back in."

I asked how they'd gotten in. Broderson said he invited them up to his apartment—"I just can't say no," he said. Personally, I suspected Broderson let them in because they came bearing a twelve-pack of beer, but then they wouldn't leave. At the end of February, Reuben and Jolena Kipp Williams moved to Helena. That left Broderson pretty much alone in Great Falls, except for his mother who was in a nursing home. He walked out to visit her several times a month. In mid-March, Broderson said he woke up in his apartment, his pillow and the wall soaked in blood.

"I must have fallen and cracked my skull on a curb," he said. "I remember they brought me home in a cab because I couldn't walk."

He staggered over to Opportunities Inc. the next day, where they told him to go to the hospital emergency room. "He needs about seven stitches, but it's way too late for that so he is going to have a bald spot for the rest of his life," said Townsend. "And I don't believe he fell off a curb either because he's got no money anymore," he added. "I think someone whacked him pretty good and took his money, but it must be someone he knows because he won't go there with me."

Broderson drank heavily all spring, and he was back in the detox center at Benefis Healthcare on April 10, when the Pulitzer Prizes were announced. When I got back to the office the next morning, I found a message from him from the evening before letting me know he was in the hospital. I went there, but was told he had been discharged hours before.

I found him in an alley behind the Lobby Bar, peering pensively into a dumpster. We went into the bar, and I bought him an orange juice. He was very shaky and had trouble talking. After half an hour or so, he asked to borrow $10.

"Bill," I said, "I'll buy you lunch for the rest of your life and I'll buy you all the orange juice you can hold, but I'm damned if I'm going to subsidize your suicide." Angry, he stood up and told me he was going to join his true friends at a bar up the street. Then he staggered out the back toward the Red Door. A couple of hours later, I got a call from the attorney who had represented Broderson in his application for Social Security disability benefits.

He wanted me to know that Broderson had been in to see him about suing me and the *Tribune* for his share of my Pulitzer Prize. "I told him to get out of my office and not to return until he was sober," said the attorney. "And I also want you to know I wouldn't touch that suit with a pole."

Later, Dirk Gibson, director of the hospital's Addiction Medicine Center, called Broderson's behavior predictable. "It shows you the power of his disease," said Gibson. "All he's concerned about is how to get his next drink."

The next Sunday, Broderson shocked me by showing up in our church, which is right across the street from his apartment. For months, I'd been inviting him to join us, but he was usually too drunk to attend the 10:00 A.M. service. Instead, he'd leave a smiley face drawn in the dirt on the driver's door of the truck as he walked down the street to buy a twelve-pack.

But here Broderson was, sitting with us in the front pew of our church. He was clean-shaven and relatively sober. The pastor looked out at the congregation and asked, "How many of you won a superior in the music competition?" Three teens stood up and received a round of applause.

"How many of you won a Pulitzer Prize last month?" he asked. I stood up.

Suddenly, the whole church was on its feet, clapping and cheering. "I had no idea there were so many prize-winners in our congregation," I later joked. When the applause finally ended, I reached down, pulled Broderson to his feet, turned him around to face the congregation, put an arm around him, and introduced him as our guest.

Another round of applause—and it may have been the first Broderson ever received. As we sat down, I put a hand on his knee. "I couldn't have done this without you," I told him quietly. He flushed with pride.

Four days later, the *Tribune* held a community reception to allow our readers to share the honor. I had invited our readers' panel and half a dozen of the folks I had written about.

Broderson showed up with Tara Fatz, but he was fairly drunk, very nervous, and didn't stay long. Most of the people I had written about did show up to celebrate with us—including the two families I had written about, the Ashbys and the Keelers.

Lissy Clark brought me some dog biscuits (her new business) and hugged me several dozen times. And the Keelers sent me an e-mail message that summed up their feelings: "CONGRATULATIONS!!!!!!! We are so very happy for you. What can one say at a time like this except that you deserve it!!!! It really couldn't have happened to a nicer guy. I am so glad we got to know you. I remember when asked to be interviewed, I thought 'Oh my God,' but you put me and my family at ease right from the start. You do have a way with people."

It was an incredible feeling, knowing that the people who could have been devastated by any mistake on my part were there celebrating with us.

The other thing that moved me deeply was that strangers began approaching me on the streets, in parking lots, in restaurants, in alleys. They told me that they were alcoholics or ex-alcoholics, that their husbands or girlfriends were alcoholics, or that their children were alcoholics. "Now you have told our stories," they said. "People finally know who we are, why we are the way that we are, and what we're going through. Thank you."

On Easter Sunday, Broderson joined us in church again, but he slipped out the back way after the service so he wouldn't have to visit with people. Later that week, I bought him lunch. He ate well, but looked fairly ragged. Someone named Butch had moved into Broderson's apartment with him, and he brought a girlfriend named Darlene.

Together, they made him very nervous, he said, but he couldn't bring himself to throw them out so he had taken to living on the street again. The previous evening, he said, he had slept in an abandoned car.

Gateway Recovery Center was talking about committing him again, he said, but he didn't see much use in it. "I'm dead anyway," he said. "Why prolong it any longer?" I told him I didn't think he'd quit drinking until he was able to take control of his own life, support himself, and make a difference in the world around him. He nodded at me. "It'll be no big loss when I'm gone," he said, "So there's really no reason to quit drinking."

On May 3, Broderson called again from Benefis detox, but this time he was in the holding cell. I went over to see him, and he looked awful—shakes, sallow skin, difficulty putting words and thoughts together. Broderson said he was beginning to feel ill on May Day, so he called Gateway Recovery Center for help. They rolled an ambulance, a rescue unit, and a couple of squad cars at him.

Brought to the emergency room, he was immediately put in restraints. "I was in them for a couple of hours," he said, "and I couldn't get out of them. I was trying to chew them off with my teeth, but I couldn't do it."

I asked if that was why he was locked up. "I walked out of here the last two times," he answered.

"You told me you were discharged," I said.

"I lied," he said.

Broderson said he didn't know how long he would be in the hospital involuntarily, but said the state was preparing to appoint a guardian for him and possibly confine him to a nursing home. "But I'll be able to walk out of that any time I want to," he said.

Dr. James Day of Golden Triangle Community Mental Health Center said that Broderson was admitted this time as a psychiatric patient, not for treatment of alcoholism. "He was in our emergency room not only drunk, but threatening suicide in a fairly dramatic and public display," said Day. The doctor said that years of heavy drinking had caused brain damage to Broderson, including dementia, which impaired his judgment.

"He's no longer capable of protecting his own safety, health, or nutrition," Day said, adding that he felt Broderson needed to be committed to the state mental hospital until the court could find a safe home for him.

But Marvin Anderson, assistant county attorney, doubted that would be possible. "He's not really mentally ill," noted Anderson. "It's the alcohol that's causing the dementia. I talked to him today, and he sounded pretty lucid to me. He told me he'd challenge the commitment, so I don't think we're going to be able to commit him."

Broderson apparently got out May 16 because I had a message on my telephone answering machine from him. I could hear a jukebox in the background, then a voice saying: "Sssssss Bill (hic) g'by." So much for a sixteen-day treatment program that cost taxpayers nearly $5,000.

A week or so later, he was complaining that he had invited three friends to move in with him, but that he had given them his key. Now he couldn't get in his own apartment unless his guests were there to let him in.

On Sunday, May 28, he called me at home to tell me he was going to begin camping out again because he couldn't stand the visitors and noise in his apartment. Angry, I told him to stay by the phone, and I quickly drove to town. Alarmed, Broderson asked what I planned to do. "I'm going to ask your guests to leave," I replied.

That scared Broderson. He just couldn't do it. We argued for ten minutes or so.

"Don't do it—please," he said. "I invited them to come, and I can't throw them out. If I go sleep in the park, it would be just one more person on the street, not three. And it's a nice night. Please...."

So Broderson slept on the lawn of our church, across from his own apartment, for the next two nights while taxpayers paid for a room 100 yards away for three other drunks.

Through June, Broderson joined us in church most Sundays, although he was drinking heavily. In late June, he called from a bar, his words slurring, to report that he was having difficulty walking and talking. "I've had a few beers," he said, "but not enough to do this. Something weird's going on with me."

So I took him to the emergency room of Benefis Heathcare. He looked bad, unable to walk without weaving and almost falling down. "This is Bill Broderson," I told the ER receptionist. "He has been drinking, but he's experiencing problems that he says are more severe than the amount he has had to drink. And he has had plenty of experience with drinking."

Doctors found no problem, though, and Broderson returned to the streets. He also began attending our church regularly, sitting with the pastor's wife, Sandy, on the Sundays that we were out of town.

After missing us for two consecutive Sundays, Broderson took advantage of a quiet moment to stand up and ask, "Where the hell's Eric?"

"I don't honestly know," replied Pastor Tim Christensen. When we returned from five days in Denver at the beginning of July, I heard about the interruption and asked Tim whether it was a problem.

"No," he said, "he didn't cause a scene or anything. And I'm going to be real angry if people don't think Broderson should be in church just because he's not entirely sober. He's the kind of person that Christ tells us to take care of. I'd rather have him here than somewhere else."

"Some people around here need to get a little more glad," opined Marlys Stuart, a pillar of the church who had been listening in on the conversation.

That Friday, I went looking for Broderson to tell him we wouldn't be in church next week either, that we would be floating the White Cliffs of the Missouri on that Sunday morning. Couldn't find him anywhere.

It was a wonderful trip, but when we got back on Wednesday, Broderson found us. He and a friend, Kelly, pulled up in Kelly's car at our home out of town; then they came in, and sat on the deck to visit with us. Broderson was in a good deal of pain, having just come out of the hospital where he had spent three days, recuperating from a fall down a staircase that broke three of his ribs.

It was an uncomfortable visit because Susie and I were drinking a beer when Broderson showed up. He wanted one, and we wouldn't give him one. It was awkward.

More than that, it put me squarely in the middle of a dilemma. I'd intruded on his life in every way, but I always had been able to walk away from it and retreat to my own home, sheltering my personal life. I was aware that Broderson had taken advantage of others, that he may have stolen from others to buy alcohol, and I wanted to build a wall around my personal life. But here he was, sitting on my back deck. And how could I turn him away or refuse him? So I sat, as graciously as I could, and squirmed inwardly until they left an hour or so later.

The next week, Broderson met us in the church parking lot and asked for $1.62 to buy a pack of cigarettes. In the past, I'd personally bought him the smokes, rather than give him the money. Susie, however, gave him $2. "Ah," he said, standing on the hot asphalt with a faraway look in his eyes, "I'll just head over to the store and get me a nice, cool— cigarette."

A few Sundays later, Bishop Mark Ramseth happened to be preaching at our church because it was the fifth anniversary of our pastor's ordination. The bishop's message was that each of us has our own calling.

As I listened, I looked over at Broderson, sitting in the front row beside me, and realized it was true. My calling was to chronicle the problem of alcoholism, and his was to demonstrate it. We were linked in the same cause, sitting side by side. It was a startling insight to me, and one that made me profoundly grateful that I had by far the lighter end of that load.

Broderson spent much of July living outside because Butch and Diane had taken over his apartment. By August 1, however, Pete Townsend had managed to talk the manager of a senior center called the Downtowner to rent him a room, and I promised to help him move. The Downtowner is an old hotel that still looks fairly good. At 8 A.M., there are a few seniors sitting in the lobby fussing about whether the door should be open or closed.

Broderson's new room was on the first floor, near the back. It had no furniture, but was filled with so much cigarette smoke it was hard to see. Broderson was horribly hung over, shaking badly, and sipping on a beer to quiet his nerves. Sitting on the floor was a young man in his twenties who didn't look at me or speak. Standing was a sun-tanned man with a shock of silver hair. His name was Nicky, and he reminded me of a rat— cunning, greedy, genial, or aggressive depending on the circumstances.

"They crashed here last night," Broderson explained. I was stunned. After all, that's exactly why he was moving out of the other apartment building. And he was setting up the same predicament.

Anyway, we went over to his old apartment. Since he had no key, he had to bang on a ground-floor window and ask someone called Little Joe to open the door for him.

On the third floor, three apartment doors were open as we walked down the hall. The carpet looked like Grant's army had marched over it. In each room, men were sitting around the living room, watching television and drinking beer for breakfast.

Broderson walked into one room, picked a beer can off the coffee table, and asked if he could borrow it. No one answered. He just opened it, took a long swallow, and walked back out. In his room were Butch and Diane.

Butch was angry. Why hadn't Broderson said something about moving out? Where had he been yesterday? What was going to happen to them? His voice was that of an aggressor, someone who pushed others around and took advantage of a situation. I could see him as a cocky, pushy crow.

Diane was very quiet, sad, subdued. She showed no bruises, but looked abused. "Here's your clothes, Billie; they're all clean," she told him.

As Broderson gathered his few belongings—clothing, a radio, the monster television set, a few books, and a framed picture of his mother—Diane looked at me and said, "We tried to take good care of him."

After it was all over, I dropped by Opportunities Inc. to chat with Pete Townsend. When I told him Broderson had roommates, he looked stricken. "They won't put up with that," he said. "He'll be thrown out of there as soon as they find out he has guests."

Townsend also said he had visited with the super at Broderson's former apartment about keeping predators away from him. The super said he had tried, but Broderson invited people to stay with him because he was unable to sleep alone. "How can you help someone like that?" the super asked. "Someone who refuses help?"

I had no answer to that. Still don't.

Early in the fall, Broderson came to join us in church. He was falling-down drunk. In fact, when he tried to sit down, he fell into my lap. He slept through much of the service, but as the rest of the congregation rose to take communion, I seized an opportunity, got him out of the church, and took him home. He sat down on the edge of his bed and took his shoes off. Then he looked up at me, eyes brimming with tears. "I'm terrified," he said softly. "I'm terrified at what I'm doing to myself. Why am I doing this?"

I could only tell him that he suffers from an illness that he can't control. Both his parents were alcoholics, and he's genetically loaded for it. In addition, everything in his environment has taught him to drink and conspired to keep him drinking.

Over the next few years, Broderson continued drinking about a gallon of beer a day. But his life got better. He moved upstairs to the fifth floor of the Downtowner, where he got a large corner apartment with windows that looked out over the town and provided cross-ventilation. Being off the street really cut down on the predators that dropped in.

There's a pocket park right beside the Downtowner with benches and picnic tables sitting on green grass beneath shade trees. When the weather was good, Broderson and his friends sat in the park, sipping beers and watching people.

He began attending church with us regularly. People accepted him, asking about his health and chatting with him. He began to develop friends without serious drinking problems. And he began to ask questions about what he was hearing on Sundays. He tried to read the Bible and some of the commentaries, but didn't have the capacity anymore to make much sense of it all. So I began to do a simple Bible study with him.

As his body began to fail under the pressure of the huge intake of alcohol, he and I visited a number of doctors. My role was to interpret the medical jargon into uncompromising language that he could grasp. The most serious problem was a bladder failure that inflated him with urine like a water balloon. The docs decided he needed an operation to put in a tube that would allow him to drain his bladder manually. He complained about that for the next couple of years—he couldn't roll over in his sleep, it was painful and it became too easily infected—but it also kept him alive.

On June 13, 2004, I sponsored Broderson for baptism at our church. He showed up clean, shaven, sober, and nervous as a cat. He tried to joke about the service, but couldn't. At the end, he was visibly shaken. Susie and I brought him out to the house for a Sunday dinner, and sat with him in the sun through the afternoon, just talking. It was almost unheard of for him to be sober through an afternoon.

Later, he told me: "That was the best day of my life."

With some stability in his life, Broderson shifted back to maintenance drinking rather than the heavy binge drinking. He never returned to the detox unit again. "I'm just amazed that he's still alive," Dr. Nauts told me a year ago. "And I'm amazed that I haven't seen him in a long time. Something is working for him in his life." And that tells me that a little effort from us can make a tremendous difference to others.

Broderson beat the odds for a long time, but he couldn't do it forever. With cirrhosis and hepatitis C, his liver was the next to go.

Dr. Julie Wood, medical director of the City-County Health Clinic, looked at him on May 12, 2006. She noted his swollen ankles and belly, and she diagnosed liver failure. You'll be dead within the next six to twelve months, she said. "I'm just trying to be honest," she told him. "I'm not condemning you for your drinking. We both know you won't stop. And with your genetic load," she added, "I don't know that I wouldn't be right there beside you."

She suggested he make his peace with those he would leave behind—a thought that clearly made Broderson uncomfortable. His brother John, for example, had pretty well written him off two decades ago. She also asked whether he wanted any extraordinary measures to resuscitate him in his final hours.

"I don't want to leave the wonderful people I've met, the people who are my friends," he answered. "But I'm ready to go anytime." As the doctor left the examination room, Broderson and I sat in silence for a moment. "God I need a drink," he said finally.

A week later, on his way back from the convenience store with a twelve-pack of beer, he collapsed and was taken by ambulance to Benefis. I stopped to see him a few times, but couldn't do much good. He was heavily sedated for the pain, and his ankle and foot were still red and swollen.

Four days later, we rolled Broderson in his wheelchair down the street to a transitional unit in Peace Hospice. He had serious doubts about the place, but they'd promised he could have a beer now and again, so he reluctantly consented. I told him that he'd be put into therapy and he'd have to work hard to be able to return to his own apartment and an independent—albeit slowly suicidal—lifestyle.

He just stared at me, eyes glazed and lips swollen. "No, this is it," he whispered. He turned out to be right. He slipped into a coma May 24, 2006, and died that evening. I was shocked by the call from Peace Hospice because he'd been propped up in bed and snoring when I'd checked in on him just a few hours before.

He left the remaining ten cans of beer and $20.91 in change. As a parting gift, I gave the booze to his friends, the ones he used to sip beers with in the small park beside the Downtowner. There were some tears when I told them of his death. And the $20.91 is being used to start the Broderson Benevolence Fund at First English Lutheran Church. It will be used to help the destitute, the alcoholics, and the addicts.

By the time of his memorial service, that fund had grown to more than $400. On June 13, 2006, about 30 of us gathered to celebrate Broderson's life. Hal Harper, now the governor's chief policy advisor, was unable to attend, but called to tell me how important it was for people to understand the tragedy of Broderson's life—and his death.

Before the service, Pastor Tim noted that Broderson lived outside the box, and that he required others to join him. "Bill forced us to live out our faith," he said, "and we did." He said a few people in our congregation were judgmental, but that they had the sense to keep their opinions to themselves. Everyone else accepted him.

"When I think of the people that Jesus hung around with, I always think of Bill," Pastor Sandy said during the service. "Two years ago today, Bill was baptized and became a child of God," she added. "And after the service, when I saw the people who came up to him and welcomed him, I thought to myself, 'This must be what God's true love looks like.'"

Broderson turned out to be the ideal "poster child" for alcoholism because he was incurably addicted to booze, but had no other complicating side effects. He was intelligent, witty, kind, even gallant in the face of massive pain. There was no malice or evil in him. We all learned a lot from him.

Over these years, I've done a lot of thinking about alcoholism. I think back to Bishop Ramseth's message, and I'm forever grateful that I got the easier of the two callings: to observe and write about an illness, rather than to live it. I also think about all the street people that I've failed to notice over the years.

Today, I know that they are all people, people who have an illness (and I'm convinced that alcoholism is a form of mental illness because its most serious forms involve an imbalance of the same neurotransmitters).

Like Broderson, their lives are tragedies, but they muddle on and try to laugh when the pain gets too great. The greatest lesson Broderson taught me is that alcoholism can strike anyone, can *kill* anyone. And we don't really know how to prevent it or cure it.

I suspect that the next few decades are going to bring about tremendous new knowledge of how the brain works. I certainly hope so. I hope we're on the threshold of an age in which we can cure these diseases and make alcoholics well.

BIBLIOGRAPHY

By the time I finished with the alcoholism series for the *Great Falls Tribune*, I had a stack of reports, papers, and documents about three feet high, filling three large boxes.

My main reference source was the 420-page "Special Report to the U.S. Congress on Alcohol and Health," prepared by the National Institute on Alcohol Abuse and Alcoholism. It examined alcohol's effect on the human body from a medical standpoint, but also looked at its effects on behavior and safety, as well as the economic costs of alcohol abuse. NIAAA also has an excellent periodical called "Alcohol World, Health and Research" which is available through the office of the Superintendent of Documents in Washington, DC.

I made good use of the Center for Substance Abuse Treatment's TIP series. Particularly useful were numbers 7, "Screening and Assessment for Alcohol and Other Drug Abuse among Adults in the Criminal Justice System"; 8, "Relapse Prevention and the Substance-Abusing Criminal Offender"; 10, "Rural Issues in Alcohol and Other Drug Abuse Treatment"; 17, "Planning for Alcohol and Other Drug Abuse Treatment for Adults in the Criminal Justice System"; 21, "Combining Alcohol and Other Drug Abuse Treatment with Diversion for Juveniles in the Justice System"; 23, "Treatment Drug Courts: Integrating Substance Abuse Treatment with Legal Case Processing"; and 25, "Substance Abuse Treatment and Domestic Violence."

There are also a number of publications available through Alcoholics Anonymous that provided useful data and psychological insights.

Here are some of the other major references that I found helpful:

"1998-99 Montana Statewide Core Data Base." Billings, MT: Montana Higher Education Network for Substance Abuse Prevention.

"Alcohol, Tobacco and Drugs." California Drug and Alcohol Treatment Assessment.

Anthenelli, Robert & Schuckit, Marc. "Genetic Influences in Addiction." *Journal of the American Society of Addiction Medicine.*

"Apparent Per Capita Alcohol Consumption: National, State, and Regional Trends, 1977-95." NIAAA.

"Back to School 1998—National Survey of American Attitudes on Substance Abuse IV: Teens, Teachers and Principals." New York, NY: National Center on Addiction and Substance Abuse, Columbia University.

"Behind Bars: Substance Abuse and America's Prison Population." New York: NY: National Center on Addiction and Substance Abuse at Columbia University.

Bernard Ellis & Associates. "The Latest View: An Updated Report on Substance Abuse-Related Social Indicators." Northwest New Mexico Fighting Back, Inc.

"Billings Area Profile." Billings, MT: Indian Health Service.

Burgess, Donna M. & Streissguth, Ann P. "Educating Students with Fetal Alcohol Syndrome or Fetal Alcohol Effects." unpublished.

Burgess, Donna M. & Streissguth, Ann P. "Fetal Alcohol Syndrome and Fetal Alcohol Effects: Principles for Educators." *Phi Delta Kappan.*

Cashin, Jeffrey R., Presley, Cheryl A., & Meilman, Philip W. "Alcohol Use in the Greek System: Follow the Leader?" *Journal of Studies on Alcohol.*

"Chemical Dependency Relapse Prevention Therapy Workbook," Montana State Prison.

"Drug Abuse Cost to Society set at $97.7 Billion, Continuing Steady Increase Since 1975." NIDA Notes.

"Fatal Workplace Injuries, a Collection of Data and Analysis." Bureau of Labor Statistics, U.S. Department of Labor.

Finigan, Michael. "An Outcome Program Evaluation of the Multnomah County S.T.O.P. Drug Diversion," Multnomah County (Ore.) Department of Community Corrections.

Hawkins, J. David, Catalano Richard F., & Miller Janet Y. "Risk and Protective Factors for Alcohol and Other Drug Problems in Adolescence and Early Adulthood: Implications for Substance Abuse Prevention." *Psychological Bulletin.*

Hayne, Bill. "FAS/E, At-Risk Children and Multiple Intelligence." Poplar, MT: Fort Peck Community College.

Howland, Jonathan. "A Randomized Trial on the Effects of Alcohol on Safety Sensitive Occupational Performance: Simulated Merchant Ship Handling." Boston, MA: Boston University School of Public Health. Unpublished draft.

Howland, Jonathan. "Effects of Low-Dose Alcohol Exposure on Simulated Merchant Ship Piloting by Maritime Cadets." Boston, MA: Boston University School of Public Health. Unpublished draft.

Kelley, Matthew & Daw, Raymond. "Outcome and Program Evaluation of a Substance Abuse Treatment Protocol Based on Traditional Native American Therapeutic Practices." Gallup, NM: Nanizhoozhi Center Inc.

Ketcham, Katherine & Asbury William F. "Beyond the Influence: Understanding and Defeating Alcoholism." New York, NY: Bantam Books.

Koob, George F. & Roberts, Amanda J. "Neurocircuitry Targets in Reward and Dependence." *Journal of the American Society of Addiction Medicine.*

Krupski, Antoinette. "The Cost of NOT Providing Substance Abuse Treatment: Prevalence, Outcomes, and Cost Offsets." Washington State Division of Alcohol and Substance Abuse.

Leshner, Alan. "Addiction is a Brain Disease—and It Matters." *National Institute of Justice Journal.*

Mangione, Thomas W. et al. "Employee Drinking Practices and Work Performances." *Journal of Studies on Alcohol.*

Mangione, Thomas, Howland, Jonathan, & Lee, Marianne. "New Perspectives for Worksite Alcohol Strategies: Results from a Corporate Drinking Study." NIAAA and the Robert Wood Johnson Foundation.

"Matching Alcoholism Treatments to Client Heterogeneity: Project MATCH Posttreatment Drinking Outcomes." *Journal of Studies on Alcohol.*

May, Philip A. "Motor Vehicle Crashes and Alcohol among American Indians and Alaska Natives." *The Surgeon General's Workshop on Drunken Driving: Background Papers.* University of New Mexico.

May, Philip A. "The Epidemiology of Alcohol Abuse among American Indians: The Mythical and Real Properties." *American Indian Culture and Research Journal.*

"National Drug Control Strategy, 1998." Office of National Drug Control Policy.

"Native American Traffic Fatalities." Helena, MT: Traffic Safety Bureau, Montana Department of Transportation.

"No Safe Haven." New York, NY: National Center on Addiction and Substance Abuse, Columbia University.

Nutt, David J. "The Neurochemistry of Addiction." *Journal of the American Society of Addiction Medicine.*

"Occupational Injuries and Illnesses: Counts, Rates and Characteristics." Bureau of Labor Statistics, U.S. Department of Labor.

O'Farrell, Timothy J. "A Behavioral Marital Therapy Couples Group Program for Alcoholics and Their Spouses." *Stabilizing Sobriety and Relationships.*

Presley, Cheryl A., Leichliter, Jami S., & Meilman, Philip W. "Alcohol and Drugs on American College Campuses." Core Institute, Southern Illinois University.

"Problem Identification." Helena, MT: Traffic Safety Bureau, Montana Department of Transportation.

"State Trends in Alcohol Related Mortality, 1979-92." NIAAA.

Streissguth, Ann P. "Fetal Alcohol Syndrome and Fetal Alcohol Effects: A Clinical Perspective of Later Developmental Consequences." *Maternal Substance Abuse and the Developing Nervous Systems.*

Streissguth Ann. P. "Fetal Alcohol Syndrome: Understanding the Problem; Understanding the Solution; What Indian Communities Can Do." *American Indian Culture and Research Journal.*

"Stress and Distress: Major Relapse Predictors." St. Paul, MN: Cator Connection.

"Substance Abuse and Federal Entitlement Programs." New York, NY: National Center on Addiction and Substance Abuse at Columbia University.

"Substance Use Disorders Needs Assessment Summary." Helena, MT: Addictive and Mental Disorders Division of the Montana Department of Public Health and Human Services.

"Supervisor's Guide on the Effects of Addiction in the Workplace." Illinois Institute for Addiction Recovery.

"The Economic Costs of Alcohol and Drug Abuse in the United States—1992." National Institute on Drug Abuse and NIAAA.

"The Medicine Wheel and the 12 Steps." Montana State Prison.

"Understanding the Occurrence of Secondary Disabilities in Clients with Fetal Alcohol Syndrome (FAS) and Fetal Alcohol Effects (FAE)." University of Washington School of Medicine.

"U.S. Apparent Consumption of Alcoholic Beverages." NIAAA.

Wickizer, Thomas, et al. "Employment Outcomes of Indigent Clients Receiving Alcohol and Drug Treatment in Washington State." Substance Abuse and Mental Health Services Administration, U.S. Department of Health and Human Services.

Idyll Arbor Personal Health books:
help for personal problems with alcohol and drugs.

Outwitting your Alcoholic
Keep the Loving and Stop the Drinking
Kenneth A. Lucas

Foreword by Eric Newhouse

Some people still love their alcoholic partner. They don't want to hear, "Just leave!" They want to find a way to get themselves *and* their loved one out of the trap of alcohol.

This book will help readers do that: outwit the alcohol that is ruining their lives.

The world of alcoholism is strange, filled with half truths and whole lies. The journey out of that world can be confusing and difficult, but people have made it. In this book, Ken Lucas provides a map of the alcoholic's world. (He lived there once.) He talks about how to get out, and bring the alcoholic out, too.

Things That Work
A No-Nonsense Guide to Recovery by
One Who Knows
By Barry Bocchieri

This book is for you if you are beginning to come to terms with your problem. It contains no generalities behind which you can hide, no Pollyanna solutions that will let you believe that you can sidestep the tough times ahead. Instead, you will have the principles that worked for the author in spite of his predisposition for, inclination toward, and background of alcoholism.

Printed in the United States
66885LVS00001B/1-102